Get the eBook FREE!

(PDF, ePub, Kindle, and liveBook all included)

We believe that once you buy a book from us, you should be able to read it in any format we have available. To get electronic versions of this book at no additional cost to you, purchase and then register this book at the Manning website.

Go to https://www.manning.com/freebook and follow the instructions to complete your pBook registration.

That's it!
Thanks from Manning!

First-Party Data Activation

Modernize your marketing data platform

ALINA D. MAGAUOVA
OSCAR KENNIS
DAVID H. JOOSTEN

FOREWORD BY MURAT GENC

MANNING
SHELTER ISLAND

For online information and ordering of this and other Manning books, please visit www.manning.com. The publisher offers discounts on this book when ordered in quantity.

For more information, please contact

Special Sales Department
Manning Publications Co.
20 Baldwin Road
PO Box 761
Shelter Island, NY 11964
Email: orders@manning.com

Manning Publications Co.
20 Baldwin Road
PO Box 761
Shelter Island, NY 11964

Development editor: Rebecca Johnson
Technical editors: Chinmay Abhay Nerurkar and Evangelos Pappas
Review editor: Dunja Nikitović
Production editor: Kathy Rossland
Copy editor: Andy Carroll
Proofreader: Melody Dolab
Typesetter: Tamara Švelić Sabljić
Cover designer: Marija Tudor

ISBN 9781633436367
Printed in the United States of America

To my children, Janine and Erika—my greatest gifts, my daily joys, and my everything.
To my mom, Alma, and my husband: thank you for your unwavering love and support.
—Alina

To my family, friends, and everyone who has directly or indirectly shaped
who I am today. I am deeply grateful and feel truly blessed.
—Oscar

To my children, Liam, Sofia, and Chloe, for teaching me more about creativity, incentives,
and the need for personalization than any marketing strategy ever could.
—David

contents

foreword

I still remember it like it was yesterday—the President of our Greater China business called a meeting with me, the SVP of the Beauty business unit, and Marketing and Finance leaders. Something different was happening in the category . . . we had started growing double digits in the last three months after several years of decline in a row. "There isn't a new product launch, a new TV ad, or a major new promotion. What is going on?" he asked. We all nodded in the meeting, agreeing that this turnaround was related to how we started using customer data and 1-to-1 marketing, with personalized product recommendations and engaging content tailored to consumers' beauty needs.

I have pioneered three generations of digital marketing and media stacks in my career, and the most challenging part was often stitching people, processes, data, and technology components into a holistic strategy and leading the change with strong execution for exceptional results. This book brings together all the parts of the puzzle in a holistic and easy-to-follow way, providing technology, marketing, and e-commerce leaders with a comprehensive guide for their journey to create superior 360 customer experiences and value, using technology, data, and AI.

Every company and brand context is different, and often change leaders need to bring together the art of what is required and the science of what is possible with tech and data. That context is rapidly evolving with generative marketing tools due to the AI/ML revolution we are in, but the fundamentals are not changing. You need to listen to your customers, understand their needs, and then respond to them with solutions, great products, and content in a timely and helpful manner, creating frictionless experiences. This is only possible using real-time, high-quality data across touch points.

I have worked with many multidisciplinary teams and signed nine-figure investments in this domain, learning to lead one of the most complex digital marketing and e-commerce transformations in the world. This transformation included a customer data lake, DMP, CDP, programmatic media, and performance marketing platforms used across 100+ countries and multiple 30+ billion-dollar brands. I wish my team had this guide when we started our journey.

—Murat Genc
CIO / CDO / CTO
P&G | Whirlpool | McLane

preface

Marketing today feels like a high-speed chase in pursuit of growth goals—one where the road constantly shifts beneath us. If you're a marketing leader, you've probably felt this too. The data, strategies, and technologies we relied on just a few years ago have quickly become outdated. The old world of third-party data, once the backbone of digital marketing, is quickly becoming unreliable. Privacy regulations are tightening (as they should), customer expectations are shifting dramatically, and AI is no longer a futuristic concept—it's here, actively reshaping how we work.

We've spent years navigating these changes firsthand. As martech professionals working across industries, we've seen companies large and small struggle with the same fundamental questions: What does a modern marketing tech stack even look like anymore? How should we think about AI's effect? And most importantly, how do we prepare ourselves—and our teams—for what's coming next?

Again and again, we found that the answer wasn't in some cutting-edge tool or secret growth hack. It was something much more fundamental: *first-party data.* Not just owning it but truly understanding how to use it effectively. It's about moving beyond the basics: rethinking data strategies, embracing privacy-first approaches, and learning how to activate data in ways that drive real, measurable effects to compound growth.

We started searching for a guide—something practical, strategic, and grounded in real-world experience. But we couldn't find the resources we needed, so we chose to write one ourselves.

This book is designed for marketing leaders, data-driven strategists, and martech professionals looking for clear, actionable frameworks in a time of constant disruption. It's divided into three core sections:

- *Part 1: Marketing foundations of first-party data*—A deep dive into the shifts driving this transformation, the critical role of privacy-centric marketing, and a roadmap for building a strong first-party data strategy
- *Part 2: First-party data building blocks*—A look under the hood at data lakehouses, composable CDPs, identity resolution, and the key technologies that power modern marketing
- *Part 3: New and upcoming technology opportunities*—A forward-looking exploration of data clean rooms, ethical data collaboration, and the rapidly evolving role of generative AI in marketing

Ultimately, our goal is to help you cut through the noise and focus on what really matters—building a marketing approach that is not only resilient but future-ready. This is a journey, and we're excited to be on it with you.

acknowledgments

Bringing this pioneering book on first-party data to life has been an extraordinary team effort. We are deeply grateful to everyone whose guidance, expertise, and faith in our vision shaped these pages.

We extend our heartfelt thanks to our wonderful reviewers—acquisition editor Jonathan Gennick, development editor Rebecca Johnson, and technical editor Evangelos Pappas—whose thoughtful insights and compassionate feedback elevated every page of this book. Their commitment to precision and clarity made our words sing. Evan has spent 17 years in the IT industry as Data, Platform and Protocol Engineer with experience in AdTech, Analytics, and Web3 industries.

We are also deeply grateful to Joe Cristee for coordinating real-world use cases with GrowthLoop, which enriched our narrative, and to Chinmay Nerurkar for his early feedback that guided our initial direction.

None of this would have been possible without Jonathan Gennick's tremendous support. His curiosity about martech sparked his strong backing of our proposal and inspired him to trust us with writing this book. We are equally thankful to our editor, Rebecca Johnson, whose eagle-eyed attention to detail kept our writing accurate, clear, and accessible.

We're also very thankful to Murat Genc for sharing his experiences and insights with us throughout the process and in the foreword to this book.

To Elizabeth Kazandzhi for additional copy editing, and to all the reviewers, Achint Kumar, Amit Singh, Brenn Hill, Carnell Greenfield III, Claudiu-Mihai Gurguță, Cristobal Gonzalez Perez, Evangelos Pappas, Gunjan Paliwal, James Black, Jeff Marcus, Karan Asher, Kay Engelhardt, Milind Kelkar, Neeraj Gupta, Nishchai Jayanna Manjula, Osama Khan, Pradeep Chintale, Pradeep Kumar Muthukamatchi, Praveen

Gujar, Prithvi Shivashankar, Puneet Gangrade, Siddharth Parakh, Sonam Kanungo, Srikanth Daggumalli, Sujay Kulkarni, Sumith Damodaran, Suvarsha Rai, Tulika Bhatt, and Vinoth Nageshwara, your suggestions helped make this a better book.

Personal thanks:

Alina: To my children, Janine and Erika—my miracles, my greatest joy, and the heartbeat of my life. Your laughter is my favorite sound, your hugs are my safest place, and your love is the purest gift I've ever known.

To my husband—my best friend, constant supporter, and favorite partner in every adventure. Your love gives me strength, your encouragement moves me forward, and your vision sparked this book. I still smile remembering our excitement when Jonathan first expressed interest—this journey began because of you.

To my parents, brother, and grandmothers—my foundation, lifelong supporters, and guiding lights. Your love shapes who I am, your wisdom lights my path, and your support inspires me every day.

To the Segment360 team—my creative partners and dedicated collaborators. Your passion and creativity lift every project higher.

I'm forever grateful to have you all in my life.

Oscar: To my wife and children—thank you for standing by me with love, patience, and unwavering support. Every step of this journey has been shaped by your encouragement.

David: I'd like to thank my co-founder, Chris, for continuously inspiring us to build the future, and the whole GrowthLoop team for bringing it to life with us. I appreciate everything our customers, advisors, and especially partners have done to help us along the journey. Most importantly, I'm grateful to my wife, Brooke, for building a warm and loving home during these demanding years.

And to you, our readers, thank you for choosing to spend your time with us as we explore the evolving world of first-party data. Your curiosity, dedication to learning, and trust in our work make this endeavor so worthwhile. We hope our shared passion for data-driven insights will empower you to innovate, connect, and make a meaningful effect in your own endeavors.

From all of us—Alina, Oscar, and David—thank you for being part of this journey.

about this book

First-Party Data Activation was written for marketing leaders seeking a strategic guide to first-party data in an environment shaped by evolving privacy standards and diminishing reliance on third-party cookies. It begins by introducing essential concepts—what first-party data is, how privacy-centric marketing works, and why these elements matter—and then moves into frameworks for modernizing your data platform and activating campaigns. You'll also find discussions of more advanced topics, such as data clean rooms and generative AI, presented at a leadership level rather than as code-centric tutorials. Throughout, real organizational examples and best practices highlight common challenges and solutions.

Who should read this book

Whether you're a CMO, VP of Marketing, Director, or marketing operations lead, this book provides the strategic context to build and refine a first-party data ecosystem. It also benefits data and analytics professionals responsible for designing scalable data architectures that support marketing, and it indirectly benefits compliance and privacy professionals by providing a clear understanding of the marketing context surrounding data privacy and governance. The emphasis is on frameworks and decision-making rather than deep technical details, making it accessible to those without a programming background.

How this book is organized: A road map

This book is divided into three parts, covering nine chapters in total.

Part 1 lays the foundational knowledge about first-party data and its strategic importance in modern marketing:

- Chapter 1 establishes the core value of first-party data, differentiates it from other data types (zero, second, and third-party data), and addresses the evolving privacy landscape.
- Chapter 2 outlines a framework for embedding privacy at every marketing stage—from data sourcing and governance to personalized activation—by emphasizing first-party data, consent, transparency, and privacy-enhancing technologies to build trust, ensure compliance, and drive sustainable growth.
- Chapter 3 offers a phased, practical "crawl, walk, run" approach to implementing first-party data initiatives, drawing from real-world success stories to illustrate key strategies.
- Chapter 4 guides you through selecting the right platform—like composable CDPs or monolithic marketing clouds—based on your objectives and existing infrastructure.

Part 2 delves into the essential building blocks for constructing a robust first-party data infrastructure:

- Chapter 5 introduces data lakehouses, composable architectures, and the medallion approach (bronze, silver, gold) for refining data and supporting real-time analytics.
- Chapter 6 details methods for unifying scattered customer data into a single enriched profile, highlighting deterministic and advanced matching approaches alongside enrichment best practices.
- Chapter 7 demonstrates how to activate first-party data, turning customer insights into effective marketing campaigns across multiple channels to drive engagement.

Part 3 explores new and emerging technology opportunities that are shaping the future of data-driven marketing:

- Chapter 8 explains data clean rooms and their role in enabling secure collaboration with partners while upholding privacy, comparing walled gardens to neutral solutions.
- Chapter 9 examines emerging AI-driven personalization methods, including generative text and image capabilities, and explains how these tools expand what's possible with first-party data.

You can read part 1 first if you're new to first-party data or skip directly to part 2 or 3 if you already have a strong grasp of the basics. The chapters do not include formal exercises; they offer key insights, frameworks, and examples you can adapt to your specific context.

About the code

Because this is a leadership-level guide, there are no step-by-step coding instructions or large code snippets. Certain chapters touch on data engineering concepts, but these references are meant to inform strategic decisions rather than provide hands-on tutorials. No code downloads are included.

If you're interested in practical experimentation, you can explore common marketing data or cloud platforms (e.g., Snowflake, BigQuery, or a CDP) to apply the discussed frameworks. Our goal here is to equip you with a deeper understanding and strategic approach to first-party data, not to teach programming.

liveBook discussion forum

Purchase of *First-Party Data Activation* includes free access to liveBook, Manning's online reading platform. Using liveBook's exclusive discussion features, you can attach comments to the book globally or to specific sections or paragraphs. It's a snap to make notes for yourself, ask and answer technical questions, and receive help from the authors and other users. To access the forum, go to https://livebook.manning.com/book/first-party-data-activation/discussion.

Manning's commitment to our readers is to provide a venue where a meaningful dialogue between individual readers and between readers and the authors can take place. It is not a commitment to any specific amount of participation on the part of the authors, whose contribution to the forum remains voluntary (and unpaid). We suggest you try asking the authors some challenging questions lest their interest stray! The forum and the archives of previous discussions will be accessible from the publisher's website as long as the book is in print.

Other online resources

Need additional support?

- Explore GrowthLoop University at https://www.growthloop.com/university for comprehensive resources on first-party data, encompassing everything from collection strategies to real-world personalization use cases, along with a wealth of articles and guides on marketing automation, data analytics, and other growth-focused marketing strategies. While it doesn't function as a Q&A community, it's an excellent way to expand your knowledge and enhance your skills.
- Please check out the step-by-step walk-through on how to build a journey for more hands-on examples: https://docs.growthloop.com/docs/build-a-journey.

about the authors

Alina D. Magauova is a brand strategist and product marketing leader specializing in privacy-focused, first-party data strategies. She has worked with Fortune 500 and Global 500 companies across Asia, Europe, and North America, guiding them in developing go-to-market strategies, bridging brand-building with performance marketing, and crafting customer-centric product roadmaps.

Drawing on her expertise, Alina founded Segment360, a martech consultancy and first-party data activation platform. Through Segment360, she helps e-commerce and retail companies unify, segment, and responsibly activate customer data in line with evolving privacy standards. She also advises companies on integrating emerging technologies and advanced analytics into marketing and product development, with an emphasis on privacy-first engagement.

Beyond her professional work, Alina is committed to education-focused community initiatives, sharing insights on martech innovation and responsible entrepreneurship. In her spare time, she enjoys nature photography and spending time with her husband and two children.

Oscar Kennis is the founder of OpsAngels Consultancy, a technology solutions firm specializing in designing and implementing high-impact data and AI strategies. With more than 18 years in the technology sector, he has developed deep expertise in architecting and managing enterprise platforms both on-premises and in the

cloud—including Google Cloud, AWS, Azure, Databricks, and Snowflake. His portfolio spans multiple industries, from fintech, telecommunications, and healthcare to media, e-commerce, insurance, retail, and martech.

In partnership with major cloud providers, Oscar has led end-to-end modernization initiatives, ranging from replatforming analytics systems to unifying business intelligence across entire organizations. He stays current with the latest developments in data management, analytics, and digital strategy, ensuring his guidance reflects advanced solutions that help organizations optimize operations, enhance customer experiences, and drive sustainable growth.

Oscar resides in the San Francisco area with his family and their furry cat, who often keeps him company during late-night coding sessions.

DAVID H. JOOSTEN is a recognized expert in first-party data and technology. He advises Fortune 500 companies in industries ranging from financial services to technology, retail, e-commerce, sports, and media. He combines a deep knowledge of data science with practical marketing applications to drive business growth.

As the Co-Founder of GrowthLoop, David has pioneered technology-first solutions in partnership with companies like Snowflake, Google Cloud, and AWS to enhance data capabilities in marketing, including advanced segmentation, measurement, and predictive modeling. GrowthLoop serves marketing teams at major companies such as Indeed, NASCAR, the Boston Red Sox, and Google.

David started his career as a Product Marketing Manager at Google. He earned his BA in Economics from Harvard and later completed a Master's in Computer Science at Stanford with a specialization in data science and cloud computing systems. This combination has helped David build bridges between marketers and technologists seeking to solve challenging first-party data problems at organizations large and small.

In his free time, David enjoys spending time with his wife and three children. He loves our national parks and spending time in Spain with family and friends. This book draws on his extensive experience and vision, aiming to equip marketers with the necessary tools and insights to use first-party data most effectively.

about the cover illustration

The figure on the cover of *First-Party Data Activation* is "La modista," or "The dressmaker," taken from *Usi e Costumi di Napoli e Contorni Descritti e Dipinti* by Francesco de Bourcard, published in 1853. Each illustration is finely drawn and colored by hand.

In those days, it was easy to identify where people lived and what their trade or station in life was just by their dress. Manning celebrates the inventiveness and initiative of the computer business with book covers based on the rich diversity of regional culture centuries ago, brought back to life by pictures from collections such as this one.

Part 1

Marketing foundations of first-party data

Digital marketing is shifting, with growing restrictions on third-party data collection and increasing consumer expectations around privacy. Marketers face tightening regulations and browser restrictions that limit third-party cookies and external tracking. Instead, businesses must focus on first-party data—information collected directly from customers with consent—to build sustainable, privacy-first marketing strategies. This part of the book lays the groundwork for understanding the role of first-party data in modern marketing.

Chapter 1 introduces how privacy laws and browser restrictions fragment third-party data and why brands must prioritize customer data to remain competitive. Chapter 2 explores privacy-centric marketing, showing how businesses can balance personalization with compliance, navigating evolving regulations and consumer expectations. Chapter 3 provides a structured approach—crawl, walk, run—to gradually implement a first-party data strategy while demonstrating effect. Chapter 4 then guides marketers in selecting the right first-party data technologies, distinguishing between customer data platforms (CDPs), marketing data lakehouses, and composable CDPs.

By the end of this section, you'll understand why first-party data is central to modern marketing and how to approach it strategically in an increasingly regulated digital landscape.

1 First-party data in the digital marketing space

This chapter covers

- First-party data and its importance
- Comparing first-party data with other data types (zero-party, second-party, and third-party data)
- Understanding how first-party data improves marketing strategies
- Challenges, potential, and opportunities associated with first-party data

First-party data is the most valuable data a company has.

— David Raab, Founder of the CDP Institute and marketing influencer

As a marketing leader, you're no stranger to pressure. The demand for growth is constant, competition is fierce, and staying ahead of the curve in a rapidly evolving digital landscape feels like a never-ending race. You're tasked with making strategic decisions, often with limited resources and under intense scrutiny. As of 2024, the marketing technology landscape—mapped annually by martech expert

Scott Brinker in his "Marketing Technology Landscape Supergraphic" (https://mng.bz/5grD)—features over 14,000 solutions (and counting). Navigating this crowded landscape can feel like stepping through a minefield, with every new platform, automation tool, or AI-powered solution promising to be the silver bullet that will propel you to success. Yet chasing these trends often feels like running on a treadmill: you're putting in the effort, but are you truly moving forward? Are you building something sustainable or simply piling more complexity onto your already overflowing plate?

That's likely why you picked up this book. You're tired of chasing fleeting trends and quick fixes. You're looking for a longer-lasting, ethical, and customer-centric approach to marketing—one that delivers real, enduring results. This book isn't about adding another "next big thing" to your tech stack. It's about using the data you already have—your first-party data—to gain a clearer picture of who your customers are, what resonates with them, and where you should focus your efforts for greater influence.

Think back to when a brand made you feel truly seen and understood. It could be a streaming service that always recommended the perfect next show or an online store that emailed you a discount on your favorite product when you needed to re-order. In those moments, you probably weren't thinking about "data." Yet behind the scenes, data—specifically, first-party data—played a crucial role in shaping that positive experience and building the kind of loyalty no competitor could replicate. It's powerful, isn't it? But let's not get ahead of ourselves!

First-party data is at the heart of this book—it's a critical asset we'll unravel throughout this chapter and beyond. For now, consider it the foundation of sustainable marketing strategies—data you gather directly from your audience, built on trust and connection. Your company's approach to its first-party data strategy is unique, shaped by the company's culture and your creative understanding of this invaluable resource.

DEFINITION *First-party data* is information your organization collects, stores, and uses directly—without intermediaries—through channels you own, such as your website, app, or customer relationship management (CRM). It includes user behavior (pages visited, items purchased), user attributes (demographics, account details), and engagement activities (email interactions, loyalty program participation). When collected transparently and with user consent, your organization exclusively owns and controls this first-party data. It is the foundation for trusted marketing strategies, personalized customer experiences, and compliance with global privacy regulations.

In this book, we'll explore first-party data from every angle—not as a technical how-to, but as a high-level strategic vision by marketers, for marketers. We'll break down its key elements, showcase its role in marketing strategies, and demonstrate how to use it as a competitive advantage. To set the stage, this first chapter focuses on why first-party data matters more than ever, highlighting its challenges and opportunities and comparing it to other data types—like zero-party, second-party, and third-party data. You'll also discover how new technologies, such as generative AI and data lakehouses, are transforming how marketers work, while also introducing new challenges in collecting, integrating, and making sense of first-party data. And, of course, we'll discuss evolving regulations like the General Data Protection Regulation (GDPR) and the California Consumer Privacy Act (CCPA), illustrating why staying compliant is just as important as staying ahead.

1.1 The evolving data landscape

Before we get into the nuances of first-party data, let's take a step back and reflect on how customer data collection has evolved. Today, as marketing leaders, you're immersed in a world of dashboards, metrics, and ever-evolving strategies. Yet the core idea behind data-driven marketing isn't new. Remember when your grandparents—or even great-grandparents—visited the local shop? The shopkeeper knew their name, what they regularly bought, and even remembered the small details, like how they always preferred a particular type of tea or the special bread for Sunday dinner. This wasn't just good customer service; it was an early form of data collection and relationship-building built on trust and personal connections.

Fast forward to today—the shopkeeper's handwritten notes have transformed into vast digital databases, but the fundamental principle remains the same. First-party data—information you collect directly from your audience through interactions with your brand—is the modern version of that shopkeeper's knowledge. It's the foundation of effective, long-lasting marketing.

Imagine you're a personal stylist helping clients refresh their wardrobe. You might start by recommending outfits based on current trends—perhaps saying something like, "Bold patterns are really popular right now!" This approach mirrors third-party data. If you're wondering, "Wait, what exactly is third-party data?" we'll cover that briefly in the following sections. For now, think of it as information borrowed from someone else's interactions, not directly from your client's. First-party data takes a more personal approach. It's based on carefully observing your client's choices, noticing precisely which clothing racks catch their eye, which styles they repeatedly try on, and what they ultimately purchase. In marketing terms, it's based on closely tracking your customers' behaviors, like clicks, browsing patterns, purchase histories, and engagement across your marketing channels. You're not guessing what might resonate with your customers; you're understanding what actually does, straight from the source.

So what's changed? The answer is simple yet profound: the power dynamic has shifted. Consumers are no longer passive bystanders in the data exchange. They're informed, empowered, and demanding a new set of rules. This shift is evident in the growing consumer awareness around data privacy and the regulations designed to protect it. Regulations like GDPR and CCPA have clarified that transparency is no longer optional. Brands that fail to prioritize privacy are risking not only legal penalties but also the erosion of customer trust—something far more valuable and harder to regain.

And the changes aren't stopping there. You've probably heard about the "cookiepocalypse"—the predicted demise of third-party cookies. But just as we were gearing up for this dramatic shift, Google announced on July 22, 2024 that they would not fully deprecate third-party cookies in Chrome as initially planned. Instead, they've shifted toward a more privacy-focused model, placing control in consumers' hands through an opt-in approach. This means users must explicitly agree to be tracked by third-party cookies, complicating data collection efforts even further. Safari and Firefox have already blocked third-party cookies by default, and with Chrome adopting similar measures, the implications are significant. Third-party data is becoming increasingly fragmented. Think about it: What will it mean for your data if most users choose not to opt in? How much of the customer picture will you be able to see? The once-reliable insights from cross-site tracking could soon become incomplete and unreliable.

As cross-site tracking faces growing restrictions, the mounting data fragmentation is challenging online advertising and analytics, leaving marketers with fewer actionable insights. However, innovative alternatives are emerging, offering viable paths forward. This book will guide you through privacy-preserving solutions such as data clean rooms (explored in chapter 8) and first-party identifiers (covered in chapter 6), focusing on ethical, customer-centric marketing driven by first-party data. This shift demands critical reflection from marketing leaders. Are your strategies built on the shifting sands of third-party data? Are you prepared to navigate a world where reliance on such data is no longer sustainable? These challenges require more than technical adjustments—they fundamentally force us to rethink how we engage audiences. Beyond new regulations, this is a call to lead the shift toward ethical, customer-centric marketing. The future of your brand depends on how effectively you adapt.

1.2 Why first-party data matters more now

You might think, "We've been collecting customer data for years—what's the big deal now?" You're right—customer data itself isn't new. But here's what's changed: expectations. Today's customers no longer simply hand over their data; they now demand transparency, meaningful value, and robust privacy protections in return. For example, think about how email sign-ups worked a decade ago—people would often submit their information without a second thought. Today, customers want to know precisely what data you're collecting, how you'll use it, and whether you respect their privacy. The real challenge now goes beyond collecting data—it's earning trust and maintaining it as you scale.

Think back to the shopkeeper we mentioned earlier—someone who knew their regulars personally, anticipating their needs and preferences. Today, the challenge for marketers is replicating that same sense of personal connection, but at scale—across thousands, if not millions, of customers—while navigating stricter privacy expectations. First-party data is the key to tackling this. It offers the accuracy and relevance that third-party sources simply can't match, and it respects the growing need for transparency around how data is gathered and shared. This shift isn't theoretical; it's accelerating rapidly. According to the Interactive Advertising Bureau (IAB), 71% of brands, agencies, and publishers actively expanded their first-party data initiatives in 2024, nearly doubling the 41% recorded two years earlier.

Additionally, organizations prioritizing first-party data in 2024 projected an average dataset growth of 35% over the subsequent 12 months, driven primarily by tightening privacy regulations and the declining reliability of third-party tracking methods. Publishers notably led this transition with an 80% adoption rate, followed by brands (67%) and agencies (64%).[1] This underscores that evolving privacy laws and declining third-party tracking have made first-party data strategies essential rather than optional. Marketers across industries increasingly recognize that transparent, consent-driven customer relationships built around first-party data are foundational for long-term success in today's privacy-focused environment.

The critical question now is this: In a landscape where consumer trust and privacy are paramount, how prepared is your organization to use first-party data to build authentic, enduring connections with your customers?

1.3 Understanding the data ecosystem

Now that we've explored the growing importance of first-party data, let's take a step back and see how it fits into the broader data ecosystem. First-party data is undeniably critical, but it doesn't function in isolation. Today's data ecosystem is multilayered, with various types of data originating from different sources, each shaping your marketing strategy in distinct ways.

To maximize the potential of your data strategy, it's essential to grasp the specific roles each type of data plays and, crucially, to understand how they integrate to support your broader plan. As illustrated in figure 1.1, the ecosystem can be categorized into four key types: zero-party, first-party, second-party, and third-party data (sometimes referred to as 0P, 1P, 2P, and 3P data). Let's break them down and see how each fits into your strategy.

Table 1.1 outlines the key differences, strengths, weaknesses, and typical uses for each data type to give you a clear, concise summary of the broader data ecosystem. In the following subsections, we'll explore each type of data individually, beginning with a deeper look into zero-party data.

Table 1.1 Types of customer data and their strategic implications

Type of data	Source	Pros	Cons
Zero-party	Shared proactively by customers (e.g., surveys, wish lists)	High consent; reveals explicit preferences and aspirations	Not always consistent with actual behavior
First-party	Directly from brand interactions (e.g., transactions, web analytics)	Highly accurate, direct relationship, privacy-friendly	Requires strong internal data governance and privacy compliance

[1] Interactive Advertising Bureau (IAB), *State of Data 2024: How the Digital Ad Industry is Adapting to the Privacy-by-Design Ecosystem* (Interactive Advertising Bureau, March 2024), p. 23.

Table 1.1 Types of customer data and their strategic implications (*continued*)

Type of data	Source	Pros	Cons
Second-party	Another brand's first-party data (via partnerships)	Extends reach with trusted data, enhances targeting accuracy, and is more accurate than third-party data	Relies on partner's data quality; requires legal and privacy agreements
Third-party	Aggregators, data brokers (e.g., cookie-based tracking), broadly collected online	Large-scale; historically easy for broad targeting	Privacy concerns, declining accuracy, often lacks meaningful context; under heavy regulation

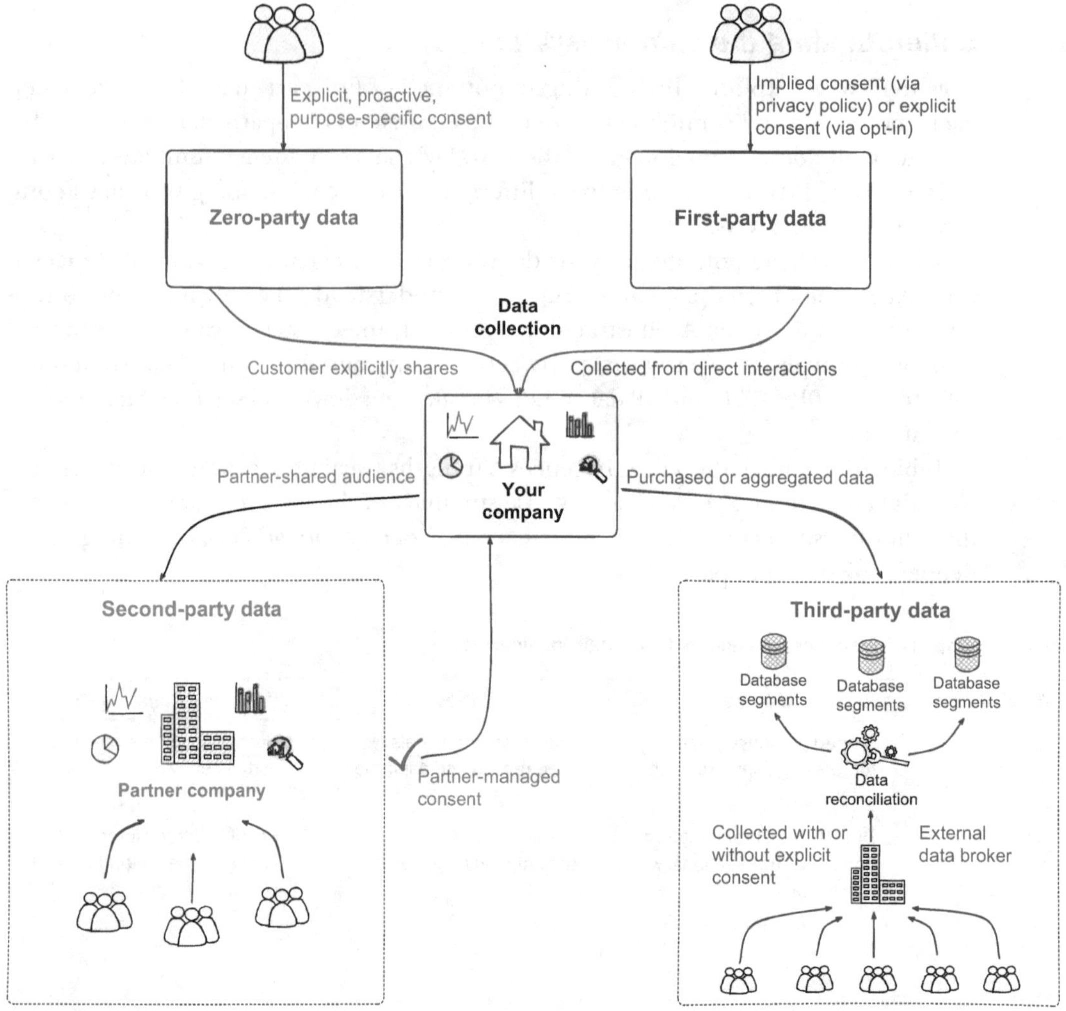

Figure 1.1 Types of data

1.3.1 Zero-party data

Before exploring first-, second-, and third-party data, let's begin with a more direct form of customer-supplied information: zero-party data. Zero-party data centers on *intentional* and *proactive* sharing, where customers *willingly* provide information, explicitly communicating their preferences, needs, and desires. This could be through surveys, wish lists, detailed profile settings, or even the app's "tell us your preferences" quizzes. It also includes actions like engaging with interactive content like videos, polls, contests, or sweepstakes, providing feedback or product reviews, and actively participating in loyalty programs. This data doesn't replace your first-party data strategy; it adds a more explicit layer of customer insight.

Here's where things get interesting: while first-party data captures actual behavior—clicks, purchases, and content interactions—zero-party data reflects aspirations or immediate preferences, providing insights into customers' intentions that range from long-term goals to actionable specifics like dietary restrictions. Crucially, the customer directly determines zero-party data, whereas your brand observes first-party data. This distinction can lead to different personalization outcomes: zero-party data may highlight what customers intend or wish to do, while first-party data reveals what they actually do. For example, a customer might eagerly share their commitment to sustainable fashion in a survey, stating that ethical sourcing is a priority. This aligns with a brand's values and seems like an opportunity to connect. However, when faced with price and convenience, that same customer might opt for fast-fashion (inexpensive, mass-produced) items. This contrast between expressed ideals and purchasing actions highlights the gap between values and practicality, influenced by price sensitivity and urgency. Recognizing this gap and understanding this dynamic is crucial for marketing leaders. You gain a holistic view of your customers by integrating the aspirational data from zero-party sources with the behavioral data captured by first-party sources. This comprehensive understanding allows you to bridge the gap between what customers say they want and what they actually do, leading to more effective personalization, segmentation, and engagement strategies.

Transparency is paramount when seeking these valuable insights. Offering genuine value in exchange—such as early access to new product lines aligned with their stated preferences, exclusive content tailored to their interests, or a points system in your loyalty program that rewards them for sharing—not only enriches your data but also cultivates the crucial element of trust.

1.3.2 First-party data

As you've already seen, first-party data—insights collected directly from how customers interact with your brand across various touch points—lies at the heart of modern marketing strategies. It serves as the foundation that enables marketers to REACH their audience by being *relevant, engaging, authentic, customer-focused,* and *high-impact*:

- *Relevant*—Delivering experiences tailored to individual needs and preferences
- *Engaging*—Encouraging genuine interactions and conversations

- *Authentic*—Building trust and transparency
- *Customer-focused*—Prioritizing customer needs and values
- *High-impact*—Ensuring every interaction drives meaningful connections and measurable outcomes

Figure 1.2, featuring Happy Dude and friends, provides a high-level illustration of data points like login times, search queries, clickstream data, and content engagement, all of which help your marketing team understand your customers better. For example, when a user like Happy Dude logs in to your platform, your platform captures data that reveals their actions, preferences, and peak interaction times. This allows your marketing team to create targeted emails or exclusive offers—like the 20% off coupon shown in figure 1.2—perfectly tailored to their browsing habits and engagement levels. By analyzing these interactions across platforms—from email to social media—your team can refine strategies to drive repeat business and enhance customer loyalty.

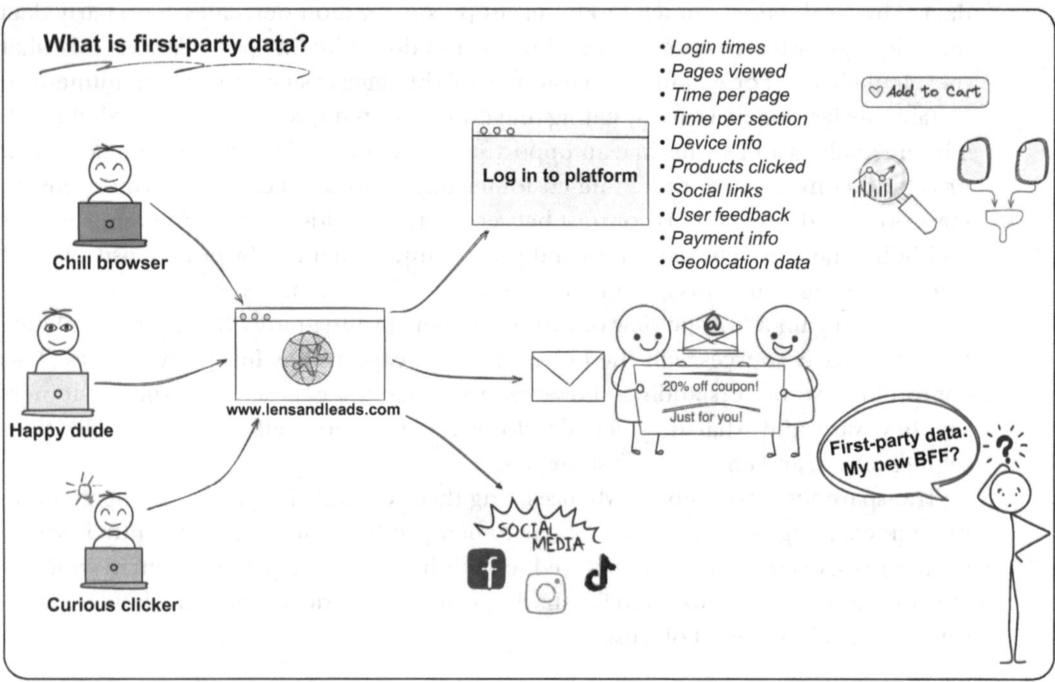

Figure 1.2 Overview of first-party data

While figure 1.2 captures some important data points, first-party data extends beyond what's illustrated. It also includes insights from customer feedback forms, purchase history, offline interactions like in-store visits or customer service calls, loyalty programs, and even in-app activities. These diverse data points provide a richer, more holistic view of your audience, enabling your marketing team to craft highly personalized strategies that resonate across digital and physical channels.

Let's explore how first-party data can transform a brand's approach to customer engagement. Let's assume an e-commerce business specializing in everyday essentials is seeing strong sales in its baby category but struggling with customer retention. Parents buy diapers and then rarely return. Recognizing the need to strengthen their connection with customers, this brand shifts focus from being just a vendor to becoming a trusted partner for parents during those challenging early years. The company introduces a dedicated baby registry to expand these relationships further, offering a small welcome gift to new parents in exchange for essential information, such as the baby's due date or special needs. By capturing these details early on, the business can proactively recommend age-appropriate products as the child grows—whether they're transitioning from diapers to pull-ups or exploring toddler-friendly meal options. This approach personalizes the customer journey and reduces churn by keeping parents engaged far beyond the initial purchase.

Analyzing their first-party data, the marketing team notices a surge in late-night website visits from parents searching for colic remedies, sleep aids, and soothing lotions, highlighting a critical moment when parents urgently seek guidance and support. Recognizing this as an opportunity, the team shifts its focus from promoting products to marketing content that addresses these high-stress needs. They create blog posts with expert tips on soothing a colicky baby, downloadable guides for sleep training, and recipes for homemade baby food. They also establish social media communities to help sleep-deprived parents connect and share experiences. This data-driven approach transforms the brand from an e-commerce site into a supportive ally for parents navigating the challenging early months of parenthood.

Building on their initial findings, the marketing team expands their analysis by integrating digital behavior with customer insights from loyalty programs and purchase histories. They identify a clear pattern: parents who opt for organic baby food often choose eco-friendly diapers and cleaning products. Seeing this connection, the team strengthens the company's sustainability focus, shaping product offerings and marketing strategies. This alignment with shared values deepens connections with existing customers and draws in new audiences who prioritize natural and sustainable choices. Then, the customer service team enriches their analysis by identifying a common concern among parents. Many are looking for gentle skincare solutions for babies with sensitive skin. The company integrates data from all channels into a centralized system to effectively use these insights, revealing actionable insights that drive the successful launch of its "Sensitive Skin" product line.

Meanwhile, the marketing team anticipates future customer needs by analyzing purchase histories. The data reveals a natural progression as babies grow, showing parents gradually moving from buying diapers to toddler snacks, potty training supplies, and products for older children. Armed with this knowledge, the company shifts from reactive to proactive marketing, implementing lifecycle-based email campaigns triggered by past purchases and predicted needs. For example, a drop in diaper purchases might prompt a personalized email with potty-training tips and discounts on related products, turning potential churn into a renewed engagement.

Beyond single transactions, the company uses these insights to craft a more engaging customer journey. Personalized product recommendations are developed based on past behaviors and engagement history, and loyalty programs reward purchases and community participation. This approach transforms the brand from just a marketplace to an integral part of customers' everyday lives, offering value that extends well beyond their products. Throughout this transformation, trust and transparency remain critical. The company implements clear data usage policies and empowers customers with control over their data and communication preferences, building a foundation of respect and loyalty. This ethical stance reinforces the brand's commitment to responsible data practices.

This example demonstrates how first-party data is a strategic asset, steering brands toward precise, customer-focused decisions across marketing, product development, and engagement. By applying these insights, companies can move beyond mere transactions, building stronger relationships that enhance loyalty and drive long-term growth.

As a marketing leader, your challenge lies in turning these insights into actionable strategies that resonate with your audience. As you think about using first-party data within your organization, consider these key questions:

- Are your loyalty programs uncovering connections between what your customers buy and what they truly value?
- What stories hide in your customer service interactions that reveal pain points or spark new opportunities?
- Are your loyalty programs actively deepening customer loyalty and encouraging repeat engagement?
- How can you shift from reacting to problems to anticipating customer needs and tailoring their experience?
- Are you spotting early signs of churn in your data, and how can you turn those signals into renewed customer loyalty?
- How are you building trust by ensuring transparency and giving customers control over their data?

1.3.3 Second-party data

As you continue using your own valuable first-party data—the cornerstone of your marketing strategy—you might wonder: Are there ways to *further* enhance those insights, reach new audiences, and drive even greater value? That's where strategic partnerships and the complementary advantages of second-party data come into play. Second-party data partnerships can be a way to enrich and build upon the solid foundation of each brand's first-party data by providing access to pooled insights from both partners. When approached thoughtfully, these collaborations can open doors to creative campaigns and potentially allow you to extend your reach and connect with a broader audience while maintaining the control and accuracy that come from using direct customer insights.

Second-party data is essentially a *trusted collaboration* between two complementary brands with aligned customer interests. These partnerships form a strategic alliance—not just a passive "data swap"—that deepens customer insights, enables tailored campaigns, and drives mutual growth through shared first-party data.

Let's say you run a healthy meal delivery service targeting busy professionals. You know your customers value convenience, nutrition, and time-saving solutions. What if you partnered with a high-end fitness studio in your city? They have first-party data on individuals who invest heavily in their fitness and wellness routines. Through a carefully crafted data-sharing agreement that explicitly defines data usage rights, privacy protections, and compliance standards—such as GDPR or CCPA—you can securely access additional insights, like fitness goals, workout routines, or dietary preferences, without compromising privacy or customer trust. Clearly defining these elements ensures accountability, protects your customers' data, and maintains trust throughout the collaboration.

Here's what this partnership could mean for you:

- *Reaching the right people more effectively*—You already target your ideal customer, but with additional insights from the fitness studio's data, you might identify new customers who are also highly likely to value your services. This extension of your first-party data helps you make your messaging even more relevant.
- *Creating joint offers that resonate*—By using both data sets, you could bundle your meal delivery service with the fitness studio's packages, allowing customers to align their fitness goals with healthy eating. This positions both brands as part of a comprehensive wellness solution, building upon the strengths of your first-party data.
- *Gaining deeper insights into your audience*—By combining relevant data points from both brands, starting from the robust understanding of your first-party data, you get a clearer, more nuanced picture of your shared customers. What drives them? How can you meet their broader lifestyle needs? These enhanced insights can guide your strategy moving forward.

While these advantages highlight the enormous potential of second-party collaborations, it's equally important to consider potential pitfalls that can undermine success. One partner's data might be incomplete or poorly governed, diluting the overall quality of your shared insights. You could also become too reliant on one data source—if your partner changes policies or withdraws suddenly, your data strategy could suffer. Overlooking legal or regulatory requirements is another common hazard; failing to define compliance obligations or obtain proper user consent is a swift route to lost trust and possible penalties. Finally, a true alliance means brand synergy as well as data synergy—if your partner's audience or values clash with your own, even the best campaign ideas may fall flat.

It's important to remember that the effectiveness of second-party data relies on the strength and quality of the first-party data contributed by all partners. It's challenging to fully use the benefits of such collaborations without a solid understanding of each brand's customers. Additionally, careful consideration must be given to data privacy, security, and the legal complexities of data-sharing agreements. In essence, second-party data doesn't replace the power of your first-party data—it *enhances* it.

Returning to our healthy meal delivery/fitness studio example, one practical way to ensure privacy and security is by using data clean rooms. Each partner can match relevant user data in this protected environment without exposing personally identifiable information. This alignment with GDPR, CCPA, and similar regulations safeguards consumer trust while enabling more targeted marketing, loyalty perks, and specialized offers for your mutual audience. By thoughtfully combining these insights, brands can create more personalized experiences, strengthen customer relationships, and drive greater marketing influence. Keeping first-party data at the core of your strategy ensures that any additional data complements and builds upon the strong foundation you've already established.

1.3.4 Third-party data

You saw in the previous section how second-party data can enhance your existing first-party insights through strategic partnerships, enabling you to reach new audiences and gain deeper insights without sacrificing trust or privacy. However, third-party data operates differently. It's the kind of data that makes you feel like someone's watching you online . . . because, well, they kind of are. Remember that time you searched for "best noise-canceling headphones for chatty coworkers" (hypothetically, of course), and suddenly, every website you visit bombarded you with headphone ads? That's the magic (or maybe "creepiness" is a better word) of third-party data.

Beyond the "creepiness" factor, third-party data also carries significant ethical concerns around transparency, consent, and how data brokers buy and sell personal information. Growing consumer unease over being tracked across the web—and uncertainty about where their data ends up—has led to increased scrutiny from regulators and the public. This heightened awareness and stricter privacy regulations, like GDPR and CCPA, are reasons third-party data is losing favor. In contrast, first-party data is seen as more ethical and reliable, gathered through direct interactions with customers who grant explicit permission. What's more, identity resolution can be a headache when you rely on third-party data. People share devices, and cookies can get deleted, causing inaccurate profiles to merge. A single user might appear as multiple "people," or multiple family members might be lumped under one. Suddenly, you're targeting Grandma Mary with extreme sports gear ads because she borrowed her grandson's laptop.

Take a look at figure 1.3, where we meet Alma, our spring break enthusiast. She's dreaming of escaping to Europe, so she fires up her laptop, types "spring break in Europe" into Google, and boom—the data trail begins. Picturesque Tuscan villas, mouthwatering pasta dishes, maybe even a gondola ride in Venice (who could resist?)—every click is tracked, packaged, and sold to advertisers eager to shower her with "personalized" (or so they hope) travel deals. Figure 1.3 illustrates how quickly those innocent searches can turn into a relentless parade of "Visit Italy!" banners.

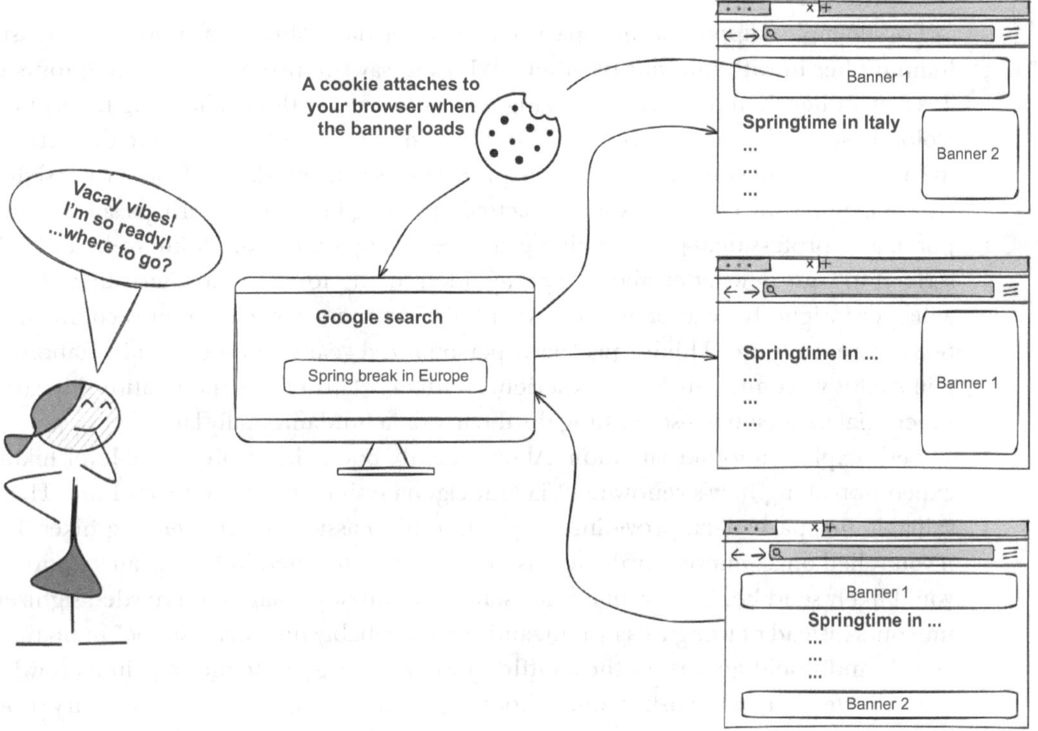

Figure 1.3 User navigates to a website

You might think, "Hey, if it means Alma sees relevant ads, what's the big deal?" And you're not alone. Plenty of marketers fall for the allure of third-party data. It promises a quick, cost-effective shortcut to targeting and personalization. But as we'll see, there are some significant downsides to relying too heavily on this type of data. Third-party data comes from organizations with zero direct relationship with the people they're tracking. Think shadowy data brokers, massive aggregators, and those sprawling databases full of browsing histories and purchase patterns, all bought, sold, and traded like commodities. It's like trying to understand Alma by peeking through her neighbor's window—you might catch a glimpse of her routine, but you're missing the full picture, the why behind her actions.

Sure, those "Visit Italy!" banners might seem appealing at first glance. However, they rely on a flawed assumption—that everyone searching for a "European vacation" shares the same interests. While basic third-party data can be overly broad, more sophisticated data providers offer detailed segments based on demographics, purchase history, interests, and online behavior. However, even with this level of granularity, third-party data is inherently limited. It's gathered through observation, not interaction. It lacks the depth of understanding that comes from a direct, permission-based relationship with your customer.

For example, suppose a third-party data vendor flags Alma as a "travel enthusiast," lumping her in with millions of others. Who's to say she prefers wine-tasting tours in Tuscany rather than professional hiking excursions along the challenging trails in the Dolomites? Or that her interest in luxury boutique hotels isn't just a one-time curiosity? You're left guessing about her true preferences without direct, first-party insights. Now imagine your brand sees Alma's actual browsing behavior—perhaps she recently purchased professional-grade hiking gear specifically suited for alpine treks and subscribed to your newsletter about expert-guided hiking tours in Northern Italy. That's a deeper insight. Instead of generic "Visit Italy!" banners, you can tailor recommendations around advanced hiking packages, personalized gear suggestions, or invitations to join exclusive communities for experienced hikers. This moves the relationship from superficial to personal—something third-party data fundamentally lacks.

Let's explore another situation: Alma recently booked a professional-level hiking expedition along Italy's renowned Via Francigena trail through your travel site. That's valuable first-party data, providing insight into her passion for challenging hikes. But if you relied on a generic third-party list of "women interested in European vacations," you'd likely send her irrelevant ads for standard tourist packages or crowded sightseeing tours instead of using this insight, and she'd probably hit "unsubscribe" in no time. Your brand would get lost in the shuffle—just another generic message in a crowded inbox. Instead, imagine using Alma's booking history to suggest complementary products and experiences—perhaps premium trekking boots designed for demanding alpine conditions or exclusive training sessions with a professional mountain guide. You could even offer her membership in an elite community for passionate hikers seeking their next challenge.

As we saw with Alma's ambitious hiking plans, third-party data offered only a superficial understanding of her interests, leaving her with irrelevant "Visit Italy!" ads rather than the advanced trekking packages she actually sought. Today's consumers aren't passive observers; they quickly recognize when brands truly understand them and when they're being targeted through guesswork and broad categorization. And this matters deeply, because trust hinges on relevance, transparency, and genuine understanding. As marketing leaders, your role goes far beyond crunching numbers or maximizing impressions. You're architects of trusted, lasting customer relationships—relationships rooted in authentic insights and respect for privacy. While third-party data can provide quick scale or broaden initial reach, its inherent limitations prevent it from delivering meaningful engagement or loyalty. True personalization—the kind Alma experienced through first-party insights—can't be replicated by third-party shortcuts.

1.3.5 From zero to third: Strategic recap and key takeaways

Before we move forward, let's briefly recap how zero-, first-, second-, and third-party data strategically fit within your broader marketing framework. Table 1.2 outlines their specific use cases, strategic roles, and measurable success indicators, providing a concise overview of how these data sources interplay to build stronger, lasting customer relationships.

Table 1.2 Types of data: strategic uses and success signals

Type of data	Strategic use case	Success signals
Zero-party	Supplements first-party data with explicitly stated customer preferences and intent	Higher engagement, improved message resonance
First-party	Central foundation for personalized marketing and retention	Enhanced retention, higher customer lifetime value (CLTV), loyalty growth
Second-party	Extends the effectiveness of first-party data via trusted partner insights	Expanded audience quality, enhanced targeting precision
Third-party	Provides broader market context (low transparency, increasing fragmentation, privacy risks; validate with first-party data)	Broader initial reach, trend validation (limited precision)

As we've navigated the data ecosystem, one truth stands clear and unshaken: first-party data is your indispensable foundation. It's your direct, accurate, transparent connection to your customer, and no other type of data can replace that. Zero-party data deepens your understanding, second-party collaborations selectively enhance your reach, and third-party data—carefully and cautiously applied—can offer limited market context but must always be secondary and subordinate to your own trusted insights.

But here's the critical reflection: Are you genuinely leading your marketing with first-party data at the core, or are you still relying too heavily on fleeting external data? As privacy regulations tighten and consumer expectations rise, the answer to this question won't just determine your next campaign but your brand's future. Prioritize first-party data relentlessly, and let everything else complement—not compromise—your strategy.

1.4 Many faces of first-party data

You live in the world of acronyms—CRM (customer relationship management), CDP (customer data platform), DMP (data management platform)—and the constant pursuit of optimizing customer lifetime value (CLTV). By now, you're aware that first-party data is at the core of any robust marketing strategy. But understanding its importance is just the starting point.

First-party data acts as a dynamic ecosystem with multiple interconnected layers, each peeling back a different view of who your customers are, how they act, and what drives their choices. These layers aren't just numbers on a dashboard—they are what we like to call the "faces" of first-party data, each offering a distinct lens into your audience's world and enabling truly empowered decision-making.

To illustrate how these dimensions come together in practice, we'll look at one apparel and lifestyle brand we partnered with—an organization that faced challenges both online and in physical locations, and that ultimately used its first-party data to enhance brand engagement and strengthen overall profitability. Let's explore these dimensions—*behavioral data, psychographic data, transactional data, engagement data, contextual data,* and *technographic data*—and see how each face contributes to your strategy.

1.4.1 Behavioral data

Behavioral data is a crucial element of predictive intelligence, covering the entire spectrum of user interactions on digital platforms: clicks, scrolls, navigation paths, session duration, and more. While "clickstream data" traditionally centers on the sequence of visited pages, behavioral data can encompass everything from scroll depth to how long shoppers linger on specific product images. For example, we noticed high cart abandonment in this apparel project—particularly for specialty jackets and premium denim. By analyzing behavioral data, we identified two main problems: incomplete product information (especially around sizing) and a mobile checkout that required too many steps. In response, we recommended more straightforward product descriptions—adding fit guides, for example—and a streamlined checkout with guest options, which sharply reduced cart abandonment and increased conversions. Beyond this immediate fix, the brand continued using behavioral signals to discover additional opportunities. Late-night shoppers hesitated on product pages without buying, so we introduced subtle retargeting reminders and limited-time offers that boosted late-night conversions. As the site evolved, behavioral data became the ongoing pulse, enabling agile tweaks to layout, navigation, and even promotion timing.

> **BUSINESS TAKEAWAY** By analyzing real-time user interactions—where users click, pause, or drop off—businesses can quickly spot friction points and respond with targeted improvements. This leads to more intuitive experiences, reduced abandonment, and ultimately higher conversions.

1.4.2 Psychographic data

Psychographic data offers valuable insights into customer *motivations* and *preferences.* These insights reveal the underlying factors that influence how customers interact with your brand, ultimately shaping their purchasing decisions, brand perceptions, and online behaviors. It's about understanding what customers do and why they do it. Our apparel client offered sustainable items that weren't selling as well as expected despite strong quality and ethics. We aggregated website analytics, social media comments, and survey responses—some explicitly shared by customers—and discovered that price wasn't the only barrier. Many shoppers sought an authentic emotional link to the brand's mission. Armed with these insights, we guided the brand to focus on genuine storytelling: highlighting local artisans, explaining the sourcing process, and encouraging customers to share photos of these ethically produced garments. A/B testing revealed that heartfelt narratives about craftsmanship resonated far more than bland discount copy. Repeat purchases for eco-friendly lines rose, and a passionate community of brand advocates emerged.

> **BUSINESS TAKEAWAY** By tapping into customers' deeper motivations and attitudes, businesses can align messaging to what truly resonates—whether that's sustainability, craftsmanship, or a shared set of values. This emotional connection fuels loyalty, repeat purchases, and positive word-of-mouth.

1.4.3 Transactional data

When collected directly by a business, transactional data is one of the most valuable forms of first-party data you can have. It provides a clear view into your customers' spending habits—what they buy, how often, and through which channels, whether it's your website, mobile app, or physical store. And because you're pulling this data from your sources, such as your website, POS systems, or billing records, you can trust its accuracy. This data, when used responsibly and respectfully—always prioritizing customer privacy and adhering to data protection regulations—gives you a real edge in understanding your customers, creating personalized experiences, and making effective business decisions.

In examining the apparel brand's transactional data, we spotted a cohort of loyal in-store customers who regularly opened the brand's emails but rarely bought online. By cross-referencing these purchase records with email engagement, we prompted the client to offer limited-edition "Sunday Sale" products exclusively online. This clever mix of offline loyalty and online exclusivity increased digital revenue and average order values. A similar pattern appeared with another client, a SaaS company, where transactional data revealed that certain mid-tier subscribers never used a key product feature. Targeted emails and in-app prompts about that feature lowered churn and lifted overall lifetime value. Across these experiences, transactional data proved vital in flagging potential growth segments.

> **BUSINESS TAKEAWAY** By studying purchase patterns and channel usage, businesses can identify high-value segments, tailor promotions, or re-engage dormant customers. This data points to upsell, cross-sell, and retention tactics that drive measurable revenue growth.

1.4.4 Engagement data

Engagement data quantifies how your audience interacts with your brand across various touchpoints—email open rates, click-throughs, social media interactions, and more. It continuously reveals what's working and what isn't, helping you refine content strategies and improve user engagement. Communication responses, such as email opens and social media interactions, directly measure how well your messaging resonates with your audience. Event engagement, including webinar attendance and participation in other events, gives insight into how actively your audience is interacting beyond digital content. Customer stickiness is another critical engagement element, especially for industries like publishing, where loyalty is key. Metrics like session duration and recurring visits are invaluable for assessing how deeply customers engage with your content and whether they will return.

For our apparel client, email open rates were solid, but click-throughs dropped whenever they promoted niche product lines (like footwear). On social media, flash-sale posts triggered quick bursts of sales, but lengthier, story-based posts sparked deeper conversations. By dissecting these engagement patterns, we advised mixing succinct calls-to-action for immediate promotions with narrative-driven posts for brand building.

Similarly, in marketing automation platforms like Mailchimp or Klaviyo, engagement data reveals how effectively campaigns capture user attention. If a newly introduced email template leads to lower-than-expected open rates or click-throughs, these platforms help marketers analyze subject lines, content layout, and even where users click most (via click maps). By making adjustments based on these insights—changing design elements, refining messaging, or optimizing send times—SaaS teams can improve campaign performance and align content with customer interests. This real-life example highlights how thoroughly examining engagement data enables immediate optimizations and longer-term strategic refinements.

BUSINESS TAKEAWAY By monitoring email opens, social interactions, and other engagement signals, companies can refine their content strategies, identify what resonates best, and maintain continuous alignment with evolving customer interests. This strengthens overall brand loyalty and retention.

1.4.5 *Contextual data*

Contextual data helps personalize experiences by connecting with users at the *right moment.* In our apparel client's case, we found that many shoppers visited on Sunday afternoons from mobile devices. Analyzing contextual signals—like time of day, device usage, and typical site path through our first-party web analytics—revealed that Sunday browsers responded well to curated style guides and "Sunday Sale" messaging. Reinforced by accurate *master data* (stable customer attributes such as name or loyalty ID) to unify identities in a privacy-compliant manner, we developed weekend-specific promotions. We used real-time inventory to highlight trending items. The result was a notable boost in Sunday afternoon checkouts and higher satisfaction rates, as customers felt the brand anticipated their weekend shopping mindset.

BUSINESS TAKEAWAY By factoring in timing and device usage—particularly from your first-party analytics—brands can deliver the right offer or content at the right moment. Industry reports also highlight unified identity practices—commonly referred to as *master data*—that tie ephemeral contextual signals to a dependable "single source of truth." Combining who your customers are (master data) with how/when they engage (contextual data) ultimately drives more relevant, higher-performing campaigns.

1.4.6 Technographic data

Technographic data offers insights into your customers' technologies—such as devices, browsers, operating systems, and software preferences. It helps marketers tailor strategies based on how and where users engage digitally, directly influencing how they experience and interact with your brand. For example, our apparel client noticed a surprising number of high-spend shoppers on older tablets. By digging into site logs and speaking with users, we learned that images were slow to load and product-zoom features felt unintuitive on these devices. We optimized image-loading speeds, enlarged photo thumbnails, and clarified pinch-and-zoom prompts to fix this. Immediately, bounce rates among this tablet group dropped, and conversions rose. We also compared desktop versus mobile behaviors, discovering that desktop users wanted more detailed product specs, while mobile visitors preferred quick-swipe image galleries. These technographic insights helped the brand tailor each interface to the user's device context.

BUSINESS TAKEAWAY By understanding the devices, browsers, and software your audience uses, you can optimize site performance and user experience for each scenario—leading to smoother customer journeys, higher satisfaction, and stronger brand loyalty.

1.4.7 Beyond these six faces of first-party data

As shown in table 1.3, these six faces of first-party data—behavioral, psychographic, transactional, engagement, contextual, and technographic—form a powerful foundation for understanding how your audience behaves, what motivates them, and how best to engage them.

Table 1.3 Core dimensions and strategic benefits of first-party data

Faces	What it captures	Core benefits
Behavioral	Clicks, scrolls, session duration, onsite pathways	Reveals user actions to pinpoint friction and improve experiences
Psychographic	Attitudes, values, lifestyle preferences	Reveals emotional motivations to tailor messaging and deepen connections
Transactional	Purchase history, frequency, payment methods	Enables revenue strategies like upselling, cross-selling, and CLTV growth
Engagement	Email opens, social interactions, recurring visits	Indicates interest and guides content strategies to strengthen loyalty

Table 1.3 Core dimensions and strategic benefits of first-party data (*continued*)

Faces	What it captures	Core benefits
Contextual	Timing, location, real-time environment	Enables real-time personalization aligned to user context
Technographic	Devices, browsers, OS, software preferences	Allows optimization of experiences across platforms and devices

Although it's not depicted in the table, supplementary data further enriches this core framework by adding additional layers of insight. For instance, customer service interactions (from support tickets to feedback surveys) can spotlight recurring problems and areas for service improvement. Attitudinal data—gathered through surveys, reviews, and testimonials—captures customers' deeper preferences and motivations, while demographic data (such as age, gender, and location) allows for more refined personalization. On top of that, geolocation data enables you to tailor messaging and offers based on where users are located, and behavioral biometrics (like typing speed or mouse movements) enhance security and personalization by analyzing subtle user behaviors.

Combining these supplementary insights with the six faces of first-party data gives businesses a more holistic perspective on customer needs, enabling them to tailor their approach and strengthen relationships over time. From an architectural perspective, emerging patterns like Data Mesh and services such as AWS Lake Formation can also play a role in unifying diverse data sources, particularly as your organization's data requirements scale. While we won't cover those in this book, we will introduce an evolving data architecture called the *data lakehouse* in this chapter and then expand on why it can be a foundation for future-proof marketing data ecosystems in chapter 5.

Now imagine the possibilities for your brand. How can your team use these different faces of first-party data and additional sources to create a more personalized and engaging experience for your customers?

1.5 Challenges of first-party data

As you've seen, first-party data stands at the core of modern marketing—it's direct, reliable, and packed with potential. However, using it effectively is not without hurdles. The challenges lie not in the data itself but in the complexities of managing it in a rapidly evolving and highly regulated landscape. For marketing leaders, navigating these obstacles is less about avoiding pitfalls and more about developing a strategic approach that turns these challenges into opportunities for growth and innovation. This book is designed to guide you through the foundational components of the first-party data strategy. From data collection and storage to governance, analysis, and activation, we'll break down each step, highlighting common pitfalls and offering practical solutions. By clearly understanding how each piece fits within the broader first-party data stack, you'll be equipped to navigate challenges confidently and unlock their full potential for your organization.

1.5.1 Unifying diverse data streams

Through our work with companies across various sectors, we've consistently observed a common challenge: data is often fragmented, scattered across different systems, and rarely in sync—ranging from customer relationship management (CRM) tools to web analytics platforms, social media channels, and beyond. This complexity is compounded in larger organizations, where data infrastructure often spans a variety of cloud providers like AWS, Google Cloud, Azure, Snowflake, and Databricks. Marketing teams are constantly juggling a complex web of systems and data sources, from CRM and analytics platforms to social media channels and beyond. And it's not just the number of sources; it's the diversity of data they hold: structured customer data, transactional records, social media interactions, images, videos, and more. This makes gaining a clear, unified view of the customer incredibly difficult.

We recently partnered with a media company that was struggling with this problem. Their primary operations were based on Google Cloud, but their mobile app attribution data was siloed in an AWS S3 bucket managed by their vendor. This dispersion created a major obstacle. They needed a unified view of user engagement across platforms to make informed decisions, but their data was telling two different stories. Back in 2021, we addressed this by building automated data pipelines to move their mobile app data from that AWS S3 bucket into their Google Cloud environment—all with a "privacy by design" approach, which included end-to-end encryption, secure access controls, and adherence to breach-response protocols to protect customer information. While this approach worked at the time, the data landscape has evolved significantly. Today, all major cloud providers offer cross-platform query capabilities, reducing the need for manual data movement. But even with these advancements, achieving true data integration remains challenging, especially for organizations with diverse and complex datasets.

Meanwhile, remember the apparel brand we mentioned earlier in the chapter? They already saw strong sales in some categories, but they struggled mightily with data fragmentation. Their in-store POS system lived on one platform, their e-commerce data on another, and loyalty purchases were captured separately in the CRM. Each channel provided only a fragment of a customer's purchase history. Once the marketing team attempted to create a "high-value buyer" segment for a special product launch, they realized several customers were either double-counted or overlooked entirely.

Unifying those siloed data streams into a single first-party data foundation was the turning point—only then could the company accurately pinpoint top spenders and avoid sending them repetitive or irrelevant messages. This is where a new approach—the data lakehouse model—is gaining traction. By blending the capabilities of data lakes and data warehouses, the data lakehouse offers a unified ecosystem that seamlessly integrates structured and unstructured data. It represents a logical evolution from traditional data lakes, emphasizing a hybrid approach that combines the strengths of both systems. The data lakehouse is emerging as a comprehensive and flexible solution designed to meet the demands of today's increasingly complex data environment. We'll explore the data lakehouse architecture further in the next chapter, examining why it could be the foundation for future-proof marketing data ecosystems.

But as you reflect on your own organization's data fragmentation, take a moment to think about your organization's data dynamics. Are you managing to connect the dots between integration and real-time insights, or is your current setup leaving gaps? Is your data architecture truly a catalyst for informed decisions, or is it quietly holding your team back? Maybe it's time to rethink your approach. Could the data lakehouse be the answer, aligning your data strategy with the ambitious goals you've set for your marketing?

1.5.2 Privacy-centric approach

We need to talk about privacy. We know, we know—it's not exactly the most thrilling topic. But hear us out, because this might just change how you think about your entire data strategy. Marketing runs on data. It fuels our insights, drives decisions, and connects us to customers. But as we get smarter with data, there's a growing tension. Consumer trust feels more fragile than ever. It's no longer just about gaining insights or personalizing every touchpoint. Headlines about data breaches and misused information are eroding the trust we're trying to build. And if you're thinking, "We've got consent forms, so we're covered," think again. Apple's App Tracking Transparency proved consumers value privacy enough to disrupt entire industries. Suddenly, granular targeting wasn't a given—it was a privilege earned through transparent, trustworthy practices.

Beyond simple cookie-consent banners or opt-in/out boxes, privacy regulations now require clear explanations of how each customer's data will be used and granular controls that let them consent to specific purposes—analytics, personalization, or marketing emails. This shift raises the bar for marketers who must illustrate what data they collect and why and how it's deployed. Regulations like GDPR's "right to be forgotten" also enable users to request permanent deletion of their data—no small task if it's scattered across multiple systems. A privacy-centric strategy addresses these complexities head-on, ensuring consent and genuine respect for users' specific purposes, preferences, and right to erase their information. After all, trust and data stewardship go hand in hand. Privacy laws like GDPR, CCPA, and others are constantly evolving, with rules that vary not only across countries but also state by state in the United States. Rather than overwhelming you with a regulation-by-regulation breakdown, we'll highlight how these laws are reshaping the marketing landscape and influencing your strategy. Our focus is on integrating privacy into every stage of your data journey—from collection through activation—so compliance becomes a strategic advantage rather than just another box to tick. After all, we love data—it's the heartbeat of what we do. But when personalization becomes invasive, it erodes trust. No one wants to feel bombarded with hyper-targeted ads after a single glance at a product—that's how you lose customers and credibility.

To move beyond a surface-level approach, we'll dedicate an entire chapter to building a privacy-first framework that involves more than just the marketing team. We'll examine the role of consent management platforms (CMPs) and show why "privacy by design" must guide every step—from data sourcing and analytics to close collaboration among legal, IT, and marketing departments, including the use of fine-grained access controls that limit data to only those who genuinely need it. This collaborative approach ensures privacy isn't an afterthought but a core principle for building trust. You'll be challenged to rethink how you handle first-party data: Are you as transparent as you should be? Do you give customers genuine control over their information? Are you prepared to exchange some data granularity for enduring trust? While these questions aren't easy, confronting them is critical in a privacy-conscious world. By embracing a privacy-first approach, you'll adapt to a changing regulatory environment while paving the way for meaningful interactions, genuine connections, and sustainable growth, making trust the cornerstone of your strategy and building loyalty that stands the test of time.

1.6 Opportunities of first-party data

Many companies we interact with recognize the importance of effectively using their data. However, a common obstacle is the belief that data must be perfect before it can be used, leading to "analysis paralysis," where progress stalls for months. Perfect data is a myth, especially in the digital age, where customer interactions generate vast data streams. We emphasize adopting a first-party data strategy without waiting for perfection. Rather than obsessing over flawless data, companies should identify key use cases that drive value with the available resources.

Instead of becoming involved in endless debates about data quality or perfect customer 360 views, businesses should objectively assess their current data warehouse and data lake. This approach helps to establish a clear understanding of what data exists today and where actionable business growth opportunities lie. While pursuing long-term goals such as building a robust customer data platform (CDP) is essential, immediate value can still be extracted from the data at hand. For instance, companies like Google have built their success partly on efficiently using data. While not every organization can replicate their approach, understanding the principles behind their data strategy can provide valuable insights applicable to your business.

At the same time, it's crucial to validate the actual effect of any first-party data initiative. Incrementality testing—whether through A/B testing, holdout groups, or other controlled experiments—helps isolate external factors like seasonality or market shifts, ensuring that improvements aren't automatically attributed to first-party data. By measuring lift or incremental revenue, you can confidently connect performance gains to your data strategy rather than defaulting to assumptions. Likewise, defining and tracking concrete key performance indicators (KPIs)—such as conversion rates, churn reduction, repeat-purchase frequency, and cost per acquisition—help tie first-party data usage to actual business results. This combination of rigorous testing and clear metrics ensures you're driving sustainable value even if your data isn't yet "perfect."

1.6.1 Acquisition, cross-sell and upsell, retention and churn winback

First-party data plays a vital role at every stage of the customer journey, from acquiring new customers to retaining existing ones. It provides deep insights into customer preferences and behaviors, allowing businesses to tailor their strategies for maximum effectiveness:

- *Acquisition*—First-party data allows for more precise audience targeting, feeding customer insights directly into your campaign strategies. By building data-driven audience models with data accuracy and continuous refinement, you can improve return on ad spend (ROAS), reduce acquisition costs, and focus on high-intent audiences most likely to convert.
- *Cross-sell and upsell*—First-party data offers actionable insights into customer behavior and engagement, identifying opportunities for targeted cross-sell and upsell strategies. By using these insights, brands can create personalized recommendations, suggest relevant upgrades, and offer bundles that align with customer needs. This data-driven approach helps optimize conversion rates and boost customer lifetime value, all powered by the precise insights unique to first-party data.
- *Retention*—Retention is where first-party data can truly transform your customer strategy. By monitoring engagement signals like product usage and interaction frequency and using predictive models, you can spot churn risks early and deploy personalized interventions to re-engage customers before they disengage. This proactive approach helps keep customers on board and builds loyalty, driving sustained revenue growth and increasing customer lifetime value over time. Moreover, by tracking key metrics such as churn-rate reduction, engagement uplift, and incremental revenue, you can measure the effectiveness of these personalized interventions. This also helps customers fully adopt your product or platform, ultimately building loyalty, driving sustained revenue growth, and increasing customer lifetime value over time.
- *Churn winback*—First-party data transforms churn into an opportunity by identifying various friction points that lead to customer disengagement, whether complicated checkouts, insufficient personalization, poor customer service, or other problems. Businesses can improve retention rates and boost customer lifetime value by tackling these challenges. These insights also shape their strategies in product development, customer service, and brand messaging, creating a more customer-centric approach.

To better visualize these four stages—acquisition, cross-sell/upsell, retention, and churn winback—the funnel diagram in figure 1.4 highlights how first-party data powers each layer of the customer journey. At the top, you'll see *acquisition* efforts focusing on high-intent audiences, followed by *cross-sell/ upsell* tactics for increasing average order value among existing customers. Further down, *retention* strategies use engagement signals to keep customers loyal, while at the funnel's bottom, *churn winback* campaigns re-engage lapsed users. Throughout each stage, we've noted key KPIs—like ROAS, incremental revenue, and churn-rate reduction—that reflect how first-party data informs more precise targeting and delivers measurable returns on your marketing investments. As shown in figure 1.4, this funnel view makes it clear how first-party data supports every phase: from broad acquisition efforts at the top to narrower, highly focused winback campaigns at the bottom.

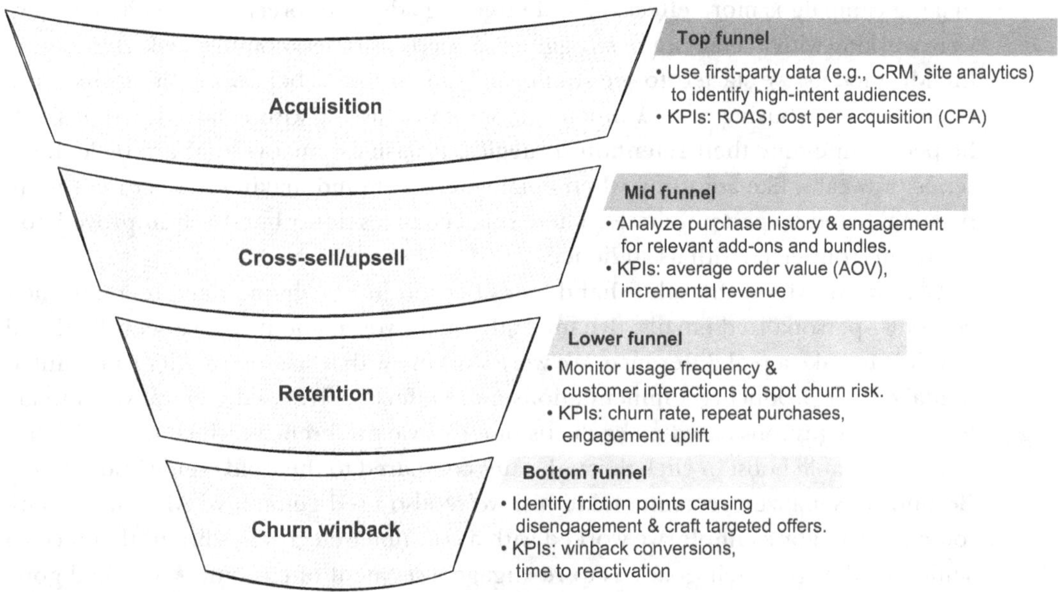

Figure 1.4 Funnel stages of first-party data-driven marketing

As you can see, first-party data transforms the entire customer journey—from attracting new customers to nurturing long-term relationships. It provides essential insights into what your customers want and how they behave, enabling you to craft strategies that genuinely resonate. Yet, as your data expands, so does the need for a robust system that effectively manages and uses it. A solid technological foundation is crucial for maximizing these benefits and getting the most out of your data.

1.6.2 Generative AI and machine learning

We're at an exciting juncture in marketing where two powerful subfields of artificial intelligence—machine learning (ML) and generative AI (GenAI)—are transforming how we interact with customers, craft campaigns, and deliver personalized experiences. Although both arise from the same overarching field, ML and generative AI each offer unique advantages for data-driven marketing strategies. These technologies are no longer futuristic concepts; they're becoming everyday tools changing how we work as marketers.

Machine learning has long been a foundational tool, especially when it comes to making predictions based on the data we already have. Its real strength is in spotting patterns that would take us humans forever to find. This helps us anticipate things like which customers might be about to leave, which ones are likely to spend the most over their lifetime, or even what someone's likely to buy next. This predictive power has been behind a lot of what marketers have been doing for a while now: segmenting audiences, making campaigns more effective, and targeting ads more precisely. A while back, we were working with a retail brand struggling to keep customers coming back. By integrating ML models, we started to see subtle shifts in customer behavior—things like how often they were buying or how much they were interacting with emails. These insights helped us fine-tune their retention strategies. It wasn't some overnight miracle, but a series of tweaks, like adjusting when emails were sent and making subject lines more personal based on past purchases. These small changes slowly but surely improved how the brand connected with its audience.

Generative AI, on the other hand, goes beyond just analyzing data; it creates new content—personalized emails, dynamic ad visuals, you name it. We've seen firsthand how it can make a real difference. We were working with a fashion retailer who wanted to make their product recommendations more effective. We used generative AI to tailor email suggestions based on each customer's style preferences, which worked! They saw a noticeable boost in click-through rates compared to their old, generic approach. Beyond personalized recommendations, we've also used generative AI to tackle customer churn. For example, we worked with a consumer electronics brand that faced a similar challenge. Their goal was to re-engage a segment of customers who had gone quiet—a familiar hurdle for many businesses. Our machine learning model, trained on purchase history and website activity, helped pinpoint a group that hadn't purchased in over 18 months. We knew that generic email blasts rarely resonated with this audience, so we turned to generative AI for a more personalized approach. The AI crafted unique emails for each customer, showcasing products related to their past purchases and offering a limited-time discount, a tactic we'd found effective in previous campaigns. This strategy, powered by insights derived from their own customer data, proved much more successful than our past attempts to re-engage lapsed customers. These experiences have shown us the potential of AI to create genuinely personalized experiences at scale, but it all starts with your first-party data.

As we continue building a data-centric foundation, we also anticipate expanding our marketing tech stack to include more advanced analytics and, eventually, AI/ML capabilities. While we'll devote chapter 9 to how generative AI and machine learning can accelerate everything from personalized content to churn prediction, it's worth noting here that our progress with first-party data sets the stage for those AI-driven insights. After all, machine learning models only become truly powerful when they're trained on consistent, privacy-compliant datasets that accurately reflect actual customer behavior.

By unifying our data, respecting regulatory frameworks, and planning early for AI and automation, we're ensuring our marketing engine is ready for the next wave of innovation and the possibilities it brings. In chapter 9, we'll explore how generative AI and ML transform the marketing landscape and how you can use their power. We'll explore how these technologies can enhance what traditional marketers do best, offering new tools without losing the personal touch. You'll learn practical strategies for integrating AI into your workflows, balancing automation with authenticity to build stronger, more meaningful customer connections.

Now that you better understand how first-party data works, let's dive into marketing with a privacy-centric approach.

Summary

- First-party data provides accurate insights into customer behaviors directly from brand interactions.
- Stricter privacy laws and the decline of third-party cookies are pushing marketers to prioritize first-party data.
- Managing first-party data involves challenges like data quality, tech complexity, and privacy regulations.
- The data lakehouse combines scalability and management features to handle diverse data efficiently.
- A privacy-centric approach ensures compliance and builds customer trust through transparency and consent.
- The loss of third-party cookies reduces targeting accuracy, requiring new marketing strategies.
- First-party data enhances marketing across the customer journey, from acquisition to retention.
- Generative AI and machine learning personalize marketing by combining data insights with creative automation.
- Adopting a growth mindset involves using available first-party data for sustainable business growth.

2 Privacy-centric marketing

This chapter covers

- Marketing with transparency and consent: a privacy-first approach
- The shifting data privacy landscape and its effect on marketers
- Ethical considerations and practical strategies for responsible data usage
- The role of evolving technologies in balancing personalization and privacy

Trust is the foundation of any successful relationship, including the relationship between a brand and its customers.

—Jim Lecinski, Clinical Professor of Marketing at Northwestern University's Kellogg School of Management

In our conversations with marketers, we consistently hear the same challenge: "How can we personalize the customer experience and drive growth while respecting consumer privacy?" It's a question that's become more urgent as consumers demand more control over their data and regulations—the General Data Protection Regulation (GDPR) in the EU, the California Consumer Privacy Act (CCPA) in the United States, and other emerging frameworks worldwide have raised the stakes. Many marketers feel caught between a rock and a hard place. They know they need to prioritize privacy, but they're under pressure to deliver results, worrying that stricter privacy practices will limit personalization and affect their bottom line.

This chapter addresses those concerns directly, showing that privacy isn't a barrier to growth but a catalyst for it—particularly for businesses already prioritizing privacy and first-party data collection. Compliance can transform into a competitive advantage for these organizations, enabling them to thrive while competitors struggle to keep pace. As global privacy regulations evolve, consumer expectations around data protection have shifted significantly. Privacy-centric marketing ensures compliance and equips businesses to stay ahead in a rapidly changing data landscape. Rather than treating consumer data as a short-term commodity, privacy-centric marketing encourages us to view it as a valuable asset. When handled carefully, responsibly sourced first-party data leads to higher-quality insights, more effective marketing campaigns, and sustainable growth.

By embedding privacy into every stage of the data flow—from collection to activation (where insights are turned into real-world marketing actions, such as personalized messaging)—you reduce risk, improve data quality, and empower consumers. It forms the foundation for more ethical and effective marketing practices.

This chapter provides a strategic framework to help you integrate privacy into your marketing architecture. We'll examine how privacy-centric marketing applies to data sourcing, management, analysis, and activation and discuss how team collaboration can support these efforts. By focusing on responsible first-party data use, this chapter will guide you in maintaining compliance and building trust with customers for long-term growth.

2.1 Understanding data privacy today

We've all been following the ongoing saga surrounding the removal of third-party cookies, with many of us expecting their complete end in Chrome. Google intended to begin deprecating third-party cookies in 2024. However, in July 2024, Google announced a further delay. The current plan is to allow users more informed control over third-party cookies, with a gradual phase-out, but a specific timeline beyond that is still subject to change. These shifting timelines may seem confusing, but they reflect both the technological complexities of replacing cookies and the need to balance business interests with user privacy.

Despite the delays, Google's Privacy Sandbox initiative still aims to replace traditional third-party cookies with more privacy-focused technologies, such as Topics and FLEDGE, which use aggregated or on-device data rather than tracking individuals. Meanwhile, Apple set the stage for privacy-forward browser design earlier with Intelligent Tracking Prevention (ITP) in Safari, illustrating a broader industry push toward more user-centric data policies.

Yet the cookie debate is only one facet of today's heightened privacy landscape. Consumers still demand transparency and control, and they hold brands accountable for how well they protect data once it's collected. This goes hand in hand with security measures—from encryption (at rest and in transit) to the prompt patching of vulnerabilities and strict access controls. The 2023 breaches at 23andMe and T-Mobile, affecting tens of millions of users, highlight how data exposures can spark regulatory scrutiny. In 2024, alleged large-scale attacks on companies like AT&T, Ticketmaster, and Dell also underscored that inadequate data protection puts brands at severe risk of reputational and financial fallout.

Privacy regulations such as GDPR and CCPA further cement the move toward "data empowerment." Under GDPR, organizations handling EU residents' data must follow strict usage rules, while CCPA grants California residents significant rights, like knowing what personal data is collected and being able to opt out of its sale. These regulatory frameworks reinforce the idea that data privacy is not optional or temporary; it's a core responsibility of modern organizations.

In this environment, consumers have become more selective about the platforms they trust, insisting on transparency and choice. While Google's updated timeline for third-party cookie deprecation might lessen the immediate urgency for new targeting solutions, it isn't a green light to revert to opaque practices. Ethical, first-party data collection remains critical for building trust and delivering the personalization users expect. By collecting only the data you need, protecting it diligently, and respecting user preferences, you stay on the right side of regulations and maintain a solid foundation for effective, privacy-centric marketing.

This signals a unique opportunity to reshape digital marketing into a more sustainable, privacy-first ecosystem rooted in trust, responsible data practices, and long-term relationships. In the next section, we'll explore the foundational principles of user privacy and learn how they support a genuinely privacy-centric marketing strategy.

2.2 Foundations of user privacy

Now that we've established the importance of a privacy-centric approach, let's turn those high-level concepts into actionable steps. The core principles of user privacy are at the heart of this effort, visually represented in figure 2.1. These principles aren't just abstract ideals—they serve as your compass, guiding you through shifting customer expectations, evolving technologies, and new legal requirements.

In figure 2.1, each principle connects to a "privacy core," emphasizing how a culture of privacy underpins every aspect of data handling. You'll notice two-way arrows, illustrating that these principles influence—and are influenced by—one another:

- *Accountability*—This principle emphasizes that responsibility for data practices isn't confined to a single department; it spans leadership, marketing, IT, and beyond. Each team should clearly understand and take ownership of how they collect, store, and use data within their specific roles. Ask yourself: Can your teams confidently explain how their systems work and what data supports them? For

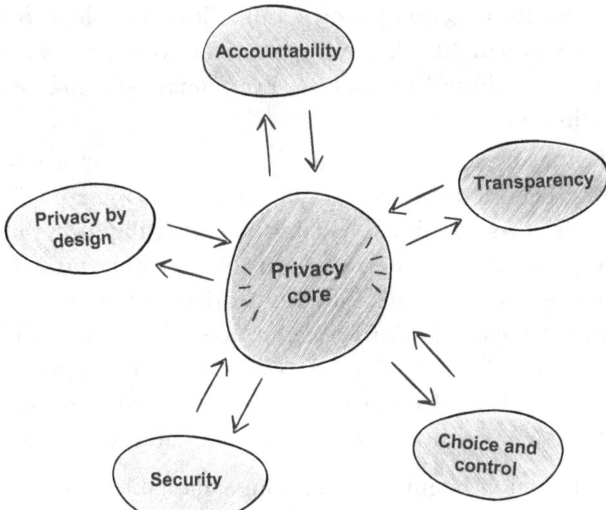

Figure 2.1 Core elements of user privacy

instance, if AI powers personalized offers, can your marketing or product teams explain which data fuels those algorithms? Establishing clear internal documentation and thorough cross-departmental training reinforces collective accountability, prevents compliance missteps, and protects your brand.

- *Transparency*—Transparency is about ensuring individuals understand exactly how and why their data is used, going beyond simply ticking legal boxes. Rather than burying explanations in dense legalese, offer tiered details: start with a concise summary, like "We use your purchase history to recommend products," and provide more in-depth information for those who want it. This proactive clarity fosters trust and meets both ethical and legal expectations, and it demonstrates your company's commitment to responsible data practices.
- *Choice and control*—Customers want the power to manage their data and preferences, and it's your job to enable that control. This principle is fundamentally user-centered, meaning it places the individual at the heart of data interactions. Individuals decide which data to share, and you must provide straightforward, easily accessible mechanisms to opt in or out. For instance, many websites now display cookie-consent banners offering "Accept all," "Essential only," or "Reject all" options. Respecting user decisions doesn't just build trust—it strengthens loyalty and long-term relationships.
- *Security*—Security forms the bedrock of all these efforts. A single breach can destroy years of credibility, so protecting user data through encryption, access controls, ongoing audits, and a clear incident response plan is critical. Security is an organizational priority, emphasizing that data protection is not just a technical problem but a core business imperative. Consider the 2017 Equifax breach,

which exposed sensitive information for over 140 million people, eroding public confidence virtually overnight. This example underscores how swiftly a weak security posture can derail brand reputation. Every team—IT, marketing, and beyond—must remain vigilant.

- *Privacy by design*—Privacy by design takes these principles a step further, embedding them into every stage of product and campaign development. This proactive approach requires cross-functional collaboration, highlighting that privacy is not solely the responsibility of one team but needs input and action from various parts of the organization. This mindset is driven by product, engineering, leadership, and legal teams working together to ensure privacy isn't just an afterthought. Before collecting any data, ask "Do we really need this? Could we achieve our goals with less data? How can we reduce risks?" These questions spark collaboration and lead to more thoughtful, privacy-conscious solutions.

Putting these principles into action begins with a strong, adaptable privacy program. Clearly define the roles and responsibilities, set measurable goals, and align privacy efforts with your business objectives. Compliance with regulations like GDPR and CCPA is only the starting point—it provides the foundation for building trust and differentiating your brand.

Most importantly, privacy isn't a solo effort. It's a shared responsibility across IT, security, HR, legal, and marketing teams. Appointing "privacy champions" in each team ensures privacy becomes part of the company's DNA. This collaborative approach transforms regulatory requirements into strategic opportunities, empowering you to build trust, stand out from competitors, and achieve sustainable growth.

2.2.1 Transparency and consent in first-party data

Managing first-party data responsibly requires adhering to the principles of transparency and consent, which are essential for cultivating trust and loyalty in an era when customers are increasingly aware of how their data is used. Transparency means openly communicating what data is collected, how it is used, and why—giving customers a clear understanding of your data practices. Consent empowers customers to decide how their data is used, shifting control to them in a meaningful way. These principles go beyond regulatory requirements; they are central to responsibly managing first-party data while building deeper customer connections.

Transparency in first-party data practices should simplify complex processes into clear, actionable customer insights. This includes providing data access logs to show when and why data was accessed, offering real-time dashboards where customers can view the data collected and its effect (e.g., personalized recommendations), and simplifying privacy settings with intuitive toggles for options like location-based services or personalized offers. These practices succeed when customers feel informed and in control without being overwhelmed.

Consent is not a one-time checkbox but an ongoing process that evolves as customers interact with your brand. Dynamic preference centers allow customers to update their data-sharing preferences anytime, such as enabling or disabling specific types of data collection. Tiered consent options—where the company gives users the choice between minimal data use strictly for essential services and an additional, optional level of data sharing for enhanced personalization—provide flexibility while maintaining trust. Additionally, analyzing opt-out rates can help refine communication strategies, as high rates may signal irrelevant messaging or an overwhelming user experience.

Technology plays a vital role in managing first-party data transparently and responsibly. Tools like customer data platforms (CDPs) centralize first-party data, while privacy-enhancing technologies (PETs) protect sensitive data. However, tools alone aren't enough; they must be paired with practices that prioritize the customer experience, such as intuitive interfaces and clear communication. Success in transparency and consent isn't just about tracking opt-ins; it's about observing how customers engage with your tools over time. Increased engagement with preference centers, reduced opt-out rates, and positive feedback on data practices are key indicators of trust and satisfaction.

By embedding actionable transparency and consent practices into every interaction, brands can responsibly manage first-party data while building long-term customer loyalty. Regularly reviewing and adapting these mechanisms shows customers that their preferences are valued, creating lasting trust. Transparency and consent are more than compliance—they are essential for building a brand that customers trust and want to engage with in today's data-driven world.

2.2.2 The value and ethics of first-party data collection

Building on the principles of transparency and consent, ethical data practices are crucial for responsibly managing first-party data. For marketing leaders, this means embedding transparency and accountability into every interaction, ensuring data collection is purposeful, limited, and aligned with customer expectations and legal requirements. Ethical data use goes beyond merely following regulations—it aligns with legal transparency and accountability to build trust, strengthen customer relationships, and ensure long-term success in today's data-driven world. At the same time, it's important to remember that ethics alone can't substitute for full compliance; failing to meet legal obligations can undermine the very trust you're working to build.

One key principle is data minimization, which means collecting only the data necessary to achieve a specific purpose or business goal. For example, if the goal is to personalize recommendations, appropriate data might include purchase history, browsing behavior, or product preferences. Asking for unrelated details like marital status or income can erode customer trust and create unnecessary risk. The same principle applies across various marketing objectives. Table 2.1 provides examples of how organizations can align their data collection strategies with specific business goals while maintaining privacy-conscious practices.

Table 2.1 Aligning data collection with marketing goals

Goal	Appropriate data to collect
Personalizing recommendations	Purchase history, browsing activity, product preferences
Improving customer support	Contact details, past support tickets
Targeted marketing campaigns	Age range, location (city/state), product interests
Fraud prevention	IP address, transaction patterns, device information

Clear and effective consent mechanisms enhance trust by empowering customers to make informed choices. These are some examples of successful approaches:

- *Granular opt-ins*—A streaming service allows users to select specific categories of personalized recommendations (e.g., "movie genres" or "trending content") instead of a blanket opt-in.
- *Dynamic preference centers*—An e-commerce platform enables customers to adjust preferences for email promotions, text messages, or push notifications at any time.
- *Interactive privacy notices*—A social media app provides visual, interactive explanations of data use with a "learn more" button for further details.

Ethical data practices also involve integrating privacy-enhancing technologies (PETs) to balance personalization with customer privacy. These tools allow businesses to extract meaningful insights while protecting sensitive information. Common PETs include the following:

- *Anonymization*—Removing personal identifiers from datasets to protect individual privacy. One well-known technique is k-anonymity, which ensures each record is indistinguishable from at least $k - 1$ other records (for example, grouping users by a broader location category rather than specific addresses).
- *Pseudonymization*—Replacing identifiable information with pseudonyms to safeguard data while enabling analysis.
- *Differential privacy*—Adding statistical noise to aggregated datasets to prevent individual identification, as seen in tools like Google's TensorFlow Privacy.
- *Homomorphic encryption*—Allowing computations on encrypted data without exposing sensitive information, as is done in solutions like Microsoft SEAL.
- *On-device computation and federated learning*—Keeping raw data on user devices rather than sending it to a central server. Model training and computations happen locally, and only aggregated updates are shared. Tools like Google's TensorFlow Federated and PySyft are gaining popularity in privacy-preserving machine learning.

By choosing and implementing the right PETs for your use case, you can unlock valuable insights without compromising user trust. When combined with thoughtful data governance and user-centric controls, PETs make it possible to deliver personalized experiences while adhering to high privacy standards.

Effective use of first-party data also requires cross-functional collaboration. Privacy isn't solely the responsibility of legal teams—it demands cooperation between marketing, IT, security, and other departments. For example, marketing teams must align their strategies with IT to implement consent mechanisms effectively, while security teams ensure that collected data is stored and processed safely. Clear communication, shared accountability, and well-defined processes are vital for maintaining consistency and ensuring privacy at every touchpoint.

Finally, measuring the effectiveness of your ethical data strategy is critical. Beyond tracking opt-in rates, monitor how customers interact with privacy settings and analyze their feedback. For instance, are users frequently adjusting their preferences? Are high opt-out rates signaling irrelevant messaging or over-collection of data? Use these insights to refine your approach in real time, ensuring alignment with evolving customer expectations.

By embedding privacy and ethical data practices into your marketing architecture, you can foster trust, strengthen relationships, and position your brand for sustainable growth. Compliance alone isn't enough—lasting success requires a strategic focus on earning customer loyalty through responsible and transparent data use.

2.3 Privacy by layer: Integrating privacy throughout the marketing data journey

In this section, we'll explore the importance of integrating privacy throughout the *marketing data journey*, focusing on the key layers of the *marketing data architecture*. As data flows through the various stages of this architecture, it is crucial to implement privacy-centric practices at each layer to protect user privacy and maintain trust. To understand how privacy can be integrated into the marketing data journey, let's first look at the marketing data architecture, which outlines the flow of data within a marketing ecosystem and the various technologies involved.

As depicted in figure 2.2, the marketing data architecture comprises five key layers: the sourcing layer, the data foundation layer, the insights and intelligence layer, the engagement and activation layer, and the media distribution layer. This architecture manages data flow across a company's marketing ecosystem, enabling organizations to optimize their marketing efforts through the strategic use of data. As data moves through these layers, organizations must identify and address key areas where ethical data practices can be implemented to protect user trust while maximizing the value derived from the data. This involves applying privacy-enhancing technologies, data minimization techniques, and transparent user controls at each stage of the data journey.

In the following sections, we will explore each layer of the marketing data architecture in detail, examining each stage's privacy considerations. By understanding how to integrate privacy throughout the marketing data journey, organizations can build a

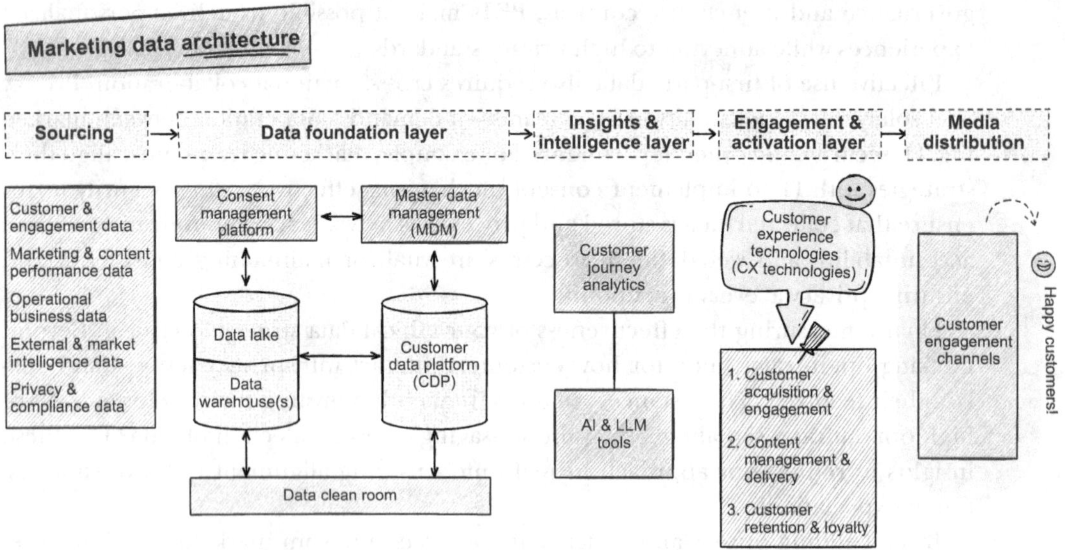

Figure 2.2 Marketing data architecture

strong foundation for ethical data management and cultivate trust with their customers in an increasingly privacy-conscious world.

2.3.1 Sourcing layer

The first phase of a privacy-centric marketing architecture focuses on *data sourcing*. As illustrated in figure 2.2, this is where businesses collect and consolidate information from internal and external sources. While some of this data includes first-party information, such as user interactions or transactional records, other data sources may come from agencies, external partners, or broader market research efforts. Figure 2.3 outlines how these data sources fall into five core categories: customer and engagement data, marketing and content performance data, operational business data, external and market intelligence data, and privacy and compliance data. Each category plays a unique role in shaping marketing decisions—whether by refining campaign strategies, improving personalization, or ensuring compliance with privacy laws.

CUSTOMER AND ENGAGEMENT DATA

Understanding customer behavior is at the heart of marketing. Customer and engagement data spans everything from demographics and purchase history to how customers interact with emails or social media channels. For clarity, we can classify these data points into distinct groups based on their source and purpose—helping marketers analyze, segment, and use them more effectively. Table 2.2 presents an overview of these customer and engagement data classifications, and one-sentence real-life use cases illustrate how each classification can drive targeted, relevant engagement.

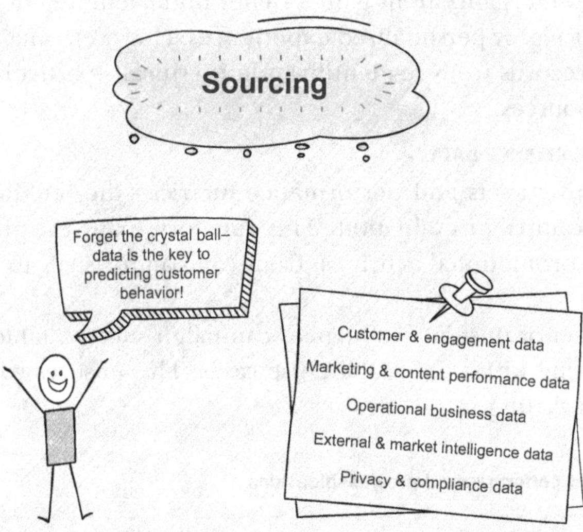

Figure 2.3 Sourcing layer: core data categories

Table 2.2 Customer and engagement data classifications

Data classification	Description	Real-life use case
Customer profile attributes	Geographic, demographic, and psychographic information	A fitness app tailors workout recommendations based on a user's location, age, and fitness goals.
Customer interaction data	Email metrics, social media comments, and customer support logs	A software company improves its FAQ section by analyzing recurring support requests and social media feedback.
Transactional data	Purchases, orders, and payment records. "Purchases" generally refer to completed transactions, while "orders" can include pending or partially fulfilled transactions.	An online retailer targets abandoned carts (orders not completed) with reminders, encouraging buyers to finalize purchases.
Customer feedback and experience data	Ratings, reviews, and survey responses	A hotel chain monitors satisfaction scores to optimize room amenities and improve the overall guest experience.
Loyalty and engagement program data	Membership details, reward points, and redemption history	A coffee shop chain sends personalized offers to loyal members who haven't redeemed points recently.
Intent signals	Site browsing patterns, wish-list additions, and behavior cues indicating intent	A fashion brand identifies users who are likely to buy new arrivals based on browsing history and wish list changes.

By analyzing this information, organizations gain a richer understanding of customer preferences and can deliver highly personalized experiences. However, obtaining consent and protecting these records from re-identification is critical—particularly when combined with other data sources.

MARKETING AND CONTENT PERFORMANCE DATA

Marketing thrives on creative assets and performance metrics—the building blocks of brand storytelling and campaign evaluation. This category spans everything that shapes and measures your promotional activities, from campaign visuals to audience engagement statistics.

To clarify how each subset of this data influences campaign success, table 2.3 provides data classifications along with brief real-life use cases. This ensures you see the data and how it's used in marketing.

Table 2.3 Marketing and content performance data classifications

Data classification	Description	Real-life use case
Creative assets	Images, videos, and text for campaigns or brand storytelling	A sportswear brand repurposes its video ads across social channels to maintain consistent creative assets while measuring engagement.
Marketing content	Website copy, banners, blog posts, and other promotional materials	A SaaS company tests different homepage headlines to see which version yields more sign-ups.
Product information	Descriptions, specs, and packaging data—often reflecting target audience preferences	An online marketplace adjusts product descriptions based on keyword trends to improve SEO and better match what customers search for.
Owned advertising campaign data	Performance metrics from brand-run campaigns (e.g., impressions, clicks, conversions)	A travel agency tracks ad conversions on its channels to understand which offers resonate best with frequent fliers.
Campaign performance metrics	Aggregated engagement statistics, ROI figures, ad spend versus results	A subscription box service compares each channel's ROI to refine budget allocation and drive more efficient ad spend.
Agency-provided marketing data	External agencies' specialized reports or creative performance insights	A retail brand reviews an agency's post-campaign report to identify new audience segments and expand future campaign targeting.

Although this data doesn't typically contain personally identifiable information (PII), it can indirectly reflect audience demographics or interests. For example, an ad campaign optimized for sustainability-conscious consumers indirectly segments users based on their values.

OPERATIONAL BUSINESS DATA

Operational data comes from the internal systems that keep a business running:

- Enterprise resource planning (ERP) data
- Order processing data
- Supply network data
- System log data
- Internal business performance data

Although it may seem less "marketing-focused," operational data often shapes customer fulfillment, experience optimization, and demand forecasting. For example, order processing data can help predict restocking needs and prevent inventory shortages, indirectly effecting marketing and the customer experience. Because these datasets may link to user sessions or transactional records, organizations must implement rigorous privacy and security measures at intake and throughout subsequent processing.

External and market intelligence data

Sourced externally, this data provides broader industry context and competitive insights, including the following:

- Third-party aggregated data
- Licensed datasets
- External partner data
- Market research data
- Competitive data
- External advertising market data (e.g., industry benchmarks, ad spend trends)

Organizations must vet providers' privacy policies, data handling practices, and security controls when using these external sources. Establishing strong contractual agreements and conducting ongoing monitoring are key strategies to reduce the risk of data misuse and non-compliance.

Privacy and compliance data

Some information requires extra care as businesses gather data from customer interactions, marketing campaigns, and external sources. Unlike other types of data, privacy and compliance data isn't just valuable—it dictates how organizations handle, store, and protect information from the start. These critical categories include

- *Personally identifiable information (PII) and non-PII*—PII can include identifiers like names, emails, geolocation data, and government-issued IDs (e.g., a driver's license or passport number), all of which may be subject to specific legal protections depending on the jurisdiction. Even so-called non-PII can become identifying if combined with other data. Businesses must be vigilant in handling both categories securely, recognizing that even anonymized information could be relinked to individuals if misused.
- *Consent management records*—Logs tracking opt-ins, opt-outs, and preference updates, ensuring companies respect user choices.

- *Data governance and compliance records*—Internal documentation showing adherence to legal frameworks like GDPR and CCPA, along with other data protection or residency requirements (such as Brazil's Lei Geral de Proteção de Dados [LGPD] and Canada's Personal Information Protection and Electronic Documents Act [PIPEDA]) and internal security policies. Because regulations vary across regions, it's crucial to maintain clear records demonstrating how your organization meets each applicable standard.

Privacy risks begin the moment data is collected—not just when it's stored. Mishandling information during sourcing can lead to regulatory fines, breaches, or eroded consumer trust. To avert these costly problems, it's critical to embed privacy practices from the outset. With data flowing in from first-party and external (or third-party) sources, each intake point must operate under a privacy-first approach. This starts with collecting only what's strictly necessary for specific business objectives, rather than gathering excessive or irrelevant information. For instance, an e-commerce brand might store only the minimal purchase data needed for processing and customer service, omitting broader demographic details that serve no immediate purpose.

Equally important is applying robust de-identification techniques—such as pseudonymization, differential privacy, or *k*-anonymity—to reduce the chances of re-identifying individuals when datasets are combined. End-to-end encryption adds another layer of defense, safeguarding information from the moment it's captured until it's archived. Meanwhile, clear and meaningful consent ensures users understand how their data will be used and that they have the option to opt out of non-essential practices. External data providers must also be thoroughly vetted through contractual agreements and regular security assessments to confirm responsible data handling and regulatory compliance. These steps do more than mitigate risk; they also build deeper trust with consumers who reward privacy-focused brands with loyalty and engagement.

Privacy isn't confined to IT or compliance departments—it's a shared responsibility. Marketing teams should openly communicate data usage policies, analysts must safeguard sensitive datasets before sharing or analysis, and technology teams must set up automated security controls to prevent misuse. Once data is sourced under these principles, it flows into the data foundation layer to be ingested, structured, and refined for further analysis and activation. Maintaining strong governance at each stage ensures the data remains accurate, secure, and compliant throughout its lifecycle.

NOTE Prioritize ethical data collection. This matters to marketers because customers are more likely to engage with brands that demonstrate responsible data practices, building trust, reducing privacy risks, and ensuring compliance from the start.

2.3.2 Data foundation layer

Once collected, data enters the system's central hub: the *data foundation layer*. Here, it undergoes a critical transformation to prepare it for analysis and use across various channels and platforms. This transformation involves gathering, cleaning, and standardizing the data, enabling effective data management, analysis, and strategic application. Figure 2.4 shows the essential components that form the backbone of the data foundation layer.

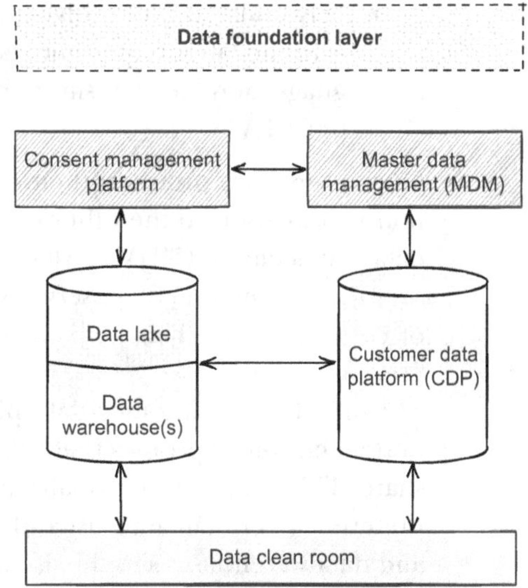

Figure 2.4 Data foundation layer overview

Let's examine each core component of the data foundation layer and see how they are interconnected. Each of these components is crucial in transforming data as it moves through the system. At the heart of the data foundation layer lies the consent management platform (CMP), a vital component for regulatory compliance and user empowerment. In addition to enabling individuals to grant or revoke consent for different data processing activities—thereby honoring their preferences—the CMP also maintains legally required documentation demonstrating how and when consent was obtained, updated, or withdrawn. This ongoing parallel work stream ensures the CMP remains compliant with evolving privacy regulations (e.g., GDPR, CCPA) by tracking consent versions, managing data retention policies, and enforcing legal requirements for data processing. Organizations can preserve transparency, fulfill regulatory obligations, and build lasting trust by uniting user-centric controls with legal safeguards.

To integrate a user-friendly CMP into your website or app, consider the following best practices:

- Granular control goes beyond simple "accept all" or "reject all" options and empowers users to choose specific data categories and purposes they consent to. For example, in an e-commerce context, users should be able to separately consent to using their data for personalized product recommendations, marketing emails, and third-party advertising.
- Transparency provides clear and concise information about data practices within the CMP. Explain how data is collected, used, and shared, and with whom. Use plain language and avoid legal jargon to ensure users can easily understand the implications of their choices.
- Integrate the CMP seamlessly into the user experience. Make it easily accessible, and allow users to manage their preferences anytime. For example, include a prominent "Privacy Preferences" link in the website footer or app settings menu.

- Stay updated with evolving privacy regulations, and ensure your CMP complies with the latest requirements. This may involve adapting consent categories, language, and mechanisms to meet the specific demands of regulations like GDPR or CCPA.

Once users have provided their consent preferences through the CMP, this information is passed on to the other components of the data foundation layer. The master data management (MDM) system, for example, will use the consent data to ensure that only the information that users have agreed to share is included in the "golden record" of customer data. This helps maintain data accuracy and integrity while respecting user preferences.

Similarly, the customer data platform (CDP) will use the consent data to create unified customer profiles that reflect the specific data points users have consented to share. This allows for personalized marketing experiences that align with users' stated preferences, enhancing trust and engagement. If used by the organization, data lakes and data warehouses should also adhere to user consent preferences captured by the CMP, ensuring that data storage and access align with user choices.

Finally, data clean rooms are secure environments that allow organizations to collaborate on data analysis while protecting individual privacy. These collaborations can occur internally—between teams such as marketing and analytics—or externally with partner companies, enabling insights without exposing individual-level data. For instance, advertisers and publishers can use clean rooms for audience matching, secure campaign measurement, and cross-platform attribution without directly sharing raw user data. Data clean rooms anonymize and aggregate information to ensure compliance with user preferences and regulatory requirements. While this section provides a high-level overview, we'll explore data clean rooms in more detail in chapter 8, including their applications for privacy-centric analytics and marketing strategies.

The building blocks of a privacy-focused data architecture we've just outlined are essential. Still, it's crucial to understand that organizations tailor these components to their unique needs and tech stacks, meaning that implementations will vary. Some companies may not employ every element described, and there's no universal, one-size-fits-all solution. However, respecting user consent is not optional, regardless of how a company builds its data systems. This foundational principle must be integral to all data-handling practices. The exact enforcement mechanisms may differ, but honoring user preferences should be a constant across all implementations. Protecting user privacy is not just about technical components but an organizational commitment to embedding respect for user choices into every aspect of data handling.

NOTE Regularly review and update your CMP to ensure it aligns with the latest privacy regulations and user expectations.

To make the concept more concrete, let's walk through an example of a user data journey to provide a conceptual understanding of how a CMP works in practice. Consider figure 2.5, which represents how a user interacts with a CMP on a website.

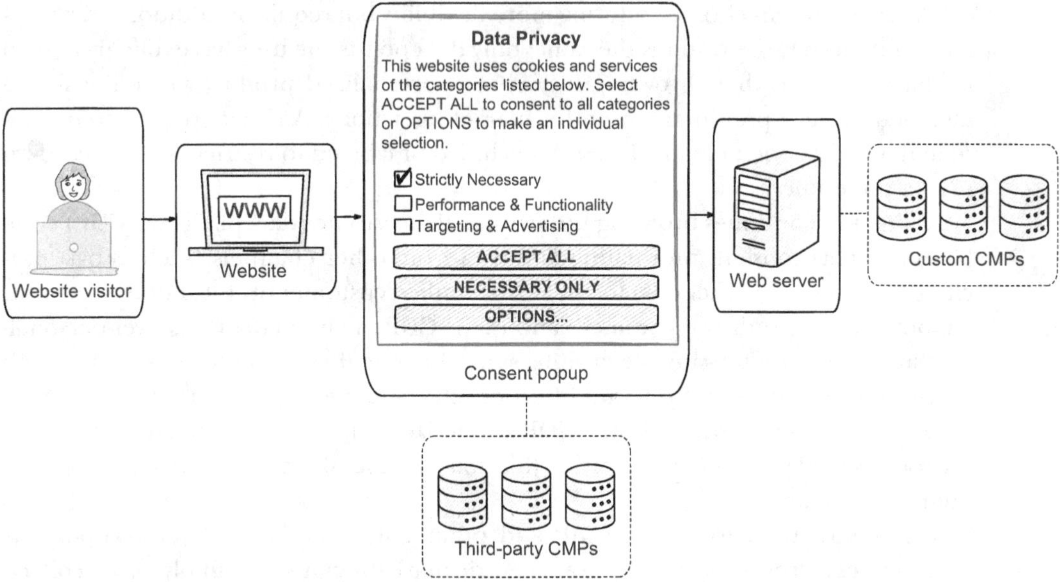

Figure 2.5 User data journey with CMP integration

The figure shows a website visitor browsing a website. This interaction typically triggers the website to present a *consent pop-up* managed by either a custom CMP or a third-party CMP. The pop-up provides clear and concise information about the brand's data practices, outlining the types of data collected—for example, browsing history for website personalization or an email address for marketing communications—and the intended uses of this data. Notably, the user is presented with granular options to consent to each use case, ensuring they maintain control over how their information is utilized. Once the user makes their choices, the CMP records them, often in a browser cookie. The website's code then reads this information from the cookie, and the web server uses it to ensure data handling aligns with the user's consent preferences. While the web server often plays a role in data handling, remember that implementations can vary, and sometimes the website's code alone will act on user consent choices.

Let's say the user consents to personalized product recommendations but opts out of receiving marketing emails. Upon clicking "save preferences," the CMP—whether a third-party platform (e.g., OneTrust or TrustArc) or a custom-built in-house solution—records these selections and communicates them to other components within the system. For example, the master data management (MDM) system, responsible for maintaining a single, accurate view of customer data, uses this information to update the user's "golden record"—the comprehensive profile within the system.

If you're using a third-party CMP, it might automatically connect to the MDM via standard APIs or pre-built integrations, streamlining how consent updates are transmitted. In contrast, a custom CMP might rely on bespoke data pipelines or direct database calls to sync consent choices, offering more flexibility but requiring additional development. Either way, the result is the same: only data points the user has explicitly agreed to share—such as their browsing history for personalized product suggestions—are included in their profile and used for marketing actions. Any data related to unconsented uses, like their email address, is excluded or labeled to restrict its use according to user preferences.

As the user continues browsing the website, the customer data platform (CDP) combines this new consent information and data from other channels (such as past purchases or support interactions) to update the unified customer profile. Because the user has opted in for product recommendations, the CDP can immediately deliver personalized suggestions on the site. Meanwhile, since the user also consented to specific email campaigns, they'll receive relevant offers or follow-up messages tied to their browsing interests. This demonstrates how a CDP synthesizes data from multiple sources under the user's stated preferences, ensuring that consent directly shapes every aspect of their online experience.

This interplay between the CMP and other data foundation layer components underscores a crucial aspect of privacy-centric marketing: it's not simply about collecting consent; it's about operationally embedding those choices into how data is processed, stored, and used throughout its entire lifecycle within the marketing ecosystem.

Later, the user might decide to change their preferences. For example, they may no longer want to receive marketing emails. They can revisit their privacy preferences—often found in the website footer or a logged-in user profile—and adjust their consent settings through the CMP. This change flows through the data foundation layer, ensuring the user's updated choices are reflected in how their data is handled. For instance, the CDP would immediately remove the user from relevant email marketing campaigns, respecting the updated preference.

This dynamic, user-centric approach lies at the heart of building a sustainable and ethical data strategy. It empowers individuals to control their information while enabling brands to deliver relevant and respectful experiences. By embedding privacy as a core operational principle within the data foundation layer, organizations lay the groundwork for lasting customer trust and a future where data-driven marketing and user privacy go hand in hand.

> **NOTE** Respect user consent and control. This matters to marketers because a well-designed CMP empowers users and helps you maintain compliance with privacy regulations. Demonstrating respect for user choices builds trust and loyalty.

2.3.3 Insights and intelligence layer

With data securely organized and governed in the data foundation layer, the next stage of the marketing data architecture is the *insights and intelligence layer*. As shown in figure 2.6, this layer transforms data into actionable insights through advanced analytics, customer journey analytics, and artificial intelligence (AI) or machine learning (ML) tools, enabling organizations to make informed decisions and refine their marketing strategies.

For example, large language models (LLMs) and ML algorithms can analyze vast amounts of structured and unstructured data, such as customer demographics, purchase history, website interactions, and external market trends, uncovering hidden patterns that might not be apparent to human analysts. This allows these tools to generate predictions and recommendations for various marketing use cases. Building on these capabilities, advanced analytics and AI/ML solutions enable organizations to apply insights effectively to enhance marketing precision. Examples include

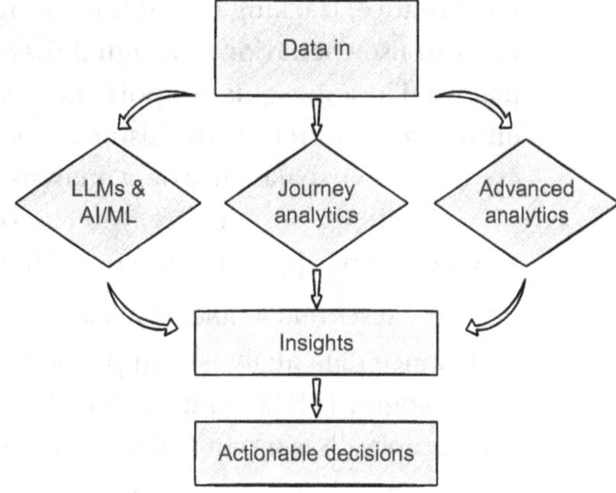

Figure 2.6 Insights and intelligence layer overview

- Predicting customer churn by analyzing historical behavior and engagement metrics
- Recommending products based on browsing and purchase patterns
- Optimizing campaign timing using real-time data to identify peak engagement windows

Complementing these AI/ML solutions, *customer journey analytics* provide a comprehensive view of customer interactions across touchpoints, helping organizations identify pain points and optimize conversion paths. By mapping customer journeys, brands can design seamless, personalized experiences that enhance satisfaction and loyalty.

In addition to customer insights, the insights and intelligence layer also measures and refines marketing performance, which is often driven by quantifiable indicators. Key metrics include

- *Campaign ROI*—Assessing the financial return of marketing initiatives
- *Customer lifetime value (CLTV)*—Evaluating the long-term value of customer relationships
- *Conversion rates*—Understanding how effectively campaigns drive desired actions
- *Engagement metrics*—Gauging user interactions, such as click-through rates and time on site
- *Churn rate*—Monitoring the percentage of customers who disengage with the brand

For instance, tracking churn rate alongside engagement metrics can help identify patterns in user behavior that signal dissatisfaction, allowing for targeted retention campaigns. These insights support the continuous improvement of marketing strategies, ensuring alignment with business goals and real-time feedback. While these insights are invaluable, balancing data analysis with privacy remains crucial.

There are several ways you can optimize the insights and intelligence layer for a privacy-centric approach, discussed in the following subsections.

PRIVACY-PRESERVING AI AND DATA ANALYSIS

To balance data analysis with privacy, organizations can implement privacy-enhancing technologies (PETs) that enable the secure and ethical use of AI/ML in marketing. These tools allow organizations to analyze data while protecting individual privacy:

- *Differential privacy*—Adds statistical noise to datasets, protecting individual identities while enabling trend analysis.
- *Federated learning*—Enables organizations to train AI models using decentralized data stored on user devices. Instead of sharing raw data with a central server, only the model updates are shared, ensuring sensitive information remains private while allowing for personalization.
- *Homomorphic encryption*—Allows computations to be performed directly on encrypted data without decrypting it first. Although full-scale analysis of encrypted data is not yet mainstream, current advancements allow specific operations, such as validation or indexing, paving the way for broader applications in privacy-sensitive industries.
- *Secure multiparty computation (MPC)*—Allows multiple parties to collaboratively analyze data without revealing their inputs, enabling secure cross-company collaborations.

For example, federated learning can train models on decentralized data, while differential privacy ensures aggregated insights remain anonymized, creating a layered approach to privacy protection. As PETs continue to evolve, they must be complemented by core privacy principles like data minimization and anonymization, which reduce risks by limiting the scope of data used for analysis.

DATA MINIMIZATION AND ANONYMIZATION

Even the most advanced analytics and AI tools should utilize only data essential for achieving specific business objectives—a fundamental principle known as *data minimization*. This practice lowers privacy risks and ensures alignment with global regulations like GDPR and CCPA. While "collect everything, just in case" may seem tempting, that approach can undermine trust and increase legal exposure. So how can marketers minimize risk while preserving analytical capabilities? Three key techniques—*anonymization*, *pseudonymization* (including *masking*), and *aggregation*—provide practical and effective solutions to balance privacy protection with insightful marketing analytics:

- *Anonymization* completely removes or irreversibly alters personally identifiable information (PII), making re-identification virtually impossible. For example, a retailer analyzing store visits might report aggregate data—such as total visitor counts or average dwell time per location—without including exact timestamps or precise geographic locations. While anonymization will help you avoid strict regulatory oversight, the trade-off can be a loss in granular insights.
- *Pseudonymization* (including *masking*) replaces or obscures direct identifiers, such as names, email addresses, or phone numbers, with artificial identifiers or partially masked fields (for example, credit card numbers shown as XXXX-XXXX-XXXX-1234). This method maintains many analytical possibilities; for example, marketers can still recognize behavioral patterns like "User1235 purchased three items last week" without directly revealing identities. However, because pseudonymized data can theoretically be relinked if original reference keys are available, it typically remains regulated under privacy laws.
- *Aggregation* groups individual records into summarized or generalized categories, greatly reducing the ability to isolate individual data points. For example, a health-focused brand evaluating fitness product sales could group customers into age brackets (such as 30–39 and 40–49) instead of storing exact birthdates. Aggregation provides valuable segment-level insights while safeguarding individual privacy.

NOTE Data minimization reduces regulatory risks under GDPR, CCPA, and similar laws, builds customer trust by demonstrating respect for privacy, clarifies analytics by eliminating unnecessary data clutter, and minimizes reputational and legal damage in the case of data breaches.

By employing these techniques consistently, marketers can ensure the insights and intelligence layer deliver robust analytics and personalized campaigns without sacrificing consumer privacy. Clearly communicating these privacy practices reinforces your brand's commitment to ethical data usage, cultivating long-term loyalty and trust.

TRANSPARENCY AND EXPLAINABILITY

Transparency is essential for maintaining trust in AI-driven marketing. Organizations should communicate how customer data is analyzed and what insights are derived. For example, an e-commerce platform might use *explainable AI* (XAI) techniques to show customers why specific products are recommended, based on factors like their browsing history or trending items in their location. XAI reinforces trust in AI systems by helping users understand how their data influences outcomes. Additionally, allowing customers to opt out of specific types of analysis ensures they remain in control of their data.

Maintaining transparency is a key element of trust, but it must be supported by robust data governance and security measures to protect sensitive data throughout its lifecycle.

DATA GOVERNANCE AND SECURITY

Establish strong data governance policies and procedures to govern data access, usage, and security within the insights and intelligence layer. Implement access controls to limit access to personal data within analytical tools and platforms. Use encryption to protect sensitive data at rest and in transit. And regularly audit access logs and monitor data usage to identify and prevent unauthorized access or misuse.

Additionally, consider investing only in analytical tools and platforms designed with privacy in mind, as many vendors now offer privacy-preserving analytics solutions that incorporate PETs and data governance features. Educate your data analysts and scientists on data privacy principles and best practices. Continuously monitor the data privacy landscape, and adapt your insights and intelligence layer technologies and practices to evolving regulations and user expectations.

To enhance our understanding of that layer, let's consider how a retail company, "RetailCo," can use the insights and intelligence layer to analyze customer journeys while respecting privacy:

- RetailCo collects customer data through various touchpoints, such as website interactions, in-store purchases, and customer service inquiries. The data is collected in accordance with the consent preferences managed by the CMP.
- Before analyzing the customer journey data, RetailCo applies data minimization techniques. They remove any unnecessary personal data and aggregate it to a level that allows for meaningful analysis without compromising individual privacy.
- RetailCo replaces personally identifiable information (PII) with pseudonyms, ensuring that the data cannot be directly linked to individual customers without additional information.
- The pseudonymized and minimized data is then loaded into a secure analysis environment, accessible only to authorized personnel. PETs like homomorphic encryption further protect the data during analysis.
- Using advanced analytics and ML techniques, RetailCo analyzes the customer journey data to identify common paths, pain points, and opportunities for improvement. The insights generated are aggregated and do not reveal individual customer journeys.
- Based on the analysis, RetailCo identifies areas where the customer experience can be enhanced. For example, they may discover that customers often abandon their online shopping carts due to a complicated checkout process. RetailCo can then prioritize streamlining the checkout process to improve conversions and customer satisfaction.
- RetailCo regularly reviews and updates its privacy practices in the insights and intelligence layer to ensure ongoing compliance with regulations and evolving customer expectations. They invest in staff training and stay informed about the

latest PETs to continuously improve their privacy-centric approach to customer journey analysis.

By applying PETs, data minimization, and secure analysis techniques, RetailCo derives valuable insights from customer journey data while respecting customer privacy.

The insights and intelligence layer enables organizations to turn data into actionable insights while respecting privacy. Businesses can refine marketing strategies and enhance customer experiences without compromising trust or regulatory compliance by implementing PETs, data minimization techniques, and robust governance practices.

NOTE Prioritize privacy-preserving AI. This matters to marketers because PETs, like differential privacy, can enable valuable insights without compromising individual user privacy. Explainable AI (XAI) allows you to be transparent about how you use AI, building customer confidence and reducing ethical concerns.

2.3.4 *Engagement and activation layer*

Now that the data is clean and all user privacy concerns have been addressed, we can move on to the *engagement and activation layer*. As illustrated in figure 2.7, this layer translates insights from the insights and intelligence layer into tangible, personalized experiences across various channels. Customer experience (CX) technologies, such as personalization engines, recommendation systems, and real-time interaction management platforms, are at the core of the engagement and activation layer. These technologies enable tailored messaging, content, and experiences that resonate with individual preferences and needs while respecting user privacy. To fully realize the potential of CX technologies, organizations must integrate these tools with privacy-centric strategies for customer acquisition and engagement.

When implementing CX technologies, organizations should emphasize privacy-preserving techniques. For example, recommendation systems can use collaborative or content-based filtering to deliver personalized suggestions without collecting excessive personal data. Transparency is critical—organizations must communicate how AI and user data are used to personalize interactions, ensuring users have control over their preferences (including the ability to opt out). As generative AI becomes more prevalent, obtaining explicit user consent and following ethical practices when using AI to personalize content and marketing materials are essential.

Beyond personalization, the engagement and activation layer empowers organizations to execute customer acquisition and engagement strategies across multiple channels—email, social media, search engines, and display advertising. Privacy-centric targeting (e.g., contextual targeting) relies on first-party data and aggregated insights rather than invasive tracking or profiling. Organizations should use privacy-preserving analytics (like differential privacy in A/B testing) to keep user data secure when measuring campaign performance. By minimizing collection and avoiding intrusive practices, businesses respect user privacy while optimizing their campaigns.

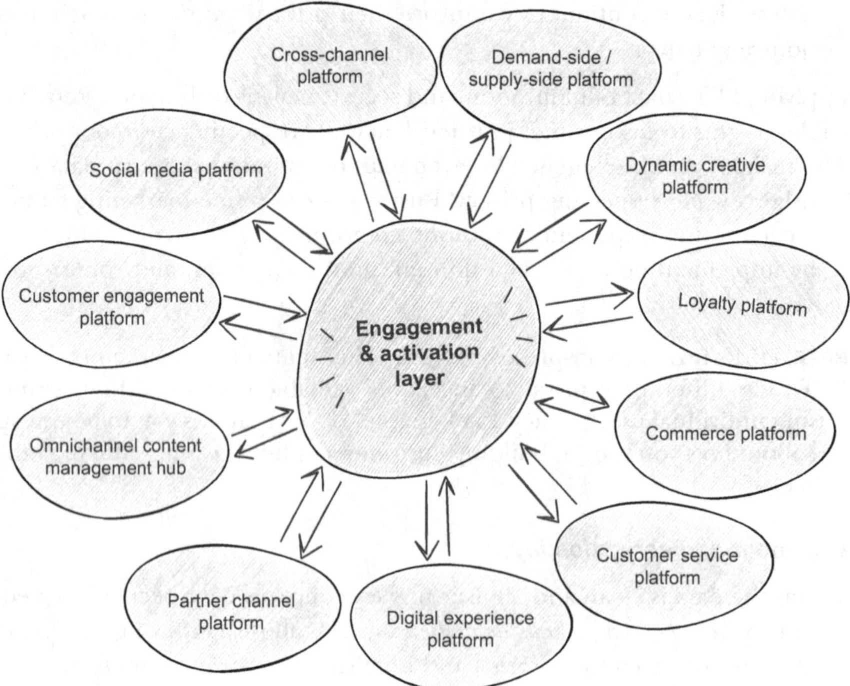

Figure 2.7 Engagement and activation layer overview

In addition, content management and delivery systems facilitate dynamic, data-driven interactions that must remain transparent to maintain user trust. For instance, privacy-enhancing technologies (PETs) such as collaborative filtering and anonymization can help personalize content without storing large amounts of personal data. When using user-generated content, particularly if it includes personal information, organizations must gain explicit user consent and explain how the data will be used. Meanwhile, customer retention and loyalty programs nurture long-term relationships and build brand advocacy. Organizations must be transparent about data use to preserve trust and ensure participants understand the benefits and privacy implications. Personalizing rewards and incentives within these programs can boost engagement while keeping data collection minimal. Finally, offering clear options for data usage and enabling opt-outs for specific practices reinforce trust over the long run.

Here are a few examples demonstrating the engagement and activation layer in practice:

- A leading healthcare provider implements a privacy-centric personalization engine using federated learning to provide tailored health recommendations without centrally storing sensitive medical information. This approach demonstrates respect for patient privacy while offering valuable personalized insights.

- A global financial services company uses privacy-preserving analytics techniques, such as secure multi-party computation, to optimize its marketing campaigns. They ensure compliance with strict financial data privacy regulations by analyzing aggregated data without exposing individual user information.
- In the entertainment industry, a popular streaming platform uses contextual targeting to recommend content based on users' viewing history and preferences. They avoid invasive tracking or profiling and provide clear opt-out options, ensuring transparency and control for users.

To see the engagement and activation layer in action, consider how a seasonal store specializing in outdoor clothing and gear might implement privacy-centric practices:

- *Data collection*—Collect user data through website interactions, purchase history, and user preferences, respecting consent preferences managed by the CMP.
- *Recommendation systems*—Implement a privacy-preserving recommendation system using collaborative and content-based filtering. These techniques provide personalized recommendations without extensive personal data collection.
- *Transparency*—Clearly explain how user data generates product recommendations, offering accessible controls for users to adjust or opt out of personalization.
- *Targeted campaigns*—Focus on contextual targeting based on the content users view, such as outdoor activities or environmental topics, avoiding intrusive tracking or profiling.
- *Privacy-preserving testing*—Use differential privacy during A/B testing to ensure individual user data is not exposed during experimentation.
- *Ongoing compliance*—Conduct quarterly audits to ensure recommendation systems comply with privacy regulations, and integrate advancements in privacy-enhancing technologies (PETs) to strengthen data security and personalization accuracy.

By following these recommendations, a seasonal outdoor clothing store can deliver engaging, personalized customer experiences while maintaining compliance and fostering trust. However, the principles of privacy-centric activation extend far beyond individual industries or use cases. Across all sectors, organizations that prioritize privacy in their engagement and activation layer strategies can achieve significant benefits, including stronger customer relationships, increased loyalty, and a competitive edge in today's privacy-conscious business environment. When designed with privacy in mind, the engagement and activation layer enables organizations to deliver personalized and engaging customer experiences while maintaining compliance and fostering trust. By prioritizing privacy-preserving techniques, transparency, and user control, companies can use data to drive business growth and customer satisfaction without compromising privacy.

NOTE Personalize with respect. This matters to marketers because customers value personalization when it enhances their experience, not when it feels intrusive or exploitative. Finding the right balance between personalization and privacy leads to stronger customer relationships and reduces churn.

2.3.5 Media distribution layer

The *media distribution layer*, the final stage of the marketing data architecture, delivers the personalized experiences and messages crafted in the engagement and activation layer to customers across various touchpoints. As illustrated in figure 2.8, the media distribution layer spans a broad range of digital and traditional channels where personalized experiences can be delivered. These channels include websites, mobile apps, social media platforms, email, online advertising networks, television, radio, print media, and out-of-home advertising, many of which remain essential.

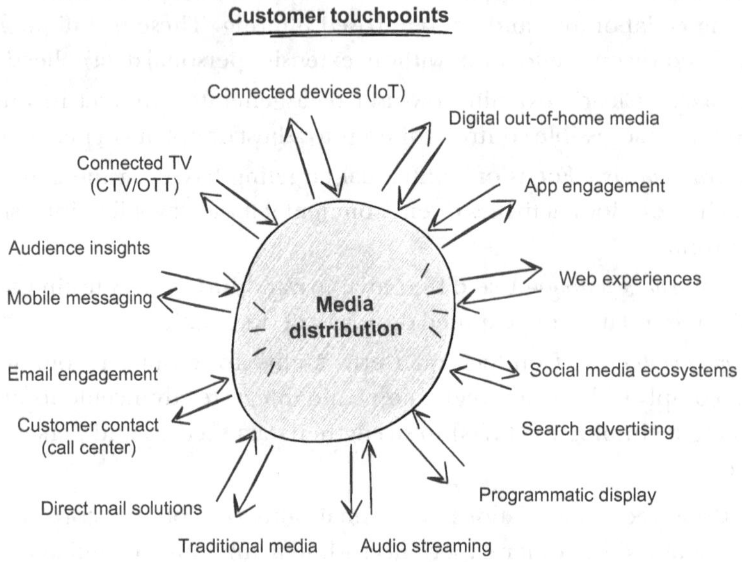

Figure 2.8 Media distribution layer: key customer touchpoints

When distributing content and experiences through various channels, it's crucial to consider the unique privacy implications and best practices for each. Privacy-focused design principles for websites and mobile apps should guide efforts—minimize data collection, ensure user consent, and provide transparent settings. Social media marketing presents its own privacy challenges, including data sharing with platform operators, managing user privacy preferences, and handling user-generated content responsibly. Email marketing campaigns must comply with consent requirements, honor unsubscribe requests, and avoid spam triggers. Even traditional channels like direct mail demand attention to data protection laws when gathering and using customer information. Data clean rooms (covered in chapter 8) can be used to facilitate privacy-preserving data sharing and collaboration with external parties. These secure environments enable joint analysis while protecting user privacy and meeting regulatory standards. Privacy-enhancing technologies (PETs), such as homomorphic encryption, anonymization, and aggregation, can minimize privacy risks when sharing data with partners and vendors.

Measuring and attributing campaign effectiveness across multiple channels while respecting user privacy adds another layer of complexity. Privacy-preserving attribution techniques minimize personal data collection, using aggregated or anonymized datasets to glean performance insights. Marketers must proactively address new data-collection and user-privacy challenges as emerging channels like the metaverse and Web3 gain traction. The metaverse involves immersive digital spaces where user interactions occur in real time, potentially capturing highly detailed behavioral data. Web3's decentralized nature may require rethinking data-sharing models and ensuring ethical practices around blockchain-based user identities. Both technologies offer innovative ways to engage customers but require thoughtful, privacy-centric approaches.

To navigate this complex environment, marketers should evaluate the privacy practices of ad tech vendors, partners, and any new channels they adopt, ensuring alignment with organizational principles and relevant regulations. By balancing robust targeting with privacy-preserving techniques, businesses can effectively reach their audiences while showing respect for user data. Ultimately, the media distribution layer of the marketing data architecture is about delivering personalized experiences across all touchpoints without sacrificing user trust. By prioritizing privacy in each channel, organizations strengthen customer relationships, protect brand reputation, and remain nimble in an ever-evolving regulatory landscape.

> **NOTE** Tailor your approach to each channel. This matters to marketers because each marketing channel has its own privacy landscape. Adapt your strategies to stay compliant and build trust. Respecting channel-specific privacy demonstrates your commitment to ethical marketing and strengthens customer relationships.

2.4 Evolving technologies and frameworks

The fading out of third-party data support and the acceleration of AI has created an unprecedented technological shift. AI undoubtedly disrupts traditional concepts, and privacy in the context of big data is a significant part of this disruption. AI-driven technologies have the potential to infer sensitive information from non-sensitive data, blur the lines between personal and non-personal information, and use data about some individuals to build models that affect others. As a result, marketers must navigate this complex landscape and adopt technologies and frameworks that prioritize privacy while enabling data-driven insights and personalization.

One of the key technologies emerging in the privacy-centric marketing landscape is data clean rooms, which we will cover in chapter 8. These secure, neutral environments allow different parties to share and analyze data without exposing individual-level information, addressing some privacy concerns raised by AI and big data. Data clean rooms come in various forms, such as on-premises solutions, cloud-based platforms, and decentralized architectures, each with their own benefits and challenges. The core features of data clean rooms include data matching, data anonymization, and secure computation, enabling marketers to collaborate on data analysis while preserving user privacy.

Data clean rooms can be used in a variety of marketing scenarios. For example, two retailers can collaborate in a data clean room to analyze customer purchase patterns across their platforms without revealing individual customer identities. This lets them gain insights into customer preferences and behavior, enabling more targeted and effective marketing campaigns. Data clean rooms also facilitate second-party data partnerships, where companies can securely share and enrich their first-party data with data from trusted partners, enhancing the depth and quality of their customer understanding.

Another area of rapid development is privacy-enhancing technologies (PETs). PETs such as differential privacy, homomorphic encryption, and federated learning enable companies to analyze data and extract insights while protecting individual privacy. Differential privacy, for instance, allows companies to analyze aggregated data while ensuring that individual data points cannot be reverse-engineered. Homomorphic encryption enables computation on encrypted data, allowing marketers to process and analyze sensitive data without accessing it in its raw form. Federated learning allows companies to train ML models on distributed data sets without centralizing the data, reducing privacy risks. The application of PETs in marketing is still in its early stages, but there are already promising examples. Some companies use differential privacy to analyze customer data and generate audience insights without exposing individual identities. Others are experimenting with federated learning to build predictive models for customer churn or product recommendations without centralizing sensitive customer data. As PETs mature and become more widely adopted, they have the potential to revolutionize privacy-centric marketing, enabling companies to derive value from data while safeguarding user privacy.

AI and ML also play a crucial role in the evolving privacy-centric marketing landscape. While AI can drive highly personalized and effective campaigns, it raises concerns about data privacy, algorithmic bias, and transparency. To address these challenges, the concept of "privacy-preserving AI" is gaining traction—techniques such as federated learning, secure multiparty computation, and differential privacy allow companies to train AI models and generate insights without directly accessing raw data. However, deleting data or "unlearning" it can be complicated for certain AI architectures. LLMs and other advanced systems often lack straightforward methods for removing personal information once it's absorbed into the model's parameters, raising questions about compliance with the "right to be forgotten" in some jurisdictions.

Beyond privacy concerns, AI in marketing also raises ethical considerations. If models are trained on biased data sets, algorithm bias can lead to discriminatory outcomes. The lack of explainability in some AI models may make it difficult for marketers to justify decisions or even understand how specific outputs are derived. To mitigate these risks, companies must prioritize responsible AI practices, such as ensuring data diversity, testing for bias, and implementing transparent and explainable AI (XAI) models. Establishing ethical AI frameworks and governance structures helps ensure that AI-driven marketing aligns with privacy principles, regulatory obligations, and broader societal values.

Emerging privacy-centric frameworks and architectures are also shaping the future of marketing. Decentralized identity solutions, such as self-sovereign identity (SSI), enable individuals to maintain complete control over their personal data by storing it in secure, decentralized environments. Users can selectively share specific data points (e.g., verifying their age without revealing their exact birthdate) with companies, offering a high level of privacy and security. Similarly, zero-knowledge proofs allow companies to verify certain attributes about individuals without accessing their actual data, enhancing privacy in customer interactions. Blockchain and distributed ledger technologies can further enable secure, transparent, and privacy-preserving data sharing and collaboration between companies and individuals.

To navigate this complex landscape of evolving technologies and frameworks, marketers must proactively evaluate and implement privacy-centric solutions. This involves conducting thorough privacy impact assessments (PIAs) and data protection impact assessments (DPIAs) when adopting new technologies to identify and mitigate potential privacy risks. Marketers should also establish clear criteria for assessing marketing technologies' and vendors' privacy and security features, ensuring that they align with organizational privacy principles and regulatory requirements. Integrating privacy-centric technologies into existing marketing tech stacks and workflows can be challenging but is essential for long-term success. Marketers must work closely with IT, legal, and privacy teams to ensure that new technologies are appropriately vetted, configured, and monitored. Ongoing training and education for marketing teams on privacy best practices and the responsible use of data are also critical.

As the marketing landscape evolves, embracing privacy-centric technologies and frameworks will be key to building customer trust and driving sustainable growth. By staying informed about the latest developments in privacy-enhancing technologies (PETs), AI, and decentralized architectures, and prioritizing responsible and ethical data practices, marketers can navigate this new landscape with confidence and resilience. The future of marketing lies in the ability to derive value from data while respecting and protecting the privacy of individuals, and the companies that master this balance will be the ones that thrive in the years to come.

Summary

- Privacy-centric marketing balances personalization and privacy, recognizing privacy as a fundamental right and business driver.
- The current landscape is shaped by eroding consumer trust, rising privacy concerns, and evolving regulations like GDPR and CCPA.
- Key principles of privacy-centric marketing include transparency, user control, data minimization, purpose limitation, security, and privacy by design.
- Ethical first-party data practices require transparency, user control, minimized collection, and robust security.
- Integrate privacy across the marketing data architecture layers: the sourcing layer, the data foundation layer, the insights and intelligence layer, the engagement and activation layer, and the media distribution layer.
- Marketers must use evolving technologies like data clean rooms, privacy-enhancing technologies (PETs), and privacy-preserving AI to balance personalization with privacy.
- Continuous innovation and adaptation to emerging technologies and frameworks are essential for navigating the changing privacy landscape.

3 Marketing first-party data: Crawl, walk, run

This chapter covers

- Phasing your first-party data strategy to maximize your team's chance of success
- Prioritizing your use cases to drive quick wins while maximizing reach
- Shifting from reach to demonstrating incremental impact
- Driving the adoption of advanced applications of first-party data

Digital transformation is not just about technology; it's about people.

—Carrie Tharp, VP of Solutions & Industries at Google Cloud and Board Member at Rue Gilt Groupe and Vera Bradley

In practice, change management is one of the most significant challenges in driving a first-party data strategy. The adoption of a first-party data strategy often represents a new way of marketing for many organizations—one that is intentionally data-driven—and it forces an organization to confront changes along several dimensions, such as the following:

- *Team focus changes*—If your marketing objectives and team are organized solely around specific channels, such as paid media marketing, email marketing, or in-product marketing, you may want to realign team members by marketing objectives or customer lifecycle stages, such as customer onboarding, cross-selling, retention, or churn winback. With the help of a first-party data solution, this can empower and incentivize your team to drive more integrated marketing campaigns across channels.
- *Process changes*—If your marketing processes are defined by your existing tools, such as customer data platforms or marketing clouds that host your data, you must adapt these to the new first-party data architecture that now hosts your single source of truth for targeting and personalization data. For example, your team should apply all targeting criteria *centrally* rather than in destination channel systems, along with reviews, compliance, and approval flows.
- *Measurement changes*—By adopting a comprehensive first-party data strategy, you can unify and standardize measurement methods across multiple channels, such as automated multivariate experimentation.

This chapter is written for changemakers—leaders who hope to improve the way their organizations use first-party data to drive growth. We will break down the steps of marketing transformation in ways that maximize your organization's chance to successfully achieve your first-party data transformation. It is based on the well-established business practice of use-case, user-driven design to find the fastest path to overall value in order to motivate a cross-functional team to take each step in succession toward the long-term goal.

What is the most common reason the companies we observed failed to achieve their vision of a first-party data transformation? Resistance to change by internal team members. By breaking down the change management into smaller steps that build upon each other, you and other changemakers can maximize your organization's chance to succeed. Table 3.1 summarizes the phases this chapter covers to drive the adoption of first-party data across your organization.

Table 3.1 Summary of key recommended stages to drive first-party data adoption

Stage	Key focus	Main actions	Outcome
Phase 1: remove barriers	Establish self-serve audience capabilities for marketers	Enable marketing teams to access and use first-party data directly, create initial use cases, and integrate audience activation tools	Faster campaign execution and early wins to justify investment

Table 3.1 Summary of key recommended stages to drive first-party data adoption (*continued*)

Stage	Key focus	Main actions	Outcome
Phase 2: experiment and measure	Implement standardized experimentation and measurement methods	Introduce controlled experiments, establish performance metrics, and automate cross-channel testing	Systematic improvement of business outcomes
Phase 3: Try advanced methods	Employ predictive segmentation, customer journeys, and multi-variate experiments	Incorporate ML-driven predictions (e.g., churn), create multistep journeys, and scale creative tests	Improved marketing effectiveness with proactive, smarter targeting

Let's dive into a well-proven glide path that successively achieves initial value, consistent measurement, and predictive personalization. This chapter assumes your team has built a marketing data lakehouse or similar customer dataset, as will be detailed in chapter 5.

3.1 Phase 1: Remove barriers

In the first phase, you need a way to enable marketers to use first-party customer data in a self-serve manner to launch campaigns at greater velocity. This ensures early reach and impact before optimization.

Many companies that have successfully aggregated their first-party data into a cloud data platform start by creating their first audiences manually, often with the help of their analytics team. By manually querying audiences with SQL, your team can effectively demonstrate some initial value of investing in your first-party data strategy before you worry about operational scalability.

The first few audiences are likely the most important, because they justify the investment in the longer-term program. Successful teams resist the urge to solve everything in a comprehensive data model before their first use case is live. While they have an overarching strategy, they realize that early wins with initial use cases generate critically important positive feedback for the data teams. Essentially, you apply value-driven design by choosing two or three use cases to focus on as representative examples. The key insight is that data models are flexible, so generalizing these data models to support dozens or hundreds of use cases is less challenging for most organizations than building buy-in from other teams.

> **REAL-WORLD EXAMPLE** In 2024, a major travel e-commerce company decided to invest in a first-party data solution after its email and messaging platform hit scalability problems. The data and marketing teams set a clear roadmap of a few use cases that answered the needs of both teams. The data team wanted to test the functionality of the first-party data solution at scale and across multiple systems (ads and messaging), while the marketing team wanted to prove value by focusing on churn and recent purchasers. This effectively set the scope of

the roadmap, which ensured the timely launch and successful adoption of their first-party data solution in two quarters.

How should you choose your initial set of use cases? We recommend you brainstorm use cases around your major marketing objectives and classify them according to two dimensions:

- *Value*—Value refers to the business impact of delivering on the use case to your organization. You should look for use cases that are not served well by existing approaches.
- *Level of effort*—This refers to the availability of the first-party data necessary to fulfill the use case you are considering. In general, it is much easier to work with data captured or generated by standard marketing and sales platforms, such as your email engagement data or your sales customer relationship management (CRM) platform. These standard platforms are normally supported by common data ingestion tools, and they typically have well-organized data schemas that make it easy to build segments on them. In contrast, complicated transactional datasets, while valuable, can be challenging for many organizations to model properly for marketing use cases.

Since this book is a practical guide, we'll include a few examples of high-value use cases requiring a relatively low level of effort. These examples apply to most organizations, and they are often overlooked by current marketing teams that do not have a first-party data strategy in place because they require unified data and cross-channel activation.

For B2C (business-to-consumer) marketers, an initial use case may focus on *engagement-based targeting* that uses email engagement data and lifetime value to target audiences on paid social channels. For example, your team may use social media ads to target customers who do not open or read your marketing email messages. Consumers use an ever-growing number of social media platforms such as Snapchat and TikTok, and it is important that your marketing team reach those consumers where they spend their time.

For B2B (business-to-business) marketers, an initial use case may focus on *account-based marketing* that uses sales opportunity data at certain stages of the sales cycle at the account level on LinkedIn. For example, your team may target all contacts at accounts that are stuck in certain sales stages in your CRM platform in order to expand the number of contacts that are engaged with your sales team. It is also an effective way to re-engage contacts who may not have engaged recently, or to further educate engaged contacts in between sales conversations with educational marketing materials to maintain sales momentum.

For B2B2C (business-to-business-to-consumer) marketers, such as those running marketing promotions to consumers via employers, an initial use case may focus on *engagement-based targeting* for the consumers represented by an individual employer. Given the importance of B2B relationships in B2B2C marketing, we recommend establishing clear shared targets and measurement methods, as discussed in section 3.2, so you can justify future marketing campaigns with your B2B partners.

3.1.1 Self-serve audience capabilities for marketers

While valuable, it is challenging to launch more than a handful of audiences per month by manually querying your first-party data for each audience. The audience design process often requires iteration to reach the right attributes and size, and the data team will soon be overwhelmed by marketing requests for audiences. Marketers find that this creates a bottleneck in their campaign execution process, and they spend more time serving as project managers than as marketers until they have self-serve capabilities. Figure 3.1 shows an example of the typical process before marketers have self-serve capabilities.

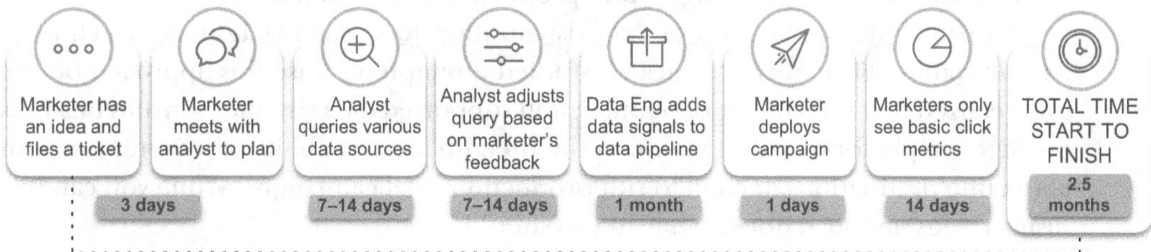

Figure 3.1 A typical manual process for audience creation

The process in figure 3.1 can be summarized as having two major parts: audience design capabilities and audience activation. Let's look at the details of each.

The term *audience design capabilities* refers to marketers' ability to use their first-party data to explore and define audiences based on criteria they set. It is essential that the marketing team easily understands the first-party data field labels to do so. Audience design capabilities must allow the marketer to set inclusion and exclusion criteria easily and then provide the marketer with immediate feedback on audience size. More advanced tools or implementations of audience design will also provide breakdowns of other attributes about the audience, overlap analysis with other audiences, and even aggregate metrics, such as lifetime sales volume at the audience level.

In the short term, some organizations unlock this capability for marketers by creating audience-specific dashboards in their data visualization tool of choice, such as Tableau, Looker, or PowerBI. The analytics team often builds the dashboard to list the most common audience selection criteria, and the marketing team uses the dashboard to apply selection criteria. The resulting dashboard may be highly customized, but it is often a challenge to scale as the number of first-party data attributes increases over time. Data and analytics leaders should consider this approach a good short-term solution to iterate on and build confidence in the data with their marketing counterparts.

The long-term solution is to invest in a marketing technology that connects directly to the first-party datasets, such as a composable customer data platform (CDP). These platforms (covered in more detail in chapter 4) are defined by the fact that they do not host and manage customer or prospect data in a predetermined customer profile or data schema; rather, they connect to the data in the customer's cloud data lake or data warehouse almost as is. This provides tremendous benefits for organizations with large and complicated data models. Most importantly, it offers the fastest time-to-value for marketing teams with quarterly targets.

In addition to audience design capabilities, composable customer data platforms provide *audience activation* to all major marketing delivery channels (such as email platforms, paid media platforms, and customer relationship management systems) or to marketing destinations. Supporting audience design capabilities with audience activation ensures there is a one-to-one connection between analytics insights and the marketer's ability to turn those insights into production-ready campaigns.

A word of caution: be wary of data visualization tools such as Looker, which offer data activation. Several companies we studied attempted to use this approach before they realized that even the most popular, well-supported data visualization and business intelligence platforms fail to maintain the breadth and reliability of integrations with marketing destinations needed to run production-level campaigns. While you can buy sushi at a gas station, it does not mean you should.

Regardless of the technology stack you choose to achieve audience design and activation capabilities, the most successful teams empower their marketers to design and target audiences directly, using their first-party data to dramatically accelerate the iteration of audience design. For many companies we studied, achieving this connected capability was the most crucial accelerator to their first-party data strategy and general marketing agility.

Successful data teams embrace the change management required at this step. The most successful data and analytics teams take the time to curate the most important marketing attributes and provide easy-to-understand data field descriptions for their marketers' benefit. They set up hands-on training sessions to familiarize marketers who may not have any experience with the organization's data models. One marketer described this experience as "seeing the data for the first time." It is transformational when done well.

This dramatically changes the process flow we described, which might take two and a half months, to one in which activation is possible in the same day, as demonstrated in figure 3.2.

The net result of unlocking self-serve capabilities extends beyond volume or velocity, which are the most obvious outcomes. Other benefits of this stage include the following:

- Marketers generally launch audiences that are qualitatively better because they have had a chance to iterate on the audience's criteria, size, and other attributes before it goes live.

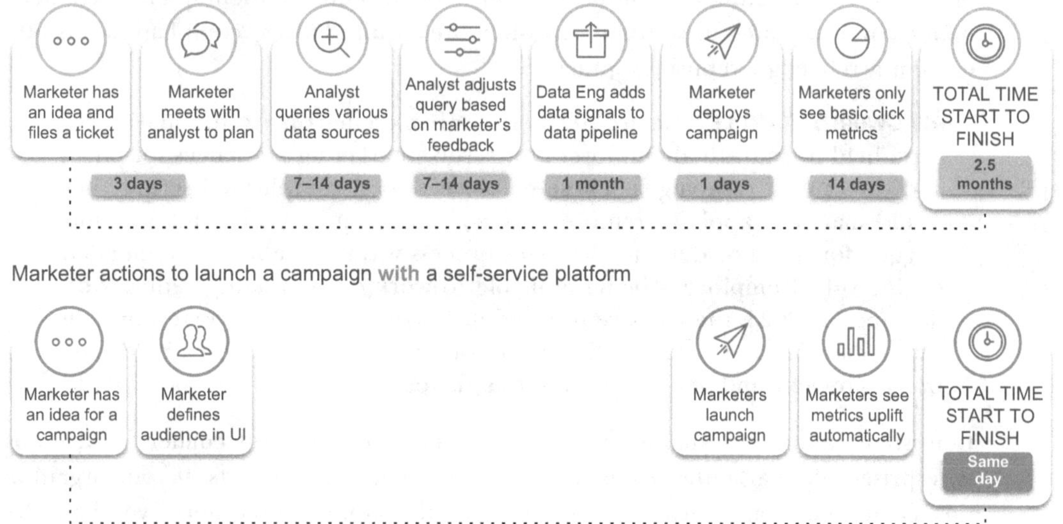

Figure 3.2 Campaign process flow shown side by side with a self-serve platform

- Data teams focus on improving and expanding the attributes marketers can use to target or personalize their audiences now that they are freed from manually delivering each audience.
- Targeting accuracy, including suppressions, improves dramatically because everyone across the company uses the same first-party data as their source of truth.

Generally, the focus of this stage of self-serve capabilities for marketers results in the greatest acceleration of data-driven marketing activity. As first-party data is democratized successfully, it's common to see a significant increase in the volume of marketing audiences at most enterprises.

REAL-WORLD EXAMPLE Indeed's marketing team achieved eight times the audience launches per quarter that they had previously by adopting a first-party data strategy that connected GrowthLoop to their Snowflake data platform. GrowthLoop gave the marketing team at Indeed a controlled self-serve way to design and launch audiences, which replaced a manual ticket-based process that had limited the marketing team to two or three audiences per quarter. According to Judy Nam, the vice president of SMB Marketing at Indeed at the time, "This has had a big impact on our team's velocity—we've been able to [increase] 8x the number of campaign launches per quarter."

3.1.2 Standardized opt-outs and suppressions

A good first-party data strategy has significant benefits for your privacy compliance. *Marketing suppressions* include all the criteria you use to remove members of your audiences from exposure to marketing campaigns. They include contacts that have opted out of marketing communications but may also include delinquent customers, minors, or other categories. Some exclusions are required to stay compliant, while others simply reflect good business practice.

REAL-WORLD EXAMPLE Before 2021, a major bank relied on institutional knowledge held by individual employees to "scrub" marketing audiences for email and direct mail campaigns. These employees used complicated scripts they would manually apply to remove minors, marketing opt-outs, and accounts flagged for fraud or delinquency. This process was unreliable and depended on individual employees being available to work on marketing requests on demand. By 2023, the bank centralized its first-party data and corresponding suppressions into a data pipeline (discussed in chapter 5), which made the process reliable and seamless for their marketers.

Consistent adoption of marketing suppressions is one of the key challenges faced by enterprise-scale marketing teams in scaling their marketing efforts. If your organization's central customer profile incorporates all the suppression criteria, you have the key ingredient to ensure your team understands and can agree upon *standard suppression criteria* that should be applied to some or all of your marketing audiences. In our analysis, organizations that set standard suppression to apply to all audiences by default dramatically increased the adoption of standard suppressions.

As an aside, it's worth noting that many organizations set up standard suppressions for specific populations (for example, differentiating between B2B or B2C targeting criteria) or for use on particular channels (for example, differentiating between direct mail and email). Consider your own organization's needs here when designing your standard suppression strategy.

The most important takeaway for marketers? Accurate audience sizing that factors in the latest suppressions answers one of the biggest questions marketers face when designing a campaign: Will this be impactful? Marketers need to know how many customers or prospects they can reach with their campaign.

Finally, for the marketing leadership at the organizations we researched, this approach resulted in near-universal application of suppressions and increased reliability in executing suppressions in production-level campaigns.

3.1.3 First automated cross-channel audience

Now that you know the basics, let's focus on developing your first cross-channel audience using a well-defined first-party data strategy.

REAL-WORLD EXAMPLE Mercari US, an online marketplace, found that the ability to automate audiences across multiple channels provided major benefits. Masumi Nakamura, vice president of engineering at Mercari, stated, "Most marketing teams own a single channel and operate on that channel—sometimes in isolation. One of the big areas of benefit of working with

GrowthLoop was the integration of marketing channels such as the CRM, User Acquisition, as well as more traditional marketing channels."

The following steps explain how to develop a cross-channel audience:

1. Choose the first few audiences from the use case prioritization exercise at the beginning of section 3.1 based on the highest value and lowest level of effort. By choosing a few audiences and focusing on the level of effort, you'll maximize your team's chances of finding a successful set of audiences.
2. Define the objective and associated success metric for each audience so that you have a measure of the business impact. For example, you may choose customer upsell as your objective and the volume of incremental sales (measured in the number of transactions or dollars spent) as your success metric. Choosing carefully is critical in building the organizational momentum for your first-party data strategy.
3. For each use case, define the data requirements as simply as possible. The *targeting criteria* includes all the data fields and rules used to define who should be included in the audience. *Personalization attributes* are any attributes you may choose to include in the content of the marketing creative you plan to deliver. Note that predictions powered by machine-learning models, such as propensities, churn prediction, lifetime value, and next-best action, can serve as a key ingredient in some of the highest-performing campaigns.
4. Map the data requirements for each use case to the available first-party data to identify gaps. Deliver the prioritized data requirements to the data team responsible for developing the customer data model, and estimate the business impact of the use case to justify the investment of effort. Note that a good composable customer data platform will allow you to dynamically create calculated fields or criteria, such as "customers who spent at least $100 on electronics in the last 90 days," without requiring a new data field to be created in your data platform.
5. Establish the automated sync to each destination channel. If you are building your own activation (not recommended), this would include developing a configurable sync application or cloud function to sync the audience and personalization data in the format needed for that destination. For composable customer data platforms, you should authenticate each destination in the application to allow for the audience and personalization data sync to be established.
6. Define, review, and export your first audience. This is the fun part. You now have everything you need in place to activate your first audience. Hopefully, you are doing so in a scalable and automated way, though manually syncing your first audiences is still worthwhile to motivate the team to continue to invest in the first-party data and associated marketing capabilities.

After your team launches its first few marketing audiences, it's very useful (or even essential) to build a mutually exclusive and comprehensively exhaustive (MECE) segmentation model to serve as the basis for audience targeting criteria. A simple lifecycle-based segmentation model, such as the one featured in figure 3.3, can focus each team member's audience-targeting criteria within specific subsegments of the customer population that avoid unnecessary overlaps with other audiences. Other common models include the Recency, Frequency, and Monetary value (RFM) in transactional business models or *k*-means clustering models.

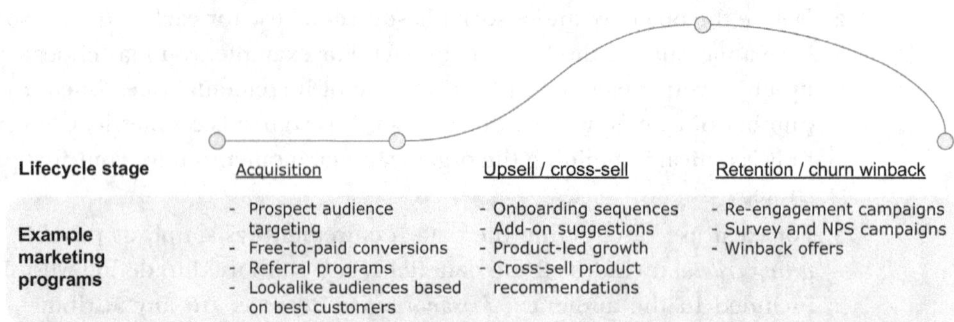

Figure 3.3 Lifecycle segmentation model

Since self-serve audience capabilities allow marketers to grow the number of audiences they create, providing a centralized view of all audiences across the team can be very helpful. Each team member gains visibility across all audiences and can follow up with each audience's creator when determining priorities between audiences that may have partial or complete overlap.

The example in figure 3.4 shows a centralized view of audiences for a marketing team. In the screenshot, you can see eight active audiences, two of which are pending approval (shown) and one of which is actively exporting to other marketing systems.

3.2 Phase 2: Experiment and measure

Many marketing leaders are asked to prove their incremental impact on the business, and there is no better way to do so than by a controlled experiment that can prove incrementality with causal, statistical significance. Now that you have audience velocity, you need a way to experiment and measure consistently to identify winners.

As organizations provide self-serve audience capabilities to their marketing teams, they remove a key data bottleneck from marketing operations. As a result, most companies we observed experienced a rapid increase in audience activation and campaign execution, followed by a new challenge: the need for optimization. Now that your team can take more shots on goal, you need a way to identify winning audiences. In the organizations we've observed, this is a good time in the change management process to introduce experiments, because there is a natural motivation to do so.

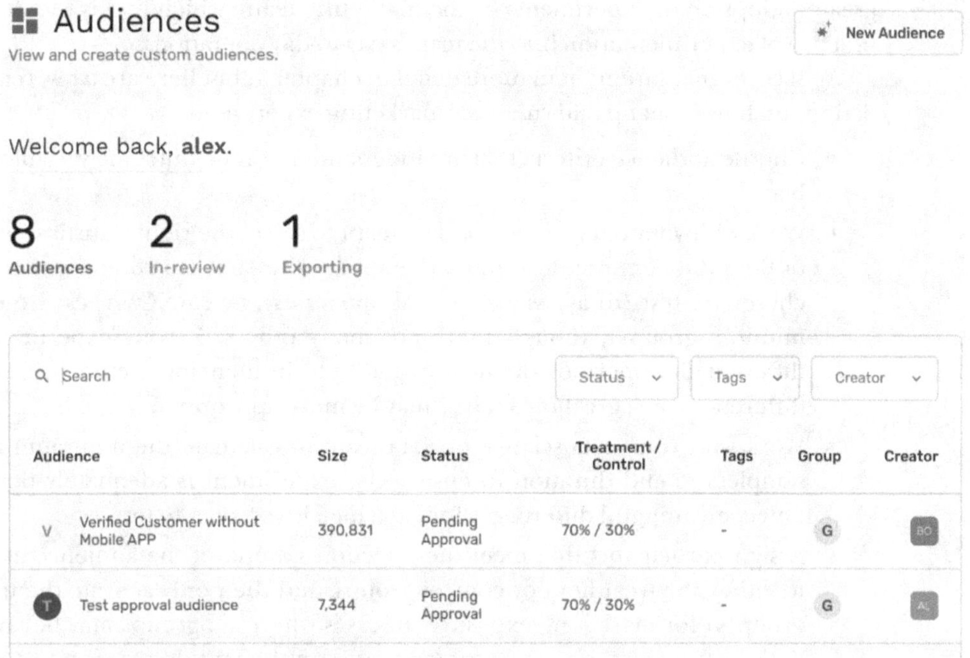

Figure 3.4 GrowthLoop example of an audience hub

As marketers launch more and more audiences targeted by campaigns, individual customers may start to belong to many audiences and reach marketing saturation (e.g., too many marketing messages). In these cases, it's time to focus on optimizing audience assignments to maximize customer lifetime value while minimizing marketing fatigue. At this stage, the focus changes from velocity to governance and optimization.

3.2.1 Automate experiments consistently

One of the key advantages of a first-party data strategy built upon an independent customer data layer is the ability to run *cross-channel* experiments. When audiences are defined in each siloed marketing tool, such as an email platform, it is very challenging to run an experiment incorporating other channels, such as paid media and mobile notifications, because the audience definition is locked into a specific channel. By applying treatment and control-group assignments to audiences on first-party data platforms *before* they are exported to marketing destinations, successful organizations scale their experiments to any set of destinations they choose for each audience.

The most effective way to do so is to suggest experiments directly into the design and activation process that marketers use to launch campaigns. This ensures all audiences use the same experimental methodology, which is essential to compare audiences' relative performance on an apples-to-apples basis. Ease of use for experiments also ensures greater adoption of experiments by the marketing team, which builds the disciplined practice of experimentation into the team's day-to-day operations.

We'll cover measurement in more detail in chapter 7, but here are a few recommendations on how to set up and run basic marketing experiments:

- Choose audience criteria that are independent of the outcome variable to avoid bias.
- Work with your data science or data team to select the right statistical test. Some of the most common tests in marketing are the *t*-test (to compare two groups), chi-square test (to assess categorical outcomes), and ANOVA test (to compare multiple groups), though there are many others. If your experiment spans different time periods or involves multiple influencing factors, difference-in-differences or regression analysis may be more appropriate.
- Work with your data science or data team to calculate the minimum required sample size and duration to ensure the experiment is adequately powered to detect meaningful differences for each metric you plan to test.
- Assign participants that meet the selection criteria of the audience at random to either the treatment or control groups, and then only activate the treatment group(s) for marketing exposure. In cases where subgroups may behave differently (e.g., new vs. repeat customers), use stratified randomization to ensure balance across key variables.
- For longitudinal studies (those over an extended period), track participant assignments to keep control group participants permanently assigned to the control group, even if they exit and re-enter the audience. Also, consider spillover effects, where treatment group exposure indirectly influences control group participants (e.g., through word-of-mouth). If this risk exists, explore designs like geo-experiments or matched-market tests.
- Wait for the duration planned for the experiment.
- When analyzing the results, avoid selection bias by keeping all participants in their originally assigned groups, even if they do not complete the experiment. Conduct the planned statistical analysis to determine incremental impact.

In a well-designed architecture, only the audience members assigned to the treatment group are exported to the marketing destinations. The members of the control group never need to be exported. This reduces the chances of any control group exposure that would ruin experimental results.

3.2.2 Measure marketing performance on any metric

As marketing campaigns go live with audiences based on your first-party data, your team should capture engagement and conversion data points for each audience member and feed that back into your central view of the customer, alongside the rest of your first-party data. Given the scalability of modern cloud-based data lakehouses and data warehouses, particularly with how inexpensive data storage costs have become, many organizations bring in as much marketing data as possible to give them the flexibility to measure results on any metric.

> **REAL-WORLD EXAMPLE** In 2020, the Boston Red Sox adopted a first-party data solution on Google Cloud. By 2021, they measured marketing performance on metrics including total sales, ticket-specific sales, email opens, and mobile app logins. This helped them assess the entire funnel of activity for each campaign.

In figure 3.5, we show a few examples of alternative metrics on which a marketing team like Indeed's could measure the incremental influence of its marketing campaigns. Some of these may be product-specific or provide deeper revenue metrics than are usually available in most marketing tools, such as email platforms.

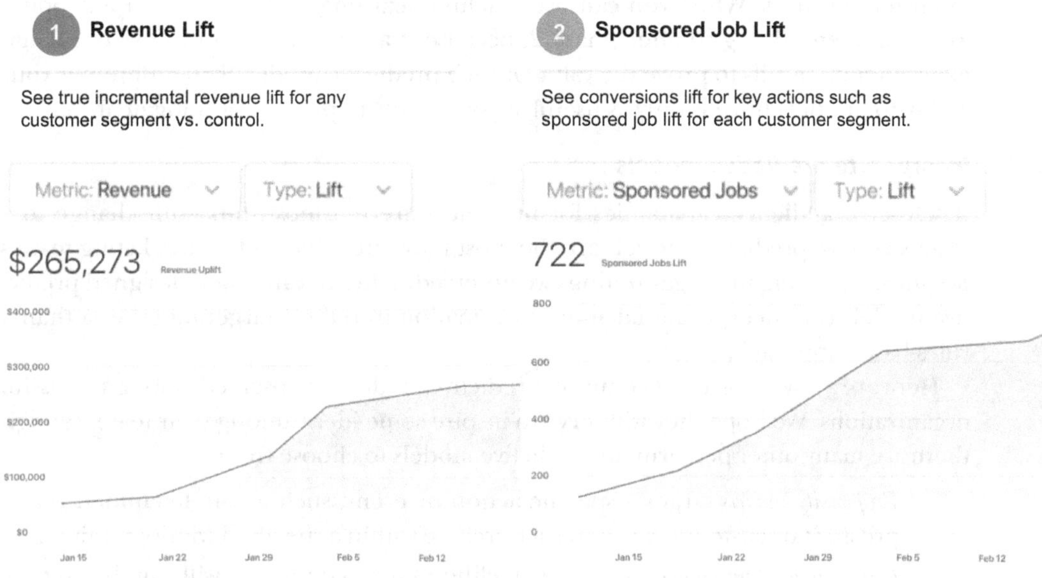

Figure 3.5 GrowthLoop measurement for a sample audience

The ability to measure audience experiments centrally on *any metric in your first-party dataset* is a major advantage to a well-designed first-party data strategy and architecture. The marketing teams we observed have used the ability to measure their experimental results on any metric to discover new insights and business impacts. For example, they look at metrics vertically across the marketing funnel to gauge the cross-channel effects of their campaigns on specific audiences. Marketers may measure changes to upper funnel engagement events, such as specific page views, to mid-stage events, like product demo views, or full conversions, such as purchases. Marketers may also look across product areas to discover synergies or cannibalization, such as when promoting one product category for an e-commerce campaign.

Many organizations struggle to adopt experimentation when it is cumbersome. By prioritizing ease of use and automation in your experimentation, your first-party data strategy should make it easy to incorporate experiments into each audience and launch many audiences and experiments so the team has a good chance of finding winners.

Once you have integrated your channels in phase 1 and established a consistent way to measure results in phase 2, it is time to explore more advanced methods, such as machine learning–based targeting, expanding audiences into multistep journeys, and multivariate experiments.

3.3 Phase 3: Use predictive models

Now that you have experimental velocity, you can incorporate predictive models and multistep journeys. While you can use machine learning (ML) models at any point, we recommend doing so after phase 2, because it allows your team to use campaign experimental results to prove the value of each predictive model. Said differently, your ability to predict churn is only as useful as your ability to prevent or mitigate it.

3.3.1 Incorporate predictive models

If self-serve audience capabilities for marketers are the most impactful change to a team's *velocity*, predictive models are the most impactful change to a marketing team's *performance*, among the organizations we observed. Why? Because well-designed predictive models can incorporate far more information into their targeting criteria than a rules-based approach.

Here are a few of the most common predictive models we observed among successful organizations. We hope they will serve to inspire some ideas among your team, though there are many other performant predictive models to choose from:

- *Propensity models* target a specific action or event, such as the likelihood that a prospect or customer will make a purchase within a specified window of time.
- *Churn prediction models* target the likelihood that a customer will stop buying the product or service. Note that the definition of churn is a prerequisite for this type of model, and it can be difficult to build consensus for a specific definition of churn if your organization has not already developed such a definition.
- *Lifetime value models* quantitatively predict how much a specific customer may be worth to the business based on initial engagement, demographic, or purchase behaviors.
- *Next best action models* predict the most effective personalized action or offer to present to a customer at a given moment, based on their behavior, preferences, and context. It's essentially about answering: "What should we do next for this customer to maximize engagement, satisfaction, or conversion?" These models are often used to personalize messaging and marketing content. Shopping cart add-on recommendations are an example of such a model.

When developing predictive models, there is an important trade-off between interpretable and non-interpretable models. By definition, interpretable models, such as linear and multivariate regression models, show which variables are the most important features in making a prediction, and some even show the magnitude and direction of each feature's impact. This is incredibly useful for marketers because it allows them to understand why the model makes predictions the way it does, which builds their confidence in its results. Interpretability also helps marketers inform their personalization strategy, including the messaging and content that best reflects the predictive model's features. This drives better campaign performance.

Given those advantages, why would a team consider non-interpretable models? The answer is predictive performance. Several machine-learning algorithms may have better predictive performance, as measured by one of several metrics, such as accuracy. Despite that, we recommend starting your team with simple interpretable models before moving on to less-interpretable advanced machine-learning models.

Driving the adoption of predictive models can be challenging if your organization's marketing team is new to the concept, but a few tactics can help. For example, to make things easier, consider converting quantitative predictions such as likelihood percentages into categorical labels such as "high," "medium," or "low" likelihood. Many marketing teams also benefit from placing data fields containing predictions alongside other data fields so that marketers can combine predictive fields with other attributes.

> **REAL-WORLD EXAMPLE** The Boston Red Sox used this approach by creating categorical labels for the highest likelihood season ticket buyers. Their team successfully combined a "high" propensity score with upcoming game purchases, providing those fans with in-person experiences and timely offers. The result was one of the organization's most effective marketing campaigns for sales.

3.3.2 *Adopt onboarding, retention, and cross-sell journeys*

Although there are some noteworthy exceptions, a common set of marketing objectives applies to most organizations. While audiences are an effective way to target prospects or customers to drive these objectives, some organizations look to build upon audiences with multistep journeys to create a personalized experience over time. Here's a list of common marketing objectives, each of which could have one or more marketing journeys associated with it:

- *Acquisition* refers to the initiatives and programs that target prospective customers to become engaged or paying customers.
- *Onboarding* includes the experience a customer has when first adopting a product or service, often defined by key milestones or a specified window of time.
- *Cross-sell* refers to the initiatives and programs that prompt customers to expand from a subset of a company's products or services to new product lines or services.
- *Upsell* refers to the initiatives and programs that prompt customers to buy or engage more with products or services they already use.

- *Retention* includes efforts to maintain a customer relationship over time, such as repurchases, renewals, and general re-engagement.
- *Churn winback* refers to re-acquiring customers lost due to churn.

It may make sense for your team to extend individual audiences with multistep and conditional journeys, but here are a few reasons that can serve as conversation starters for your marketing team:

- *Cost optimization*—Many marketing teams look to market to customers via "free" channels like email and mobile notifications before considering paid media. Journeys allow you to set this up automatically with conditional branching to activate paid media channels only if low-cost channels have failed to convert customers.
- *Narrative selling*—For complex sales (such as many B2B offerings), multistep sequences allow marketers to educate their audiences step-by-step and to escalate to conversion-oriented messaging or sales referrals as soon as lead scoring reaches certain thresholds.
- *Personalized channel engagement*—Customers and prospects engage more or less with different marketing channels, so it can be useful to lay out the possibilities on a single journey using each engagement touchpoint to determine the next channel to be used with that customer or prospect. Some organizations we observed referred to this as "meeting the customer where they're at."

Figure 3.6 shows an example of a customer journey in GrowthLoop connected to first-party data in a cloud-based data warehouse. The original criteria for the "entry" node of the journey is itself an audience that has been defined, and the connected nodes below it serve to further refine subsets of the "entry" criteria for the originating audience. Note that journey orchestration is relatively difficult to find in a composable customer data platform. Outside of composable customer data platforms, journeys are most commonly found in messaging platforms (such as email platforms or mobile notification platforms), where the marketing team is required to load data into the platform in order to use it, and the journey is limited to the messaging platform itself.

We recommend introducing journeys after predictive models because journeys require greater marketing maturity and coordination than audience-based targeting. At larger organizations, marketing teams that embrace this fully may organize their team by objective rather than by the channel they serve, such as a retention marketer, acquisition marketer, or an onboarding marketer who may use any channel to meet their objective.

3.3.3 Try multivariate splits

There are virtually an infinite number of things your marketing team can test, including the target audience, content, channel, timing, and offer. The most successful marketing teams recognize that these are interrelated and should be tested collectively. Furthermore, prior exposure can play a major role in how impactful a new marketing

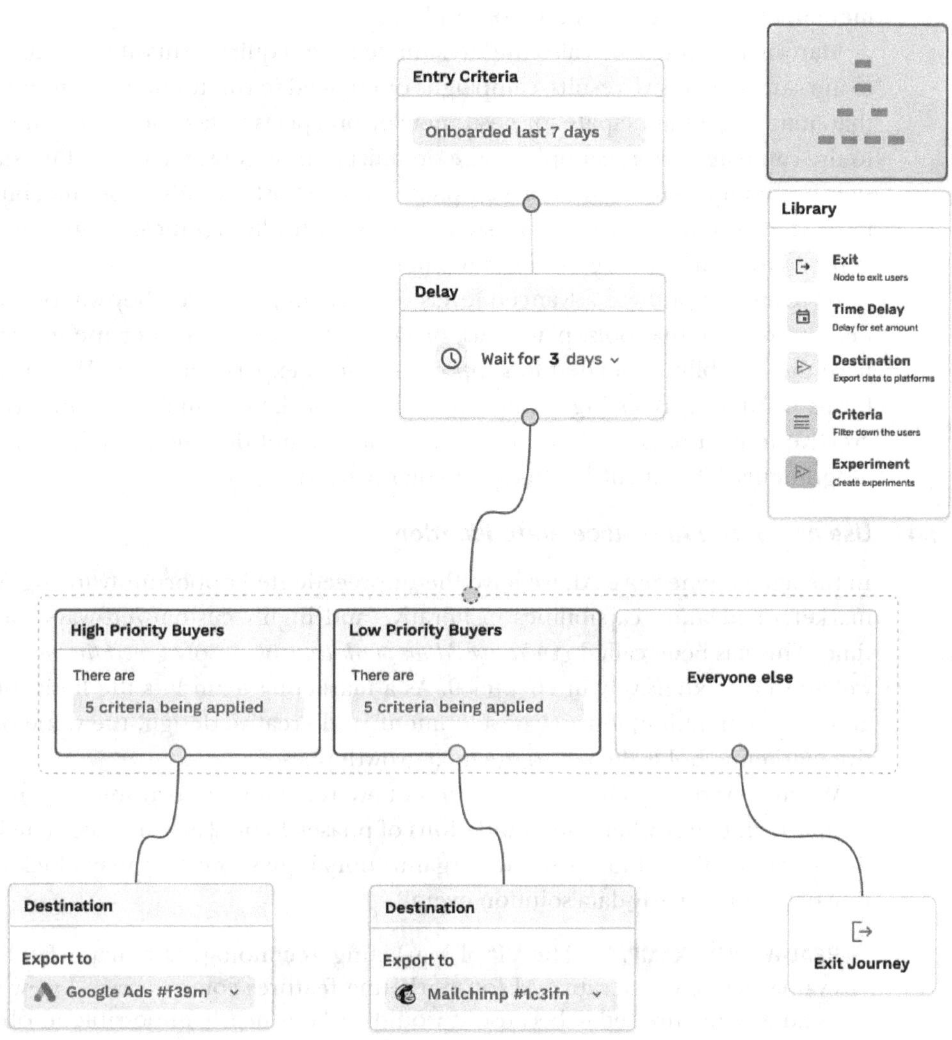

Figure 3.6 An example of a customer journey

campaign may be, so marketing teams that use journeys often use multivariate splits within those journeys to generate the most reliable test results. Thus, marketers can optimize the impact of the entire buying experience by informing it with all the first-party data and campaign structure available to them.

At this stage, it is important to note that statistical significance matters, and this often requires prior planning. The variant groups in a multivariate test within a journey may otherwise be too small to come to any definitive conclusion on the relative impact of the campaign compared to the control group. Many try to establish baseline assumptions about the expected direction and size of impact to ensure consistency in the experimental setup and interpretation of results.

Many marketing teams also underestimate time requirements at this stage. In order to measure conclusive results, campaigns often need to run for weeks or months longer than many teams anticipate for customers or prospects to take action on the exposure to the campaigns. For example, some organizations we observed found no statistically significant impact of a retention campaign within shorter windows of time, but months later, they found that long-term spend was statistically significantly greater in those exposed to a particular retention campaign.

As teams adopt these advanced levels of marketing science, they will often find the need to replace the tools, platforms, or destination channels they use to ensure they have the capabilities needed to support advanced experimentation. While some platforms provide A/B testing within the confines of the channel they support (such as creative tests in paid media), many platforms are not designed to apply multivariate assignments defined outside that particular platform.

3.3.4 Use generative AI to accelerate ideation

In the age of generative AI, we have the unprecedented opportunity to augment each marketer's ideation capabilities in iterative and highly customized ways for the first time. This has been called *generative AI for marketing*, or simply *generative marketing*, and we'll cover it extensively in chapter 9. As a marketing team hits the limits of manual audience generation, journey development, and creative design, the value of generative marketing holds the key to the next growth phase.

When considering change management, we recommend focusing on generative AI for marketing only when the foundations of phases 1 and 2 are in place. The introduction of generative AI raises several organizational questions that may block the adoption of your first-party data solution overall.

> **REAL-WORLD EXAMPLE** The VP of Marketing Technology at a major US bank evaluating new generative AI for marketing features commented, "I view that as an anti-feature today because it would make it nearly impossible to obtain compliance approval at the bank."

Given that caveat, the potential of generative AI to greatly accelerate the integration of insights into ideation is immense. Generative AI models can provide suggestions that factor in each organization's first-party datasets, destination channels, and marketing objectives, as well as contextual information about the organization. This makes suggestions much more relevant and often immediately actionable by the marketers who interface with the generative marketing models.

Further, generative AI is capable of *conversational design* that allows a marketer to iterate on the suggestions provided by the generative AI in a dialogue of step-by-step feedback (see figures 3.7 and 3.8). This is critically important to making generative marketing useful and contextually relevant (e.g., localized, brand-specific, etc.) since the possibility of model "hallucinations" creating errant suggestions will still exist for some time as the field of generative AI advances. Additionally, current generative marketing models can often explain why they make each suggestion, which aids marketers in their decision-making process to drive buy-in.

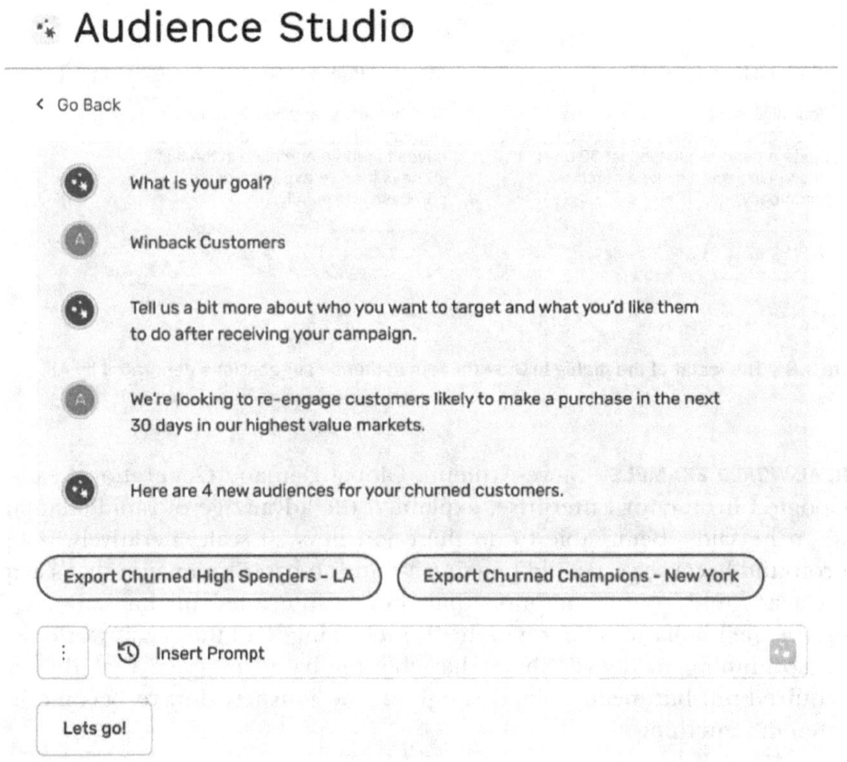

Audience Studio

< Go Back

What is your goal?

Winback Customers

Tell us a bit more about who you want to target and what you'd like them to do after receiving your campaign.

We're looking to re-engage customers likely to make a purchase in the next 30 days in our highest value markets.

Here are 4 new audiences for your churned customers.

Export Churned High Spenders - LA

Export Churned Champions - New York

Insert Prompt

Lets go!

Figure 3.7 A generative marketing dialog for a specific audience in GrowthLoop

Beyond *audience suggestions,* generative AI can already suggest full *customer journeys* and *creative assets,* such as email templates, paid media ads, in-product messaging, and more. In isolation, these are useful to a degree, but what makes generative AI powerful at this stage of organizational maturity is the ability of the models to incorporate learnings (e.g., campaign engagement, customer lifetime value, and experimental results) together in a virtuous feedback loop. This can drive continuous, compound improvements in an entirely new way for marketing teams ready to adopt it.

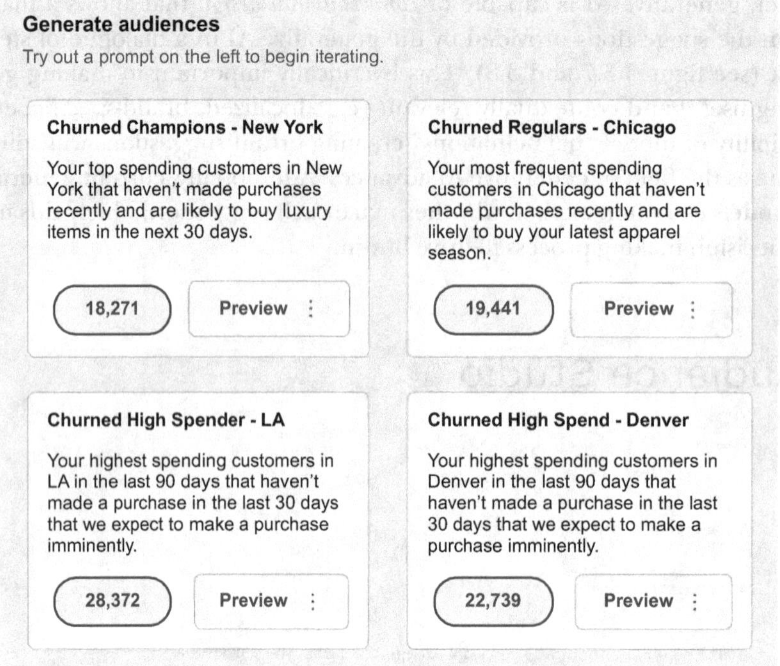

Figure 3.8 The result of the dialog in GrowthLoop: audience suggestions generated by AI

REAL-WORLD EXAMPLE Steve Armenti, Global Demand Generation Leader at Google Chrome for Enterprise, explained the advantage of rapid adaptation when he said, "Being able to do these journeys, at scale, iteratively, is really profound because you could imagine a solution-based campaign that's acquiring leads under an assumption that they're interested in that solution but maybe their behavior later on in the funnel changes. In the classic world, you'd be continuing to deliver them that solution-based message that they were acquired on, but meanwhile, throughout the journey, they've become interested in something else."

In the next chapter, we'll dive deeper into the marketing technologies available to accelerate your team's success with first-party data, including some incorporating generative AI.

Summary

- Change management is often the most challenging part of a first-party data transformation, and success relies on thoughtfully designed phases that deliver valuable wins along the way.
- In the first phase of change, organizations should focus on bridging the data between teams with self-serve capabilities for marketers.

- In phase 2, the focus should be standardized experimentation and measurement that ensure you accurately identify wins.
- In phase 3, you can use the foundations your team has built up to that point to introduce predictive models and multichannel journeys.
- Your team can introduce generative AI to assist with ideation and decision-making to spark further innovation.
- Changemakers at successful organizations design with the current people, processes, and systems in mind to minimize friction in driving change.
- Changemakers find ways to motivate transitions and use user-centric design to achieve change.

4 Choosing your first-party data solution

> **This chapter covers**
> - Core technology capabilities for first-party data platforms
> - Comparing the major marketing technology solutions by category
> - Considerations and recommendations based on recent marketing technology offerings

Marketing technology is no longer just a department; it's the foundation for how businesses grow.

—Scott Brinker, "Godfather of Martech" and VP of Platform Ecosystems at Hubspot

Many of you reading this book may face a confusing set of options and time pressures to find the right first-party data solution for your organization. According to the CDP Institute (a vendor-neutral organization dedicated to helping companies manage customer data) in their 2024 member survey, "The industry faces old challenges in deploying customer data systems." With statements like that, it's natural to feel intimidated when parsing the myriad options. After all, "everyone says they do everything, but they don't or don't do it well," as a marketer at a large accounting software firm stated as they navigated first-party data solutions.

This chapter aims to demystify first-party data solutions and focus on what matters most: how you and your team can use your organization's strengths to prioritize and map capabilities to the right set of use cases. We aim to explain concepts like *customer data platform* (CDP), *composable*, and *activation* and use the learnings of others to avoid the most common pitfalls.

After reading this chapter, you should have a practical evaluation framework your team can apply immediately to choose your first-party data supporting technology (including any vendor selection process), key first-party data capabilities you may need (and their relative importance to most organizations), and examples that illustrate some of the key trade-offs to consider.

We'll start with an overview of the role marketing technologies play in addressing the core challenges marketers face regarding first-party data. Then we'll cover our primary recommendation: a marketing data lakehouse activated via a composable CDP. We'll explore strong alternatives and then introduce a framework for evaluating your team's needs.

4.1 Why marketing technology is necessary

Modern marketing teams face a significant challenge in determining the right first-party data strategy and implementing that strategy with marketing technology (martech) tools. Several important industry trends, such as the following, are creating an urgent need for smarter, more capable first-party data solutions to achieve marketing that is competitive with industry best practices:

- *Privacy regulations*—The collection, management, and use of personally identifiable information (PII) have been scrutinized in recent years, particularly when the data is sold, licensed, or used by third parties. Massive fines have been levied against companies that have failed to abide by privacy regulations, so it has become urgent for organizations to invest in building their own first-party data to target and personalize their marketing. For example, third-party cookie tracking has been deprecated by major web browsers or made configurable by each user, and marketers need a solution that will work everywhere. (It is such an important topic that we covered privacy compliance in more detail in chapter 2, in case you've skipped ahead.)
- *Channel proliferation*—Consumers and business prospects are engaging with brands on more and more marketing channels. From humble beginnings across email and direct mail, marketing teams must now reach prospective customers via mobile notifications, chat applications, paid social, and many new advertising platforms. The breakneck speed of integrations has escaped virtually all home-grown solutions we've encountered, and even popular solutions like

Adobe Experience Cloud and Salesforce Marketing Cloud have failed to keep up with the proliferation of marketing integrations required of modern marketing teams.

- *Personalization acceleration*—The most effective marketing teams today are generating rich insights about their customers and applying those insights to highly personalize the targeting and messaging of their marketing. Customer lifecycle stages, discount sensitivity based on purchase history, propensity to purchase certain product categories, and even marketing touchpoint history are highly effective dimensions for targeting and personalizing content. Generative AI for marketing is already accelerating this trend toward individual personalization.
- *AI decisioning*—Those brands that most effectively use AI to determine the optimal channel, delivery time, and next best action for each customer stand to make significant gains over competitors that send marketing messages using a one-size-fits-all approach. AI models that look at each user's engagement patterns can use them to make more effective choices about when, how, and what to deliver for each individual user.

Given these challenges, why is marketing technology necessary to solve first-party data solutions? For most organizations, the right marketing technology can deliver incredible time-to-value, a rich capability set, and built-in uptime and support that can be hard to come by with home-grown solutions. Add in the complexity of regulatory compliance requirements, like the following, and the case is even stronger for marketing technology solutions that can be specialized to meet those needs on your organization's behalf:

- *Privacy compliance*—Most marketing technologies that store or process PII come with privacy compliance features like the ability to mask PII, sanitize (i.e., delete) PII, and report on PII upon request. Many also offer audit logs of access to PII and a high level of security to protect PII certified by third-party auditors. It is difficult to get these guarantees when working with PII manually or with in-house solutions.
- *Cross-channel campaigns*—The marketing technology solution you choose can allow you to define a target audience once and make it available seamlessly across all your channels or downstream marketing systems automatically. There are dozens of important marketing, sales, and product systems or destinations your marketing team may want to integrate. Note that each marketing channel will have its own protocol to sync data, and in the case of APIs, it will require your team to keep up with new API versions and handle destination-specific responses. Your team risks reinventing the wheel or experiencing failures by trying to maintain data integrations with all these systems.
- *New capabilities*—There are so many valuable capabilities offered by marketing technology services in the first-party data space that your team risks missing out on if you try to go it alone—for example, visual audience builder capabilities,

automated experimentation, journey building, AI features, and more. We'll cover many of these in the framework later in this chapter.

- *Support and guaranteed uptime*—Compared with in-house builds, marketing technologies are provided by third parties whose reputation and financial success depend on reliability. Obtaining support and uptime guarantees is much easier with these products than with internal builds. Many companies offering marketing technologies have mature monitoring and alert systems built into their products, along with 24/7 on-call rotation from their engineering teams to ensure their guarantees are met.

Framed differently, all of these integrations, regulatory requirements, and new capabilities represent a major competitive advantage for organizations that use marketing technologies successfully. Some companies, such as startups, may simply lack the team and capabilities necessary to build their own solutions from scratch. As we'll see, new composable technologies blur the distinction of traditional "build versus buy" decisions by promoting "build and buy" hybrids that achieve the best of both worlds. The most effective companies evaluate their core competencies and focus their efforts on the points of highest leverage with respect to first-party data.

The good news is that marketing technology is a mature and dynamic industry. There are many viable solutions to consider, with trade-offs we can describe and evaluate in straightforward ways. This chapter focuses on several of those considerations.

Let's start with the basic component parts that apply to most solutions so we can use a common language across the solution space. If you squint enough at the architecture diagram for any solution, you will usually find three common parts, as shown in figure 4.1:

- *Collect*—Some capabilities help you collect first-party data in secure, scalable, and compliant ways.
- *Manage*—To create a unified customer profile, there must be a way to manage and combine datasets from various sources. This includes identity resolution, among other data management capabilities.
- *Activate*—Prospects and customers are found across an increasingly large number of channels or media. Modern marketing technology needs to help your team sync targeting and personalization data across platforms and systems to reach those prospects and customers.

How first-party data solutions accomplish each capability has major consequences for your team's marketing. For example, some marketing technology solutions will integrate with other technologies at your organization, such as your data, while others will try to consolidate those capabilities in an end-to-end solution. Some of these solutions will prioritize simplicity to serve small businesses, while other systems will build in smarter capabilities for measurement and artificial intelligence that support larger enterprises.

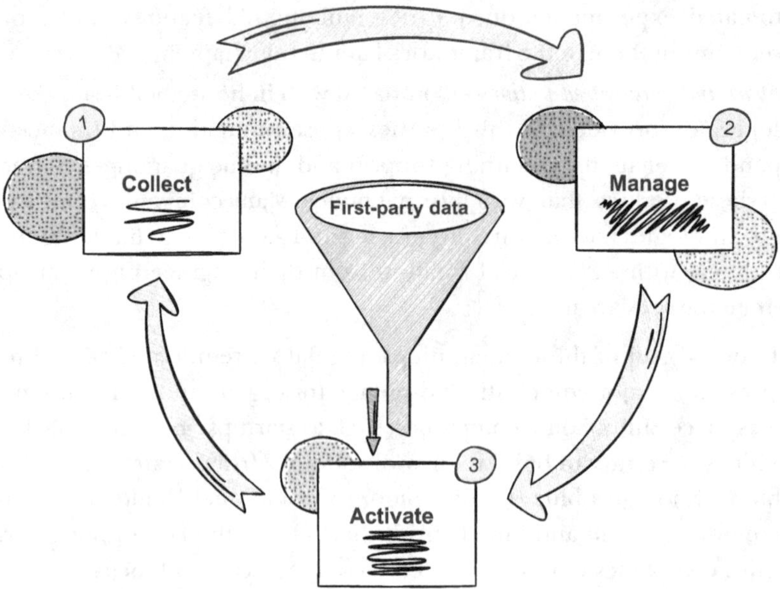

Figure 4.1 Components of modern marketing technology solutions for first-party data: collect, manage, activate

In the next section, we'll start with our primary recommendation based on recent innovations in marketing technology for first-party data. Then we'll review all the alternative options and determine when each is situationally the better choice.

4.2 Why choose a composable customer data platform

Let's consider the example of a major retailer that relies on both in-store and, increasingly, online orders to drive sales. The retailer engages current and prospective customers via email, direct mail, a mobile application with push notifications, personalized web experiences, and targeted paid media ads. They use incentives and offers to drive conversions around major events throughout the year, but they also have a robust loyalty program that rewards customers for more frequent purchases.

The marketing team's objective is to increase customer lifetime value by 8% while reducing the use of discounts by 20% (discounts that many customers have gotten used to). The marketing analytics team has built a new segmentation model using centralized customer data to greatly optimize offers and reduce the cost of marketing incentives. The marketing team would like to test it segment by segment with refreshed creative. Time is of the essence because the targets for customer lifetime value start the next fiscal quarter.

Given this scenario, the marketing team needs a solution that can do the following:

- Launch next quarter to influence their annual goals this year

- Use the segmentation models and all the attributes built by the marketing analytics team to personalize messaging
- Reach all current marketing channels to drive multichannel campaigns
- Support segment-level, cross-channel experiments to measure the incremental effect of the new creative and offer combinations applied to each segment

The marketing and marketing technology teams evaluated their options and chose a composable customer data platform (composable CDP) because it allowed them to meet all of these objectives. They successfully launched their first campaign in less than three months by connecting it to the marketing analytics datasets they already had, rather than building a unified customer profile somewhere new.

DEFINITION *Composable CDPs* are first-party data solutions that activate your unified customer profile to many marketing destinations by querying your data warehouse or lakehouse in place.

4.2.1 Why consider a composable CDP?

Let's dive into more details on why this approach works well for most organizations, and then we'll explore the cases where other approaches may work better. But first, let's define our terms:

- *Marketing data lakehouse*—This term refers to the marketing datasets of your enterprise data warehouse, data lake, or data lakehouse. We'll cover marketing data lakehouses in more detail in chapter 5, but for now, you can think of this as where your marketing analytics team queries and stores its data.
- *Composable CDP*—We use the term *composable* to refer to solutions that do not host your first-party data but rather connect directly to your first-party data inside your marketing data lakehouse, much like data visualization tools do. This gives them several distinct advantages, which we cover in the following subsections.

THE BEST OF "BUILD" AND "BUY" COMBINED

Fundamentally, centering your first-party data strategy around a marketing data lakehouse with a composable CDP works well because it combines the best attributes of "build" and "buy." It can be customized to your organization and built to be extensible for custom integrations and to unify your marketing and analytics or data science. Architecturally, it also provides agility to avoid lock-in with downstream systems, takes advantage of the scalability and security of the cloud, and is poised to take advantage of the rise of generative AI capabilities in the cloud.

Customization is key to making first-party solutions work well for your organization. Composable solutions allow your organization to define and control the data layer while using best-in-class activation for scale and reliability. This approach supports custom data models for your unified customer profile in ways that reflect your organization's full complexity. For example, conglomerate corporations may need to combine some shared central data with brand-specific datasets in complex ways. Banks often have complicated household and account hierarchies across business and consumer accounts. Marketplaces may have overlap between buyers and sellers with different data models. All these organizations can create a marketing data lakehouse that represents the complicated relationships between various data entities connected to their first-party data for marketing activation.

Extensibility is a second advantage of composable solutions that create point-in-time data copies (data snapshots) of their audiences and data for your marketing data lakehouse by default. This creates a historical record of audiences and personalization attributes that your team can reference. In fact, the seamless integration between marketing capabilities, such as audience creation and the marketing data lakehouse, means that you can use your composable solution to create *cohorts for analytics purposes* by connecting audience membership history to key metrics over time and then visualizing the results. Bespoke product integrations that drive personalized experiences are easier to implement when snapshots are available in the marketing data lakehouse for use elsewhere across your organization. Finance teams may even use marketing segmentation models to provide more granularity to the revenue composition in their reports. These are all examples of the extensibility of a unified data layer underpinning your first-party data strategy.

Unifying your marketing operations with marketing analytics, data science, and machine learning development is a third advantage of composable solutions driven by a shared source of truth. When the analytics team produces a segmentation model with individual customer-level labels, or the data science team produces a predictive model for customer churn, the marketing team can put them into live campaigns almost immediately because the composable CDP is connected to the same set of data tables in the marketing data lakehouse. Similarly, data science and analytics team members have direct access to every live audience, including each audience's membership and experimental labels. They can use this audience information to produce additional insights or features for new predictive models. In short, there are many organizational advantages to ensuring a shared source of truth between teams.

> **TIP** Having a single source of truth ensures that your team spends less time resolving conflicting facts. When you find an error, your team only needs to fix it once, and it will appear correctly everywhere.

ARCHITECTURAL ADVANTAGES

Agility in your marketing technology stack comes from your marketing team centralizing its intelligence in the marketing data lakehouse. Every audience definition, personalization field, calculated attribute, and experiment configuration is independent of any individual marketing channel or destination. This provides your organization huge leverage in changing your marketing technology solutions, such as email platforms or CRMs downstream of your composable CDP. You can adopt a "best of breed" system for each channel and reach new channels as they emerge without any vendor lock-in.

Scalability and security are built in by design in a composable architecture because they are natively available with the data lakehouse solution you choose, along with backup and recovery. Rather than hope that an individual marketing technology vendor, like Adobe, will solve your data scalability challenges as your company grows or you connect large new data sources, modern data platforms like Snowflake (featured in chapter 5) are constantly innovating to find more performant and cost-effective ways to scale querying on ever-increasing magnitudes of data. Many organizations hit data size constraints with their email and messaging platforms as they grow, and the best long-term solution is to keep your targeting data in your marketing data lakehouse and send only audience membership lists to your email or messaging platform (along with any personalization fields). Security is also paramount to these data platforms. They provide granular access controls, audit logging, and networking protections and uphold the highest security standards to stay competitive. This has enabled organizations in highly regulated industries such as banking, healthcare, and government to adopt the latest marketing technologies for the first time.

Innovative new capabilities, such as generative artificial intelligence, the latest machine learning tools, and business intelligence applications natively found in each major cloud platform or hyperscaler, are readily available in a composable architecture. Your team can connect or deploy an entire ecosystem of partner applications, giving you a competitive advantage over other organizations in your industry that are limited by the capabilities of an individual marketing technology that hosts first-party data. For example, Google Cloud launched generative AI capabilities for BigQuery in October 2023, so organizations with a composable marketing architecture could create custom messaging for each user within hours of the release of this new capability.

We believe today is the "App Store moment" for enterprise software because the composable architecture allows for near-zero implementation timelines and software purchases directly through the cloud marketplaces. If your organization adopts a composable architecture with a marketing data lakehouse at its center, it can take advantage of innovations in any of these fields.

COST ADVANTAGES

Finally, let's discuss the cost implications of composable CDPs and how organizations can build a business case for purchasing one.

Traditional monolithic marketing systems require you to host your data inside them to function. It is generally more expensive, because you must pay to host many copies of your data (one copy inside each marketing system). Since composable solutions centralize your data on a cloud data platform like Snowflake, which is built to be very cost-effective and fast, they are often half the cost of traditional marketing systems that must host your data.

How do you justify such a purchase? We recommend you prepare a business case that shows a strong return on investment of at least 2–3x. There are two key ways to build such a business case: *revenue-based* and *cost-based* arguments.

TIP Since your composable CDP is not tightly tied to your marketing data lakehouse, you can always switch to a less expensive solution with minimal migration effort.

Revenue-based (opportunity cost) arguments include how investing in your first-party data solution will help you grow sales or revenues. The strongest arguments are based on finding new campaigns or use cases that your recommended solution will make possible for the first time. Still, you can also find optimizations to your current campaigns or use cases. The math is simple, but it requires research into your business, marketing performance, or industry benchmarks when no internal figures are available.

Here's a real-life example: a travel site selling flights and hotel bookings was forced by its email platform to host only active user profiles because of the scale and cost implications. This meant the marketing team could not run churn winback campaigns (or retention campaigns focused on lapsed users). By estimating the size of the churned customer universe (say, 15 million churned users), the conversion rate for marketing outreach to those churned users (say, 2% or so), and a customer lifetime value (say, $25 per reactivated user), your team could estimate the effect of ongoing churn winback campaigns by multiplying the factors:

15,000,000 churned users × 2% reactivation rate × $25 lifetime value = $7,500,000

Most teams find several campaign examples like this to justify the revenue effect that a strong first-party data solution could provide their business, and they add them together to calculate a return on investment for their leadership team.

Your team can make an even stronger business case by pointing out the potential increase in customer lifetime value, which is the total revenue from a customer across all their lifetime purchases. If your team is better equipped to intervene early in a customer's impression of your brand, you may be able to have an outsized effect on their lifetime spending.

Cost-based, labor-saving arguments are all about saving the company money. Can you estimate the number of hours saved by the team by adopting a first-party data solution that offers marketing automation? If you can estimate the number of hours each campaign takes to run manually across teams, the number of campaigns you'd like to run each year, and your labor costs, your team could estimate the effect of cost savings by multiplying these factors:

30 hours per campaign × 120 campaigns per year × $60 per hour fully loaded labor cost = $216,000

Cost-based, media-saving arguments, such as ad suppressions, are often more compelling for companies that spend a lot on paid media. For one-time purchases (such as purchasing a car), your team should immediately remove the customers who have purchased from your paid media campaigns, or you risk wasting media dollars on customers who are no longer in the market for a car. Marketing teams that only update customer suppression lists with their advertisers once per month by delegating it to their media agency, or those that forgo this optimization, often waste hundreds of thousands or millions of dollars on over-targeting their ads, decreasing their return on ad spend (ROAS).

If you can estimate the share of your total media spend that you would save with more up-to-date suppression and track your total media spend, your team could estimate cost savings by multiplying these factors:

$$3\% \text{ ad suppression} \times \$30{,}000{,}000 \text{ paid media spend} = \$900{,}000$$

We cover integrations with paid media ad platforms to drive suppressions like this in more detail in chapter 7.

4.2.2 How does a composable CDP work?

Since activation from the marketing data lakehouse is relatively new, let's dive into how it works at the architecture level. The composable CDP emerged from organizations' attempts to build their own activation on the marketing data lakehouse—composable CDPs are like the productized version of an organization's efforts to build its own capabilities.

Figure 4.2 shows a high-level marketing systems architecture diagram from data source to destination (left to right). Our intention is to show how a typical organization might put the pieces of its marketing stack together to create the best solution. Note how much control over the data the architecture in figure 4.2 maintains for the organization as we break this down into data collection and ingestion, customer profile unification and management, and activation.

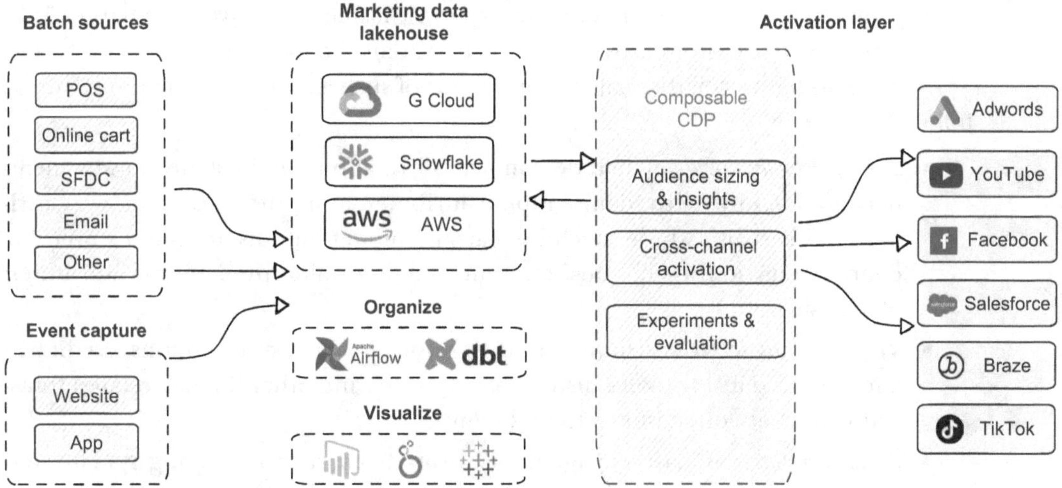

Figure 4.2 Architecture diagram for a marketing stack

DATA COLLECTION AND INGESTION

The goal of the data collection and ingestion component is simple: to bring all your organization's data sources of various types into your marketing data lakehouse in any form. This component varies widely by organization because it is often built in-house by the analytics or data teams. We'll break it down further into two types of data collection and ingestion:

- *Event collection*—This refers to website, mobile application, and other engagement data sources often collected in real time by analytics software such as GA4, Adobe Analytics, or Twilio Segment. These sources can usually be streamed into a bucket storage such as AWS S3 or Google Cloud Storage and queried directly to give you the most up-to-date data. Some data is purely anonymous and non-targetable, some is pseudonymous data that creates individual records and can be matched only with specific ad platforms, and some is personally identifiable data that can be matched with the rest of your marketing data lakehouse.
- *Batch data ingestion*—Most data sources, such as transactional data, are found in the backend of other important systems across the organization. The good news is that many of these are now well-supported by data ingestion tools such as Fivetran and Matillion to keep records in sync between your marketing data lakehouse and the original data source.

CUSTOMER PROFILE UNIFICATION AND MANAGEMENT

Customer profile unification and management refers to a system that combines various data sources to create a unified customer profile. It may also include audience segmentation and journey orchestration capabilities for your marketing team.

While monolithic CDPs require your organization to adopt a specific customer data model, a marketing data lakehouse allows your team to choose your own customer data model. You can apply data engineering in a stepwise fashion (discussed in chapter 5) to create a very flexible customer (or prospective customer) data model.

As shown in figure 4.3, the major components of such a customer data model are as follows:

- *Direct customer attributes* include contact information, opt-in status, loyalty membership, identity fields, demographic attributes, and other customer-level attributes. This is also where machine learning model outputs are often stored for churn prediction likelihoods, customer lifetime value predictions, and upsell propensities.
- *Transactional datasets* include purchase history, product subscriptions, credit balances, refund history, sales history, offer history, and other finance-related transaction datasets, often linked to timestamps.
- *Activity datasets* include engagement history from each marketing system, web analytics platforms, mobile analytics platforms, product session datasets, and other activity-related datasets that record customer events at specific timestamps.

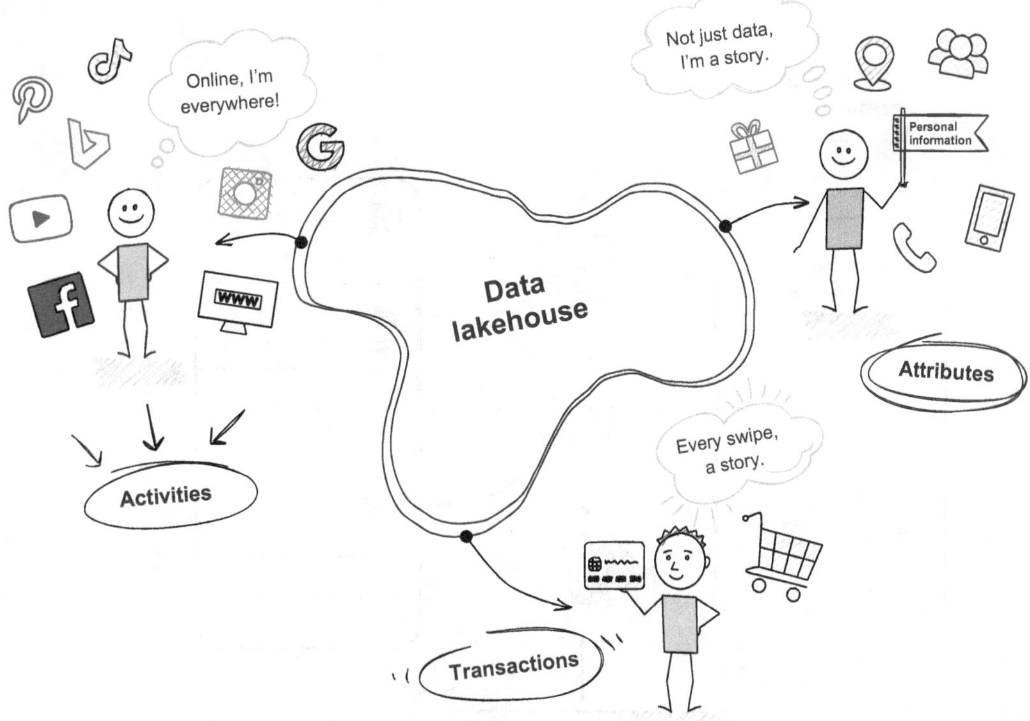

Figure 4.3 Customer data model: attributes, transactions, activities

Many organizations create a base table of all direct customer attributes and then use one-to-many relationships to help create dynamic calculations of aggregations across transactional and activity datasets to answer targeting questions like "Which customers spent $200 or more last year on shoe-related products but have not logged into their account or clicked on an email in the last thirty days?" or personalization questions like "What are the total savings from redeemed offers for each customer last quarter?"

These targeting and personalization questions can be written in SQL statements or by a composable CDP on the unified customer profile. However, they are limited to data visualizations and noncompliant CSV downloads unless programmatically integrated with downstream marketing channels or destinations.

Activation

The activation component's goal is to drive the successful sync of all audience membership and personalization attributes to marketing and sales destinations. It is the most engineering-intensive component to build and maintain, which is why composable CDP platforms are often worthwhile investments (see figure 4.4). The export of first-party data to destinations downstream consists of a few major categories, each following its own integration design pattern (covered in more detail in chapter 7).

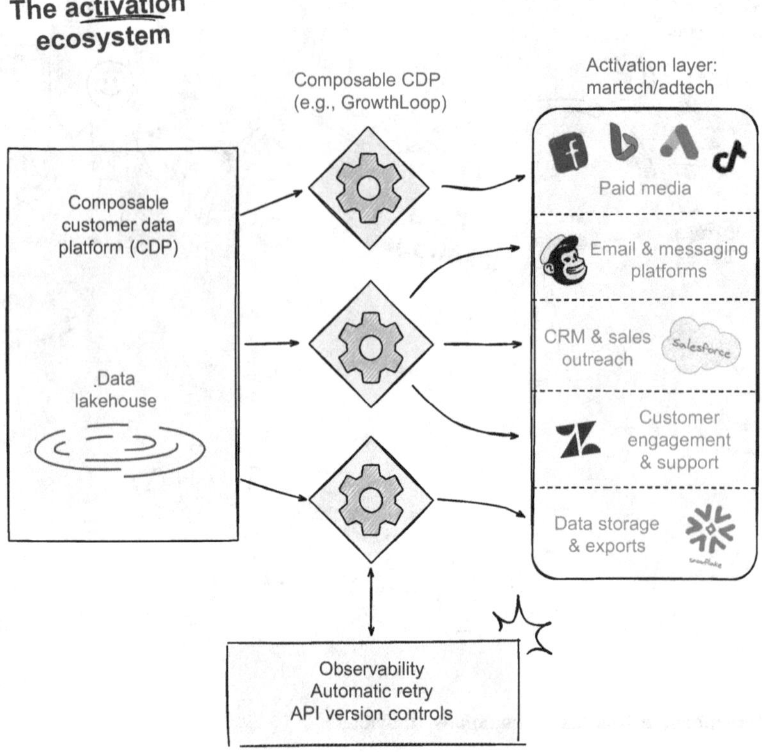

Figure 4.4 Composable CDP dynamics for seamless first-party data activation

Good activation capabilities include the following:

- *Observability*—Audit logs to monitor for data sync errors (such as duplicate record updates, key mismatches, or API authentication problems) with corresponding alerts to catch problems as soon as they arise. You'd be amazed how many organizations find marketing campaign problems in production weeks or months too late due to poor observability.
- *Automatic retry*—To overcome connection or networking problems, it's important to have destination-specific retry protocols, such as exponential backoff.
- *API version controls*—Destination APIs are often updated in ways that are not backward-compatible, but this can be easily remedied with proactive API version control monitoring and updating.

Other capabilities

There are a variety of other components that you can develop or search for in a composable CDP to enhance your team's capabilities further. Here are just a few, illustrated in figure 4.5:

- *Measurement capabilities*—These include automated experimentation, such as the dynamic assignment of individual audience members to treatment and control groups, and experimental evaluation to determine corresponding results. Some teams build attribution models on their marketing data lakehouse to view aggregate performance by marketing channel.
- *AI capabilities*—Predictive models and recent generative marketing capabilities enhance targeting effectiveness, and product recommendation models can enhance personalization. The native cloud capabilities available to a marketing data lakehouse make it much easier to apply AI to marketing at scale.
- *Reporting capabilities*—Audience-level insights such as sizing, audience overlap, and other attributes are incredibly helpful for marketers in the design and ideation phase of campaign implementation. Experimental results are often visualized for marketers so they can interpret and adapt their campaigns. These can be expressed as data visualizations or reports directly on the marketing data lakehouse for in-house-built solutions and composable CDPs—a significant advantage of this architecture for most analytics teams.

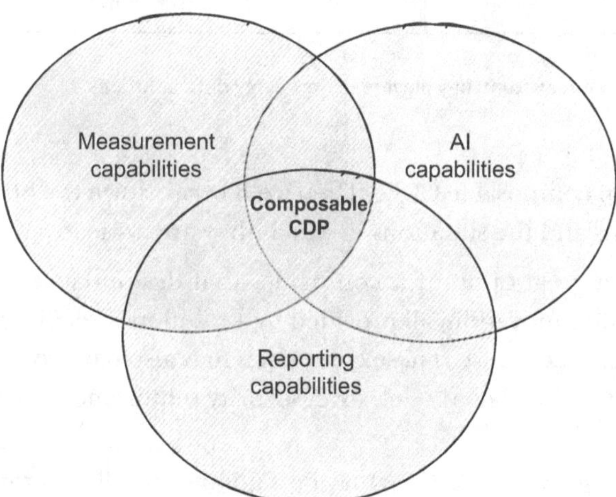

Figure 4.5 Composable CDP capabilities

4.3 Comparison of major solution categories

Marketing technologists today have several options when considering first-party data solutions. As figure 4.6 shows, there are monolithic solutions that attempt to provide an all-in-one approach, CDPs that focus on integrating systems, in-house custom builds that solve organization-specific requirements, and new composable solutions that use their customers' data cloud directly.

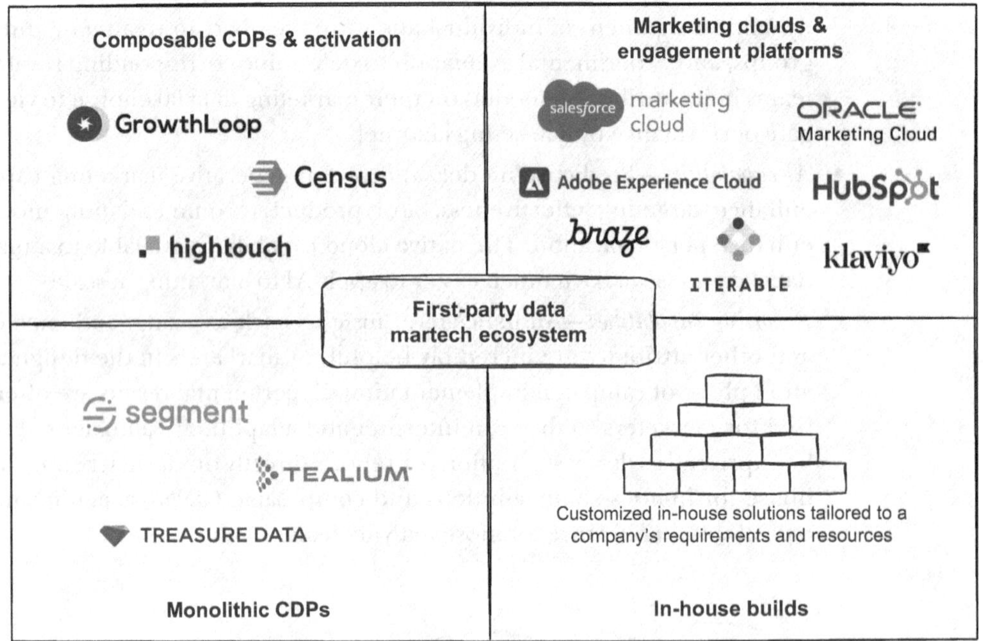

Figure 4.6 Marketing technology ecosystem: key players in first-party data solutions

We'll start with a summary of composable CDPs. Then we'll break down the other three major categories of solutions and the situations in which they are most advantageous:

- *Composable CDPs* are a great option for companies that desire data unification, extensibility, and cloud innovation, all provided by a solution directly connected to their marketing data lakehouse. These companies may also have complex data needs that require a flexible data model, strict security requirements, or massive data scalability.
- *Marketing clouds and engagement platforms* may be a good option for organizations that do not need many destination integrations or much data customization but want a blue-chip name to own product integrations for them. These are generally the most expensive options since they are offered as integrated suites of products by Adobe and Salesforce, but they are optimized for enterprise environments.
- *Monolithic CDPs* that host a unified customer profile may be a good option for web and mobile-first companies that have lower data maturity (for example, no

marketing data lakehouse) and therefore desire an end-to-end first-party data solution. These platforms provide an opinionated customer profile and offer many destination integrations out of the box.

- *In-house builds* are best suited for companies that have very simple needs, such as a single channel integration to support, or that have no marketing technology alternatives for their bespoke needs. This was commonly the path for the most data-mature companies before the availability of composable CDPs. This option may have been chosen due to regulatory needs, bespoke product integration requirements (where build solutions shine), or other organization-specific considerations.

We'll provide a detailed breakdown of each of the primary considerations in the following sections, but we'll start with a helpful summary of the benefits and trade-offs for each category, along with which companies each is best suited for, in table 4.1.

Table 4.1 Marketing technology ecosystem comparison: benefits and trade-offs

Marketing technology	Best for	Key benefits	Trade-offs
Composable CDPs	Data-mature companies needing scalability and tight integration between analytics and marketing	Data unification, extensibility, cloud-based, direct connection to marketing data lakehouse	Requires strong data infrastructure and expertise
Marketing clouds and engagement platforms	Large organizations needing an all-in-one solution with consultant support	Simplifies the tech stack, certified consultant support, ease of implementation	Higher cost, limitations in marketing destinations
Monolithic CDPs	Web and mobile-first companies with lower data maturity needing built-in real-time capabilities	Unified customer profile, preset identity resolution, many destination integrations	Difficult to implement, less flexibility
In-house builds	Organizations with highly bespoke needs or minimal data integration requirements	Fully customizable, control over data infrastructure	High development and maintenance effort

4.3.1 Composable CDPs

Let's revisit our example of the major retailer from section 4.2. Recall that the retailer needs to combine in-store and online orders to launch cross-channel campaigns on a customer segmentation model built by their marketing analytics team. Marketing teams like these began to demand a more unified first-party data solution, and they found it in a new category of composable CDPs, such as GrowthLoop, which is used by major technology companies like Indeed.

As a quick reminder, we use the term *composable* to refer to solutions that do not host your first-party data but rather connect directly to your first-party data inside your marketing data lakehouse, much like data visualization tools do. We'll cover marketing data lakehouses in more detail in chapter 5, but for now, you can think of this as where your marketing analytics team queries and stores its data.

Composable platforms generally support an open and flexible data model: you set the primary key (unique data field) to target customers and then add or link other tables to it as they are found in your data. This allows your organization to keep any complicated data models virtually unchanged while taking advantage of the full scalability and security of your organization's chosen data cloud platform.

This makes composable CDPs a good fit for larger enterprise organizations that need scalability and those in highly regulated industries with high-security requirements. Trade-offs include the need to invest in a marketing data lakehouse as the basis for activation and some limitations in real-time capabilities.

4.3.2 Marketing clouds and engagement platforms

Imagine you are a marketer at a traditional consumer packaged-goods company selling diapers. Ninety-five percent of your sales are made through retail partners such as supermarkets, pharmacies, and convenience stores, and those sales channels do not provide information about your customers. The company's IT department lacks marketing technology experience, and the analytics team is focused on consumer and product research rather than marketing performance or segmentation modeling.

Your team helped launch a direct-to-consumer website to sell busy parents subscriptions to regular diaper deliveries. This means it is now possible to collect first-party data for a small subset of your customers. The marketing team's goal is to expand the direct-to-consumer business from 5% of total sales to 10% over the next 12 months by launching a referral program with various offers for subscribing parents.

Given this scenario, the marketing team needs a solution that

- Will be easy to manage, including through support from outsourced, certified consultants
- Focuses on a single channel (email) to reach subscribing parents
- Provides a simple direct-to-consumer customer profile

This would be a great scenario for introducing a marketing automation platform that scalably delivers email and mobile messaging campaigns to customers.

We use the terms *marketing clouds* and *engagement platforms* to describe monolithic first-party data solutions that offer an all-in-one approach to collecting, managing, and activating your first-party data in a fully hosted model that often executes delivery as well (e.g., email delivery). Historically, several of these solutions were developed by integrating different marketing technologies to offer a more holistic solution to marketers, which has led to clunky integration experiences for their users.

DEFINITION Marketing clouds and engagement platforms (sometimes referred to as MCs) are first-party data solutions that offer a fully hosted customer profile with embedded delivery capabilities (e.g., email or mobile notifications).

Once they're implemented, marketing clouds provide an integrated capability set that reduces the complexity of your technology stack. The significant trade-off to marketing clouds is that your marketing team is locked into the limited capabilities in AI, measurement, data management, and destinations that the marketing cloud provides. They are also sold at some of the highest prices for first-party data solutions.

The two most popular marketing cloud solutions are the suite of Adobe Experience Cloud products and the Salesforce Marketing Cloud. Several email and mobile engagement platforms, such as Braze, Klaviyo, and Iterable, have begun to compete in this space by expanding their integrations.

4.3.3 Monolithic CDPs

Let's imagine a company that offers access to electric vehicle charging stations through a mobile app. The marketing team reaches customers through SMS, mobile push notifications, emails, and paid media. To achieve the right economies of scale, the team hopes to drive 10% greater in-network usage per customer (compared to out-of-network charging at home). While the mobile application has a data engineering team, it focuses solely on serving the product team and not the marketing team.

Given this scenario, the marketing team needs a solution that can

- Tightly integrate with customer interactions on the company's mobile application
- Use customer events instantly, such as geolocation near a charging station
- Reach all current marketing channels to drive multi-channel campaigns
- Operate entirely independently of the data engineering team

A monolithic CDP like Tealium, which is focused on capturing, unifying, and activating mobile events, may be a great first-party data solution for this marketing team, especially if they have software engineering to support its implementation. Let's review what a CDP is and the most important considerations to remember.

According to the CDP Institute, a customer data platform (CDP) is "packaged software that creates a persistent, unified customer database that is accessible to other systems" (www.cdpinstitute.org/cdp-basics/). Similarly, we define a CDP as a first-party data solution that integrates various sources to create a fully hosted, unified customer profile that you can activate to many other destinations, such as email platforms, ad platforms, and other marketing destinations. Many CDPs began by specializing in a particular feature set, such as web personalization, identity resolution, or customer segmentation. However, most have attempted to offer a more holistic capability set over time to address all the major areas related to first-party data solutions.

DEFINITION Customer data platforms (CDPs) are first-party data solutions that integrate various sources to create a fully hosted, unified customer profile that you can activate to many marketing destinations.

The main difference between a monolithic CDP and a composable CDP is in its architecture—specifically, how it collects data and who hosts the customer data. A monolithic CDP collects customer or prospect engagement data directly by integrating with web and mobile applications (like many web and mobile analytics platforms), whereas a composable CDP often relies upon existing web and mobile event collection. More importantly, a monolithic CDP will store all your customer data, while a composable CDP will connect to your marketing data lakehouse or similar data platform rather than host your data itself.

Once implemented, monolithic CDPs provide strong integrations to various marketing, sales, customer success, product, and other systems (sometimes numbering in the hundreds). While you are subject to the lock-in of your customer profile and business logic (e.g., audience definitions), monolithic CDPs allow you to migrate or change your downstream systems or channels more easily from one vendor to another than marketing clouds do.

Other trade-offs of monolithic CDPs are their long implementation cycle, limited ability to support complicated customer profiles (especially regarding data scale), and the siloed nature of the customer profile. We recommend CDPs for companies that do not have a marketing analytics or data science function but that wish to reach more destinations than marketing clouds provide. There are many monolithic CDPs, some of which are unreliable, so we recommend focusing on the best-supported ones and evaluating each carefully. The most prominent ones are Tealium, Treasure Data, and Segment.

4.3.4 *In-house builds*

In our collective experience, we've seen two scenarios in which it makes sense to build your own first-party data solution from scratch:

- There is no marketing technology that meets your organization's needs, and you have the resources to build your own (or to hire a consultancy such as Deloitte or Accenture to do so).
- Your organization's needs are so simple (for example, you only intend to use a single marketing channel) that the available marketing technology is an unjustifiable expense.

Let's start with the first category. Before composable CDPs were available, many of the most data-driven organizations began to build their own marketing activation capabilities connected directly to their marketing data lakehouse. This choice made sense because it allowed these companies to orchestrate their marketing campaigns from their central source of truth or unified marketing data lakehouse. No other marketing technology option at the time would have allowed them full control of their data.

The problem for these organizations is that they fall behind the frontier of capabilities offered by marketing technology companies with far more product and engineering resources for developing new capabilities. One of the most acute areas where we've seen this limitation is in channel proliferation, both in terms of breadth (i.e., new channels) and depth (i.e., new integration patterns for existing channels, like Meta's CAPI). As a result, many of these organizations have begun to adopt composable CDPs and have renewed their focus on their internal efforts to build a stronger data layer and deeper first-party product integrations where they have a distinct advantage over third-party solutions.

The second category represents the opposite end of the spectrum because it refers to companies with very simple marketing needs. There may only be a single data sync from a marketing data lakehouse or analytics dataset to a single email platform or sales customer relationship management (CRM) platform, so the team decides to build and maintain that single sync in lieu of purchasing third-party software. While this approach is inherently limiting, it may work perfectly well for simple marketing stacks.

In sum, the advantage of a custom in-house build is that you can pursue use case requirements that perfectly match your organization's needs. The disadvantage is that you may find yourself reinventing the wheel as the need for new channels and capabilities grows. Thus, many organizations underestimate the cost of ongoing development and maintenance.

4.4 Core capabilities and considerations

In this section, we'll offer an evaluation framework for marketing technologists that includes the most common considerations for and capabilities of first-party data solutions. We'll also include some anecdotes of lessons learned by our clients in recent years.

When reviewing these capabilities and considerations, be wary of evaluating solutions by checking boxes against everything your organization may want to do. At first glance, that seems like a reasonable approach—it feels defensible to show your team you've comprehensively evaluated the options. The problem is that first-party data solutions have strengths and weaknesses, just like any other solution. When you prioritize breadth, you sacrifice depth and ignore the fact that most solutions are extensible. Instead, prioritize the most common and important use cases your team has today and tomorrow, and look to extend the solution's capabilities for the remaining use cases.

4.4.1 Time-to-value

Many marketers we've met have experienced long implementation delays and even implementation failures with their marketing technology purchases. For those marketers and others, the following questions are key: *How long will it take your team to begin seeing value? How much software or data engineering support does the solution need?*

Many marketers have quarterly and annual growth targets to hit, and they need technology solutions that will be ready to use quickly. Accruing growth gains large enough to move the needle on quarterly or annual targets may take months, so every week of implementation required by a new marketing technology is critical and affects your targets.

Nearly every solution advertises a fast time-to-value, so how should you assess whether that's truly the case? The most common mistake technologists and marketers make is to neglect their current strengths. Do you have a strong marketing analytics team? Great! Use it by finding composable solutions that connect directly to the analytics team's data layer so your team can seamlessly turn their insights into campaigns. If not, do you have strong web and mobile application development teams? Fantastic! Consider a monolithic CDP that provides web and mobile SDKs for them to collect data directly from your web and mobile applications.

In the same vein, what kind of support do you expect to receive from other teams in terms of implementing and supporting your first-party data solution? A well-known media and entertainment organization we worked with purchased a composable solution only to get stuck in implementation because the marketing technology team failed to secure support from their data team before the purchase. By the time they realized their mistake, it had become a political deadlock, causing them to lose 12 months. The lesson? Drive stakeholder alignment *before* you commit to a first-party data solution. At this point, you have the greatest agility to change direction and to include key people in the decision-making process.

Regardless of the type of support a marketing technology requires, most teams avoid buying solutions that require a lengthy implementation or onboarding process—you don't want to spend 9, 12, or more months building, configuring, or learning to use the new solution. There are many partially implemented customer data platforms whose organizations were never able to fully realize their implementation.

What's the best way to find out what an actual implementation cycle looks like? We recommend you speak to other customers who have purchased the solution you are considering. The solution provider should be able to provide customer references, which are inherently biased but nonetheless useful—your team can ask probing questions about the complexity of the implementation process.

As a starting point for your team's search for a solution, we summarize time-to-value considerations for each marketing technology category in table 4.2.

Table 4.2 Time-to-value considerations

Solution	Considerations
Composable CDPs	(+) If your organization has its first-party data available in a marketing data lakehouse or somewhere similar, implementation usually only takes a few weeks.
Marketing clouds/ engagement platforms	(+/-) MCs often have long implementation cycles because they need to load and transform data to match their predetermined customer profile structure. While support is expensive, the good news is that plenty of implementation partners are available.

Table 4.2 Time-to-value considerations (*continued*)

Solution	Considerations
Monolithic CDPs	(-) Monolithic CDPs often have long implementation cycles due to the need to load and transform data to match their predetermined customer profile structure. Only a handful of monolithic CDPs are well-known enough to have experienced implementation partners.
In-house builds	(-) Builds often have long implementation cycles because they require product development, software implementation, and data implementation.

4.4.2 *Marketing execution speed*

Once you have a solution implemented, the next question becomes ease of use: *How easily can marketers use the new technology to serve their needs?*

Marketing execution speed is one of the most important factors in choosing a marketing technology solution for your first-party data, because a good solution multiplies your marketing team's ability to execute campaigns. While time-to-value is essential, it only represents a one-time event. In contrast, marketing execution speed represents the effort your team will need to expend every time your team wants to launch a new campaign.

When using your company's first-party data, you'll likely run into challenges navigating the intersection between data and marketing. The first-party data at your organization may be large and inherently complicated due to multiple lines of business, poorly integrated systems, or multiple classes of buyers. One of the primary goals of your implemented marketing technology solution should be to simplify this as much as possible for your marketing team, ideally to the point where marketers are able to self-serve for nearly all their use cases.

In the long term, you also want to choose a solution that does not require ongoing support from software engineering teams or solution specialists. Ideally, the solution should be well-designed enough that only marginal data needs (e.g., the integration of new data sources) require support after the initial implementation is complete. For example, a good solution should not require your team to perform data engineering for calculated fields, such as targeting "customers who have made at least three purchases in the last 90 days," which could be calculated on the fly. Without these capabilities, your marketing team will be bottlenecked by supporting teams nearly every time your team wishes to prepare and launch a campaign.

The best way to determine whether a solution will require ongoing support is to ask for demonstrations of the solution for your specific use cases (especially the more complicated ones) or the closest approximation to your specific use case. Some solution providers will offer technology pilots or proofs of concept that your team can use to gauge how easy or difficult it would be for your marketers to self-serve on the application. Be wary of canned demonstrations that do not reflect your industry or the complexity of your organization, and be sure to include your least technical marketers in evaluations. They are often the best judges of what constitutes a truly self-service solution from a user experience point of view.

In table 4.3, we summarize the most common advantages and disadvantages of each marketing technology category based on marketers' ease of use.

Table 4.3 Marketing execution speed considerations

Solution	Considerations
Composable CDPs	(+/-) Most are purpose-built for marketers, but those built for data teams may not be.
Marketing clouds/ engagement platforms	(+) MCs are purpose-built for marketers. Assuming data engineering is complete, an incremental campaign is relatively easy to execute.
Monolithic CDPs	(+) Monolithic CDPs are purpose-built for marketers. Assuming data engineering is complete, an incremental campaign is relatively easy to execute.
In-house builds	(-) Most builds focus on providing essential capabilities for data teams but lack good user experiences for non-technical marketers.

4.4.3 *Audience portability (cross-channel campaigns)*

If your organization reaches its customers and prospects across multiple communication channels, you'll want to find a solution that helps you deliver consistent targeting and messaging across all your channels: *How well does the solution integrate with your current channels, or potential future channels? How easily does the solution allow your team to launch a single campaign on multiple channels?*

Audience portability means that the marketing technology solution you choose should allow you to define an audience once and make it available across all your channels or downstream marketing systems automatically. For example, a marketer on your team may define an audience of recently churned customers whose membership will likely change daily. A good first-party data solution should automatically add and remove members, based on your latest first-party data, from the audience in your organization's email service provider, any paid media platforms your team uses, customer relationship management tools, or any other channel you plan to use to engage those customers.

Consumers and businesses are on an ever-growing number of social media platforms and device types, with new expectations for personalized engagement methods. If your solution is constrained to only a few channels or only offers certain limited integrations with those channels, your organization risks falling behind competitors. Most marketing teams find that prospective customers who convert require multiple marketing impressions before conversion, so reaching those prospective customers across several channels is crucial for performance.

How should you judge whether a solution meets your team's audience portability needs? You should prioritize and cross-reference your channels with those provided by the solution and then negotiate to ensure the vendor adds any missing channels within a reasonable time frame of your purchase. This will ensure the right *breadth* of channel integrations. Then, with each of your destination channels, map your use cases to all the types of integrations your team may need (e.g., for Google Ads, you may need to sync audiences via Customer Match and Enhanced Conversions for individual conversion events). This will help your team assess the *depth* of channel integrations.

Be wary of comparing the sheer volume of channels supported by platforms on their websites. What matters most is that your chosen solution can provide the channels *your* organization and *your* team need. In the long run, it is far more important to find an agile marketing technology provider that can grow with you to add new destinations that may not even exist now. Ask the vendor about the process and timeline for adding a new destination, and make sure you have an "escape hatch" for custom destinations, such as a bucket storage option (e.g., AWS S3 or Google Cloud Storage).

Assessing and driving value using several cross-channel campaigns at once is paramount to marketing success. Ensuring the right breadth and depth of integrations and the ease of adding new destinations will be a key factor in your organization's success with first-party data.

Audience portability is one area that varies widely across marketing technology categories, so we've summarized which technology categories serve this capability well and which don't in table 4.4.

Table 4.4 Audience portability (cross-channel support) considerations

Solution	Considerations
Composable CDPs	(+) Like all CDPs, composable CDPs offer some of the most extensive integration sets for destinations across several categories.
Marketing clouds/ engagement platforms	(-) MCs often lack destination integrations that are well supported by other categories.
Monolithic CDPs	(+) Monolithic CDPs offer some of the most extensive integration sets for destinations across several categories.
In-house builds	(+/-) Builds can support bespoke integrations that other solutions may not support, but each additional destination requires a heavier lift than third-party solutions.

4.4.4 Data trust and reliability

Creating a reliable, unified repository of customer data is hard. Maintaining multiple reliable, unified repositories of customer data in different systems is nearly impossible for most companies. This makes it essential that you find a solution that proactively addresses the risk of unreliable data. *How well does the solution use your organization's single source of truth on customer data? How accessible is the data in the marketing technology to your marketing analytics team?*

Data trust and *reliability* refer to the degree to which your marketing team can count on a marketing technology solution to represent your customer data accurately and to reliably deliver it to campaigns in production. Good solutions will provide flexibility, monitoring, and consistency to your data management to ensure reliability and trust in your prospect or customer data.

Your organization may have complex data needs. Perhaps there are multiple product lines or lines of business that each have their own data structure. You may have complicated business account relationships with multiple contacts, or you could consolidate households in some cases but preserve individual contacts in others. Flexibility in your data management means your solution does not lose the ability to represent the full complexity of your data.

Robust monitoring and alerts are the next capabilities you should consider for catching things such as duplicate fields, stale data, or logical inconsistencies, all of which are symptomatic of poor data reliability. These alerts help you identify data problems before they affect campaigns in production, so they are essential to preserving trust with your audience.

Most importantly, it's essential that whatever solutions you choose to use can help you use a single source of truth that is shared across your marketing team (and hopefully other departments). Trust breaks down when separate teams use different definitions for things like customer churn, different sources for primary contact information, or different suppression criteria that affect who receives marketing. If your organization has a managed data lakehouse or data warehouse for your first-party data, why create copies in other tools that introduce latency or that are constrained to hosting a partial customer profile instead of a complete profile?

If you choose solutions that require you to maintain multiple customer profiles, you risk creating more data silos. In this case, you immediately lose the value of a unified and organized customer profile. When prospect or customer data is siloed from its primary source, it can become inaccessible to your data team, making it virtually unmanageable. This can lead to duplicate, noncompliant, or stale campaigns and, ultimately, a loss of trust with your audience. Instead, pick solutions that rely upon a single customer profile that is visible and accessible to your data team.

However, what if that's not possible at your organization for political or technological reasons? In that case, the next best approach is to prioritize a central source of truth and keep your various customer profiles in sync based on that central source. For example, a travel company worked around this by maintaining a central customer profile in their marketing data warehouse, modeled to match their email platform's customer profile. Although this introduced data latency, and they eventually faced problems scaling this approach, this hub-and-spoke approach did meet the needs of the day.

No system is fail-safe, but good solutions are designed to take advantage of smart data architectures to help your team achieve strong data reliability by design. We've summarized which categories of marketing technology tend to do this well in table 4.5.

Table 4.5 Data trust and reliability considerations

Solution	Considerations
Composable CDPs	(+) Composable CDPs focus on connecting directly to your central customer profile rather than creating a secondary customer profile. Alerts and monitoring can be delegated to the marketing data lakehouse, which is helpful.
Marketing clouds/ engagement platforms	(-) While there are virtualized views, MCs require teams to manage a hosted customer profile, which may add latency and discrepancies compared to a primary customer profile used by analytics teams.
Monolithic CDPs	(-) While there are virtualized views, monolithic CDPs require teams to manage a hosted customer profile, which may add latency and discrepancies compared to a primary customer profile used by analytics teams.
In-house builds	(+) Build solutions often connect directly to the organization's unified first-party data, which means they work on the same source of truth as analytics teams and other functions at the organization. This is often the deciding factor for companies that choose to build.

4.4.5 *Artificial intelligence*

Even before the latest advances in generative AI, predictive models for marketing were in heavy use by the leading brands to target and personalize their communications. *How well does the first-party data solution incorporate predictive models? What generative AI capabilities does the solution provide your team?*

Predictive marketing is here; the best teams are already applying it at scale. The solution you choose to better use first-party data should be able to grow alongside your marketing team's adoption of artificial intelligence.

Why is artificial intelligence so important to creating highly performant campaigns? The short answer is that it can encode more information in a single set of predictions than a human could. For example, a human can use a mix of analytics and intuition to define an audience of customers most likely to churn in the next thirty days using a handful of rules-based criteria. An AI model, on the other hand, can incorporate hundreds of features, handle transformations and interactions between features, and then prioritize their weightings with a high degree of granularity to produce predictions for each customer.

If you have an analytics or data science team to support marketing, you should prioritize first-party data solutions that allow you to incorporate your team's models seamlessly into your marketing team's natural workflows. Marketers benefit greatly from an interface that allows them to combine prediction attributes with other direct attributes to set the targeting criteria for audiences.

More recently, generative AI has introduced an entirely new dimension of innovation in marketing, and marketing technology solutions are finding new and exciting ways to incorporate it. You should evaluate your first-party data solutions in the light of your team's generative AI strategy. In short, generative AI for marketing is much more effective if it can use a unified dataset, the list of all your team's available channels, and your organization's objectives, so your architecture matters. Note that your organization may have policies governing the use of generative AI for marketing. We'll cover this topic in much greater detail in chapter 9.

Select a first-party data solution that supports your AI strategy and any upcoming initiatives. It will likely be more future-proof than platforms that incorporate AI in limited ways. In table 4.6, we summarize each marketing technology category's typical approach to AI.

Table 4.6 Artificial intelligence considerations

Solution	Considerations
Composable CDPs	(+) Composable CDPs can connect directly to your team's predictions, and the cloud-native architecture makes it easier to incorporate new AI capabilities provided by your cloud platform.
Marketing clouds/ engagement platforms	(-) MCs often provide limited prebuilt AI capabilities that focus on ease of use but lack integrations with major cloud platforms that offer more-advanced AI capabilities.
Monolithic CDPs	(-) Monolithic CDPs often provide limited prebuilt AI capabilities that focus on ease of use but lack integrations with major cloud platforms that offer more-advanced AI capabilities.
In-house builds	(+/-) The applications of AI and the availability of best-in-class AI capabilities are subject to the design of the in-house build, and they vary widely from one build to the next.

4.4.6 Security and compliance

These days, security and compliance concerns are front and center for many organizations, and your compliance and security teams may prevent you from onboarding solutions that do not meet certain industry standards. While there are many aspects to those topics, this section will focus on how potential solutions store, process, and transmit first-party data. Key questions include the following: *How do different solutions demonstrate built-in support for security? Will your CIO/CTO/CISO allow you to copy sensitive data into a third-party marketing system? Does the solution you are considering support your organization's compliance goals?*

Let's start with security. There are now widely recognized international standards audited by third parties to serve as a baseline assurance of security best practices. Some of the most common ones are SOC 2 in the United States (developed by the American Institute of CPAs) and ISO 27001 internationally (developed by the International

Organization for Standardization). These standards include data encryption in transit and at rest with organizational controls to minimize the chance of data breaches or security incidents, which is critical to upholding trust with your brand.

Many organizations seek additional security in how solutions are designed. In recent history, most marketing technology platforms have required organizations to load and host their data inside third-party systems. However, as discussed in this chapter, a new breed of composable marketing technology solutions has allowed companies to host their data and authorize limited data sharing instead. This data hosting model has allowed highly regulated companies—like banks, healthcare providers, and higher education institutions—to take advantage of the latest marketing technology capabilities by using the robust security of major cloud data platforms. These solutions process first-party data in place so that it never has to leave your organization's cloud infrastructure until it's "exported" to marketing destinations for delivery.

One key insight that composable solutions have brought to market recently has had major benefits for both security and scalability: your systems may not need to share data fields used for targeting (which may be sensitive) to execute campaigns. By sharing only audience membership and necessary personalization attributes to marketing channel destinations (such as email systems or paid media platforms), your solution can significantly reduce the amount of data sharing, which is great for scalability. This also respects the well-established security principle of least privilege, because downstream systems have access to only the information necessary for their legitimate purposes.

Moving on to compliance, consider whether a particular solution helps you achieve your organization's compliance goals. Privacy compliance concerns, such as user consent, are critical to a first-party data solution, which is why we covered this in more detail in chapter 2. Consider other forms of compliance that may be industry-specific. For example, if you're a bank, does this solution help your marketing team comply with fair lending practices? If you're in the healthcare industry, can the solution be configured to ensure compliance with the Health Insurance Portability and Accountability Act (HIPAA)? Many marketing technology providers will not sign a Business Associate Agreement (BAA), which may rule them out for healthcare companies.

In table 4.7, we summarize the most common advantages and disadvantages of each marketing technology category based on its architecture, common approaches to security, and industry-specific considerations.

Table 4.7 Security and compliance considerations

Solution	Considerations
Composable CDPs	(+) Most composable CDPs maintain very high standards of security (SOC 2 and ISO 27001 certifications), and some will meet industry-specific regulatory requirements. No third-party data hosting is a major benefit to security.
Marketing clouds/ engagement platforms	(+/-) MCs maintain very high security standards, but they may not sign BAAs for healthcare customers or meet other industry-specific regulatory requirements.

Table 4.7 Security and compliance considerations (*continued*)

Solution	Considerations
Monolithic CDPs	(+) The leading monolithic CDPs maintain very high standards of security, and some industry-specific CDPs will meet industry-specific regulatory requirements. Since CDPs must host your data, be wary of second-tier or third-tier CDPs that are not SOC 2 or ISO 27001 certified.
In-house builds	(+/-) The fact that first-party data is hosted in the organization's own systems is a considerable advantage, but security implementation varies widely from one build to the next. It is critical to factor in ongoing maintenance for all API integrations and application patches, or vulnerabilities will likely emerge over time.

4.4.7 Standardized measurement frameworks

The most successful marketing teams consistently apply the scientific method to improve the effectiveness of their marketing over time. Your first-party data solution should support your team's efforts to measure marketing performance. When you evaluate a first-party data solution, you should ask *How well does the solution help your team standardize marketing performance measurements? Can the solution be easily integrated into your organization's marketing analytics efforts?*

Controlled experiments, from simple A/B tests to more-complex multivariate tests based on stratified samples, help your team find the effectiveness of a marketing approach incrementally or on the margin. *Aggregate measurement models*, like attribution and media mix models, look across marketing campaigns more broadly to find approximations of marketing influence on outcomes.

Consider how the first-party data solution supports experiments at the audience level (one-time and longitudinally for long-term, dynamic audiences) by creating experimental assignments (e.g., control versus treatment labels per customer) or by allowing you to bring your own experimental assignments into production campaigns.

New composable solutions grant your marketing analytics team direct access to everything from audience membership snapshots to experiment assignments and export logs. These composable platforms are huge enablers allowing marketing analytics to collaborate with marketing because they break down data silos, bringing key data back into the same data lakehouse used by the marketing analytics team for all its other initiatives.

If you take this concept further, the rise of the marketing data lakehouse allows teams to connect their experiments to their data lakehouse at the user or customer level, which makes it incredibly extensible for measurement. For example, you may find that a campaign affects usage or purchase behaviors in other areas than you originally expected, or it can estimate potential cannibalization across product lines (for example, when the promotion of one product to create incremental purchases actually decreases the purchase of another product).

Choosing a first-party data solution with built-in measurement capabilities accelerates the design-launch-iterate cycle that drives highly performant marketing programs. The more you standardize the approach and make it easy for marketers to adopt experiments, the more your team's efforts will be integrated. We summarize the most common measurement capabilities by marketing technology category in table 4.8.

Table 4.8 Standardized measurement framework considerations

Solution	Considerations
Composable CDPs	(+) The leading composable CDPs offer experimentation and measurement capabilities, and some can measure outcomes on any metric found in your marketing data lakehouse.
Marketing clouds/ engagement platforms	(+/-) MCs will often support experiments, but only on metrics that they host. As of this book's publication, they do not yet support the ability to run experiments on any metric in your marketing data lakehouse.
Monolithic CDPs	(+/-) Monolithic CDPs will often support experiments, but only on metrics that they host. As of this book's publication, they do not yet support the ability to run experiments on any metric in your marketing data lakehouse.
In-house builds	(+/-) Longitudinal multivariate experiment frameworks are generally complicated to build, so it is less common for organizations to build them, but global controls and global stratified sampling are certainly possible.

4.4.8 Cost

When you consider cost, think beyond the initial price or build effort and instead consider the long-term cost associated with scale. While the initial price tag is obvious, many vendors that provide first-party data solutions charge on usage, data volumes, integrations, or some combination of all of those to scale pricing over time with the vendors' cost and value to your organization. It's important to ask *How expensive is this solution to start? How does the cost of the solution scale with usage? How do you evaluate the long-term ROI of the solution?*

We recommend calculating small, medium, and large scenarios for your organization with any vendor to find out what the long-term costs could be so that you can protect your team from unsustainable long-term cost increases. Monolithic CDPs and marketing clouds are more expensive because they must pay to host your data, while composable solutions do not. Of course, composable solutions drive additional costs inside your marketing data lakehouse, but this is generally more economical and efficient than hosting multiple separate data systems.

For example, a major university had been using Tealium (a monolithic CDP) for three to four years when it began to evaluate a composable solution to provide greater transparency in its identity resolution. Since the composable solution would allow it to centralize its targeting outside of Tealium, it figured that its cost savings on Tealium would more than pay for the composable CDP! This made the purchase of the composable CDP budget-neutral while adding capabilities.

If you hope to drive your organization's first-party data transformation, consider positioning the cost relative to the value-generating opportunity it represents. Determine how your first-party data strategy may affect the key metrics by which your marketing team's efforts are measured (e.g., conversion rates or customer lifetime value). Then estimate what a reasonable increase to each of those metrics could mean for the organization's value, which will help you place any cost in perspective.

In table 4.9, we summarize the major cost considerations that correspond to each marketing technology category so your team can probe the most relevant areas of expense.

Table 4.9 Cost considerations

Solution	Considerations
Composable CDPs	(+/-) Composable CDPs are generally less expensive because they do not need to pay to host your first-party data. Instead, the cost of hosting data is borne once, centrally, for your entire organization, usually in a cost-efficient cloud data platform or data lakehouse utilized by multiple departments.
Marketing clouds/ engagement platforms	(-) MCs are generally the most expensive first-party data solutions, especially once you factor in usage-based pricing models and implementation consultant expenses.
Monolithic CDPs	(-) While less expensive than MCs, monolithic CDPs are generally expensive because they must pay to host your data and often require higher-tier support models. Due diligence on how costs scale with data volume is highly recommended.
In-house builds	(-) While third-party costs are low, the true cost of all product management, developers, and ongoing support resources tends to exceed third-party solutions except in simple builds.

4.4.9 Real-time capabilities

Real-time refers to the capabilities necessary to provide instant or near-instant marketing messaging, usually applied in web personalization, mobile notifications, and sometimes email or other messaging platforms. Many marketing teams overestimate the importance of real-time, but it is worth addressing in any list of considerations for first-party data solutions. *How well does the solution serve your team's specific real-time use cases, such as web personalization?*

When you consider the importance of real-time capabilities, take the time to generate the use cases needed and your best alternative for each use case. For example, you may want to personalize web pages based on the lifetime value of a customer, but lifetime value may simply be passed to your web personalization solution from your first-party data solution. The lesson? Use each marketing technology for what it does best, and don't over-engineer your first-party data solution to try to replace other well-established marketing technologies.

For example, the marketing technology leader at a large marketplace platform chose a first-party data solution that supported real-time capabilities. They purchased it, connected the first-party data solution to their customer data, and then approached the product team about integrating the real-time capabilities into the web application. The product team refused to integrate with the first-party data solution purchased by the marketing team because they already had a solution to serve real-time personalization and messaging built into the product, and more importantly, they considered web personalization part of the product team's domain. After a difficult reset in conversations, the marketing and product teams eventually agreed on a hybrid approach that would allow marketing segments to be synced to the product personalization platform. This negated the real-time features provided by the first-party data solution.

Many marketing teams migrate real-time use cases to product teams (similar to "Forgot password?" communications) or other marketing technology solutions at the edge of the marketing technology stack, such as web personalization solutions or content management systems.

These days, many monolithic CDPs, marketing clouds, and composable CDPs can provide updates in minutes, so the vast majority of use cases are met. For those that require real-time down to the milliseconds, the most common design pattern is to collect and act upon a customer's activity in the web or mobile application itself, sometimes in conjunction with saved segment memberships.

While many vendors claim to have real-time capabilities, the specific limitations of each marketing technology require careful review. We recommend listing out each real-time use case and mapping that use case to its required capabilities to avoid missing any gaps. As a starting point, we summarize the typical real-time capabilities of each marketing technology category in table 4.10.

Table 4.10 Real-time capabilities considerations

Solution	Considerations
Composable CDPs	(+/-) The leading composable CDPs offer real-time segmentation or personalization APIs, and some have begun to offer end-to-end real-time capabilities (though such capabilities are usually an add-on, since the marketing data lakehouse forms the data layer of the architecture).
Marketing clouds/ engagement platforms	(+/-) MCs that focus on web personalization offer real-time capabilities, but you should apply a healthy degree of skepticism to real-time claims for MCs' CDP offerings.
Monolithic CDPs	(+) Several leading monolithic CDPs focus on real-time use cases, though this is not universal.
In-house builds	(-) Most organizations find the complexity of real-time architectures too challenging to build if such an architecture is not already a core competency for the organization.

4.4.10 Identity resolution

Identity resolution is one of the key things your team will need to solve if you want to unify multiple sources of customer data. Depending on your use cases, you may want to ask *How well does the solution help you combine customer or prospect identities from multiple sources into a unified record? How transparent and understandable are the assumptions that go into unifying identities across data sources? Does your team need third-party enrichment or anonymous-to-known tracking?*

Let's revisit the example of the major university that looked to unify current and prospective student identities into a single unified record. The marketing team invested in a traditional CDP that provided built-in identity resolution for their website, and this seemed to work well until their first false-positive case came to light. Higher education is a highly regulated space, and matching sensitive information to the wrong person can result in liabilities and reputational damage. The team realized they needed a fully transparent way to unify or merge identities from various data sources to minimize the chance of any incorrect false-positive matches.

The team began to search for alternative solutions that allowed them to control the way identities were merged step by step. Given their strong analytics team, they realized they could use this to their advantage and take control of their identity resolution.

This example highlights a common problem in evaluating identity resolution capabilities. In our experience, most organizations seek more control, or at least greater transparency, in the assumptions that drive the unification of various contacts into a single unified customer or prospect record. They are most comfortable with ambiguity when acquiring new customers because reach matters (for example, with anonymous-to-known tracking), and they are least comfortable with ambiguity for active customers who may be mistargeted or receive incorrectly personalized communications.

Identity resolution is such a deep topic in first-party data that we have dedicated chapter 6 to it, but it is a critical component in the creation of a unified customer profile that will serve as the foundation for all your targeting, so it should be a central point of conversation. We recommend including your analytics and data team members in this portion of the conversation. We have summarized the typical advantages and disadvantages of identity resolution offered by each marketing technology category in table 4.11.

Table 4.11 Identity resolution considerations

Solution	Considerations
Composable CDPs	(+) Similar to in-house builds, organizations can build their own first-party identity resolution directly in their marketing data lakehouse and then activate it with a composable CDP. Recently, composable CDPs have begun to offer identity resolution built in, similar to monolithic CDPs.
Marketing clouds/ engagement platforms	(+/-) Most MCs offer integrations with third-party identity resolution providers, but they do not incorporate data engineering pipeline support for your team's in-house identity resolution models.

Table 4.11 Identity resolution considerations (*continued*)

Solution	Considerations
Monolithic CDPs	(+) Most monolithic CDPs offer a form of identity resolution, but they do not incorporate data engineering pipeline support for your team's in-house identity resolution models.
In-house builds	(+) Most builds succeed in creating strong first-party identity resolution by incorporating it into their marketing data lakehouse.

4.4.11 Technology stack agility and lock-in

What if you need to migrate from one email provider to another? One key advantage of a good first-party data solution is that it gives your organization *agility* (the ability to make changes to or replace) with respect to the rest of your marketing technology stack. For example: *How well does the solution support other changes you wish to make to your marketing technology stack? What happens if you choose to offboard the first-party data solution itself? In what ways could you be "locked into" the solution?*

First-party data solutions that unify your prospect or customer profile, including all the targeting and personalization data, allow you to easily direct audience membership and personalization attributes to new systems. This means your team can migrate, consolidate, or specialize other systems in your marketing technology stack more easily. This can save your organization money, give your marketing team new capabilities, or simplify your marketing technology stack to make it easier to maintain. It's a welcome change from the era in which organizations were locked into each tool they onboarded because it held all of their business logic hostage.

Here's an uncomfortable but necessary question to ask any vendor: What happens if things don't work out and we need to offboard the solution? While you hope the solution you choose is the right one for your organization, it's important to understand how much "lock-in" there is. As your team builds its business logic into a platform (such as audience criteria), is it locked into that specific first-party data solution, or is it accessible in your marketing data lakehouse thereafter?

We summarize the typical technology stack agility and lock-in considerations for each marketing technology category in table 4.12.

Table 4.12 Technology stack agility and lock-in considerations

Solution	Considerations
Composable CDPs	(+) Composable CDPs are easier to offboard than most solutions because they snapshot most of their data back into your marketing data lakehouse. Like all CDPs, they also help you migrate downstream systems more easily.
Marketing clouds/ engagement platforms	(-) MCs are difficult to offboard because you build your business logic and first-party data into them in ways that cannot be easily ported to other systems. The limited integrations do not facilitate agility in changing out other solutions in your marketing technology stack.

Table 4.12 Technology stack agility and lock-in considerations (*continued*)

Solution	Considerations
Monolithic CDPs	(+/-) Monolithic CDPs are difficult to offboard because you build your business logic and first-party data into them in ways that cannot be easily ported to other systems, but they do offer you flexibility to migrate or change downstream systems.
In-house builds	(+) Builds are specifically designed to avoid third-party lock-in, though migrations away from in-house builds can be challenging.

There are so many considerations that it can be nearly impossible to meet all your needs. If you focus on your most common use cases and err on the side of open and extensible systems, you will likely get what you need (with patience).

In the next chapter, we'll cover the building blocks of a modern first-party data solution, including the data foundations, identity resolution, and marketing activation.

Summary

- The combination of new marketing channels, increasing privacy regulations, and rising consumer expectations for smart personalization creates considerable complexity.
- The good news is that there is a large, diverse, and highly dynamic set of marketing technologies, including new composable solutions, that can be applied to this challenge.
- Composable customer data platforms (CDPs) are an excellent option for companies that desire the data unification, extensibility, and cloud innovation provided by a solution directly connected to their marketing data lakehouse. They may want a tighter integration between their analytics and their marketing teams. This best supports more data-mature companies that want a solution that will scale.
- Marketing clouds and engagement platforms may be a good option for larger organizations that do not need to customize or host their own first-party data independent of their marketing technology platform. They are also a good solution for organizations that struggle to manage a large portfolio of marketing technologies and prefer an all-in-one solution with certified consultants to support implementation. These organizations are willing to accept limitations in marketing destinations and greater costs for simplicity's sake.
- Monolithic CDPs that host a unified customer profile may be a good option for web and mobile-first companies with lower data maturity who prefer built-in real-time capabilities or a preset identity resolution feature. Although monolithic CDPs may be more difficult to implement, they offer many destination integrations out of the box.

- In-house builds may be a good option for organizations with very bespoke needs. They were the primary option for large, data-mature enterprise companies before the availability of composable CDPs. They are also a good solution for organizations at the opposite extreme—those that only need to integrate a single marketing destination and feel they can develop and maintain that integration themselves.
- As a team, your mission is to find the first-party data solution that best connects your organization's most valuable use cases while using its strengths (e.g., marketing analytics or mobile app engagement). We reviewed several scenarios to help guide your decision-making.

Part 2

First-party data building blocks

Once a first-party data strategy is in place, the next step is to ensure that data is structured, enriched, and activated for marketing effect. This section explores the foundational components required to achieve that goal, from building a unified customer profile to executing personalized, data-driven campaigns.

Chapter 5 explains how modern marketing data platforms, specifically data lakehouses and composable CDPs, unify structured and unstructured data while enabling flexible segmentation and scalable personalization. Chapter 6 covers identity resolution and enrichment, a crucial process that stitches together fragmented customer data across devices, channels, and touchpoints to build a complete customer profile. Chapter 7 focuses on first-party data activation, demonstrating how to turn insights into action across paid media, CRM, email, and other engagement channels.

By the end of this part, you'll have a structured, scalable approach for managing and activating your first-party data—ensuring your marketing is both data-driven and future-ready.

5 Modernizing the marketing data platform: Data lakehouses and composable CDPs

This chapter covers

- How a data lakehouse unifies structured, unstructured, and semi-structured marketing data
- Why composable CDPs serve as a real-time activation layer for targeted campaigns
- How the medallion architecture (bronze, silver, gold) refines data for analytics and personalization
- A practical roadmap for modernizing your marketing data stack, with an eye on realistic constraints, costs, and risks

Data silos are the enemy of effective marketing.

—Chris O'Neill, CEO of GrowthLoop,
Board Member of Gap, and marketing influencer

Data is at the heart of every marketing strategy. Yet with customers interacting across so many channels—websites, social platforms, email campaigns, call centers, and customer relationship management (CRM) systems—your teams might feel like they're trying to piece together a puzzle with missing pieces. Each platform, department, or vendor solution offers only a narrow slice of the data needed to fully understand customer behavior.

At the same time, today's marketing leaders are under pressure to prove ROI more quickly and deliver highly personalized campaigns at scale. You need real-time insights and the flexibility to pivot fast, whether you're retargeting abandoned carts or launching AI-powered recommendations.

That's where two converging trends are transforming marketing data management:

- *Data lakehouse*—A single, scalable environment that merges the strengths of data lakes (cheap, flexible storage for unstructured and semi-structured data) and data warehouses (high-performance analytics on structured data). A data lakehouse handles all data formats, giving marketing teams a holistic view without requiring separate systems for each data type.
- *Composable customer data platform (composable CDP)*—A lightweight, modular platform that taps into your existing data environment, letting you quickly build targeted segments and campaigns without creating another data silo.

Together, data lakehouses and composable CDPs can streamline how you handle customer data, offering a faster, more cost-effective way to unify and analyze data and to act on the resulting insights.

So why does this matter to marketing leaders? Marketing teams routinely ask, "How do we pull together data from so many sources without hiring an entire data engineering department?" or "How can we spin up personalized segments—and even one-to-one recommendations—in minutes, not weeks?" This chapter will answer those questions directly. By understanding the lakehouse approach, you'll be better equipped to

- Expand your analytics capabilities to include machine learning and real-time segmentation
- Reduce data replication and complexity so you're not managing the same data in ten different places
- Accelerate campaign rollouts, using a composable CDP to seamlessly sync audiences with your marketing channels

By the end of this chapter, you'll know how to unify the chaos of scattered data and accelerate your marketing outcomes, even if your current systems are less than ideal. It's not just about understanding "the new way"; it's about making the shift happen in your real-world context, with all its constraints, budget limits, and urgency.

Let's get started.

5.1 Understanding the data lakehouse

In the introduction, we noted how data fragmentation—from CRMs, website logs, call centers, and social media—can hamper your marketing potential. We also introduced two powerful solutions: a data lakehouse (combining data lake flexibility with data warehouse performance) and a composable CDP for real-time activation. Let's take a closer look at how a data lakehouse unifies structured, semi-structured, and unstructured data for marketing teams and at how composable CDPs dovetail with lakehouses to create a modern, scalable marketing stack.

5.1.1 Combining flexibility and performance

A data lakehouse merges the best aspects of traditional data warehouses (fast queries on structured data) with data lakes (flexible, cost-effective storage for any format). In practice, this means a single environment where you can handle multiple types of data:

- *Structured data*—Your CRM tables or transactional data in rows and columns (e.g., customer IDs, purchase amounts)
- *Unstructured or semi-structured data*—Call center transcripts, social media feeds, JSON logs from your website, and more

This convergence doesn't claim to replace every other system; rather, it reduces the friction of working with many siloed platforms. From a marketing standpoint, that can translate into quicker campaign insights and less overhead for your data team.

NOTE Many organizations add lakehouse capabilities on top of existing data warehouses or operational databases. That way, they can gradually integrate new data types—like call center audio transcripts—without overhauling everything at once.

5.1.2 A single place for every customer touchpoint

With today's customers engaging across multiple channels, marketers often struggle to stitch together a coherent view. A data lakehouse helps by ingesting all the relevant data into one location, as shown in figure 5.1.

By combining structured CRM details—often including personally identifiable information (PII) like names or email addresses—with unstructured text from call centers or social media, you create richer customer profiles. This unification is what enables advanced segmentation, real-time analytics, and machine learning models, all without needing a separate platform for each data type. Of course, these data types must be handled in compliance with relevant privacy regulations.

However, just piling all your data into one place isn't enough; you also need consistent, reliable access to that information. Let's see how lakehouses handle data integrity and why that matters for your marketing campaigns.

5.1.3 Ensuring consistency and reliability

When multiple teams update data simultaneously, accuracy can slip. In technical terms, lakehouses often support transactional integrity, also known as ACID compliance

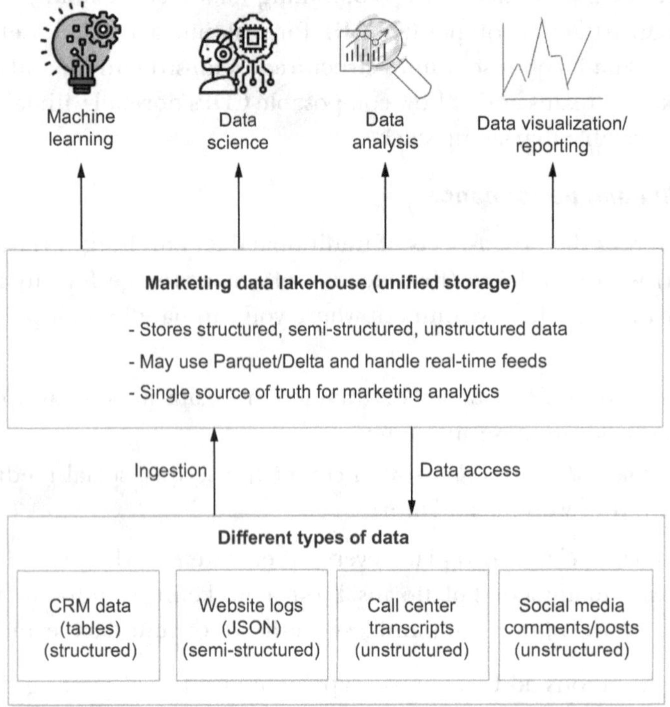

Figure 5.1 A simplified view of a marketing-focused lakehouse

(atomicity, consistency, isolation, and durability). While it might sound too database-heavy, this concept helps marketers by ensuring the following:

- *Up-to-date segments*—You won't send "first-time buyer" emails to repeat customers.
- *Accurate real-time offers*—Pricing and promotions won't break if data changes in the middle of a campaign.
- *Fewer campaign errors*—By giving your internal stakeholders a single source of truth, you eliminate mix-ups over purchase history or visit counts.

This reliability is key when you're trying to personalize messages, run A/B tests, or trigger notifications based on the latest customer interactions.

Even with consistent data, you may wonder why you'd choose a lakehouse over your existing data warehouse or CRM. Let's explore how lakehouses fit into the broader marketing ecosystem and whether they complement or replace what you already have.

5.1.4 Fitting into your existing marketing ecosystem

A data lakehouse is not a silver bullet. If your data warehouse is meeting your needs for structured queries and basic reporting, you might not see an immediate reason to switch. On the other hand, maybe you're encountering problems like the following:

- Juggling disparate tools for unstructured data (like social media or call center transcripts)
- Paying high costs to move data around between multiple platforms
- Missing real-time insights because your existing systems can't process streaming events quickly enough

If so, layering a lakehouse approach onto your current environment could solve these specific pain points. You could, for example, store large volumes of raw customer interactions (videos, transcripts, logs) in a low-cost system and apply analytics without needing an entirely separate pipeline.

In short, lakehouses don't demand a "rip and replace" strategy, but they can extend what you already do by simplifying data ingestion and enabling more flexible analytics. Of course, adopting a data lakehouse also brings its own challenges, including the learning curve for new tools, ensuring robust governance and security for large volumes of data, and managing potential cost spikes, especially during parallel migrations. Let's recap the main marketing benefits before we see how a composable CDP brings it all together:

- Data lakehouses unite structured and unstructured data in a single environment.
- Marketers gain a more holistic customer view, reducing silos and accelerating campaign analytics.
- Reliability matters. Lakehouses help ensure consistent, real-time data for segments and personalization.
- Incremental adoption is possible. You can complement your existing warehouse or CRM without starting from scratch.

Next up, we'll explore composable CDPs—the real-time activation layer that sits on top of a lakehouse. While the lakehouse stores and organizes your customer data, the composable CDP helps you quickly build segments, personalize campaigns, and push that data into any channel you choose.

5.2 Composable CDP

In the previous section, we focused on data lakehouses and how they bring all your customer data—structured and unstructured—into one environment. But unifying data is only half the story. How do you turn that data into real-time, personalized marketing campaigns? That's where the composable CDP comes in.

5.2.1 A more flexible approach to customer data

A composable CDP represents a significant leap in marketing technology. Unlike traditional CDPs that rely on copying data into their own silo, a composable CDP reads from the tools and platforms you already use (such as CRMs, social media accounts, or even your lakehouse). By layering on top of existing systems rather than duplicating them, it offers marketers these benefits:

- Immediate access to up-to-date records.
- Reduced data chaos since you avoid creating yet another data store.
- Real-time activation—segmentation and personalization can happen on-demand, provided you have real-time data ingestion (e.g., streaming pipelines) feeding your lakehouse or data warehouse. This setup ensures new events, such as website clicks or cart abandonments, are instantly available for analytics and can trigger personalized marketing responses.

"Composable" means that each function (data ingestion, modeling, or campaign activation) can be swapped or upgraded without overhauling the entire marketing stack.

> **NOTE** You don't have to abandon your current data repositories. The composable CDP simply layers on top of them, querying or streaming data in place.

5.2.2 How composable CDPs evolved

For years, marketing teams tried to fix data fragmentation by centralizing everything in one monolithic platform. Early marketing clouds and traditional CDPs offered some level of unification, but they also came with drawbacks:

- *Limited flexibility*—Adapting to new channels (like TikTok or chatbots) was cumbersome.
- *Vendor lock-in*—Once your data was in a particular system's format, switching providers became difficult.
- *Data duplication*—Copying every record into a proprietary silo meant dealing with syncing delays and extra costs.

Composable CDPs emerged to address these problems. Rather than forming yet another closed ecosystem, they layer on top of your cloud infrastructure, whether that's a data lakehouse, a data warehouse, or multiple software as a service (SaaS) tools. This architecture provides the flexibility to add or replace components without recreating the entire platform, ultimately driving greater agility in your marketing efforts. Table 5.1 shows how traditional CDPs compare to composable CDPs across key features.

Table 5.1 Traditional vs. composable CDP

Feature	Traditional CDP	Composable CDP
Data storage	Stores data within the CDP platform itself	Sits on top of your existing data warehouse (Snowflake, BigQuery, etc.)
Data duplication	Copies data from original sources, creating redundancy	No duplication—accesses data directly from your warehouse
Implementation time	6 to 18 months for full implementation	Can be set up in minutes to weeks
Flexibility	Limited to prebuilt data points and structures	Works with your existing data structure and models

Table 5.1 Traditional vs. composable CDP (*continued*)

Feature	Traditional CDP	Composable CDP
Integration complexity	Requires frequent code and integration updates	Simpler integration with existing data infrastructure
Real-time activation	Limited real-time capabilities for complex data	Better real-time activation via direct connections to your data store
Data control	Data stored in a third-party platform	Data remains in your warehouse under your control
Marketing channels	Often locked into a limited set of destinations	Can use any preferred marketing tools or channels
AI/ML capabilities	Limited to the CDP vendor's AI features	Can integrate with any AI technology in your data warehouse
Data view	May struggle with complex or unstructured data	Complete access to all data in the warehouse
Engineering resources	Significant engineering support for setup and maintenance	Reduced engineering dependency
Data security	Customer data moved to a third-party platform	Data stays within your security perimeter
Regulatory compliance	Can pose challenges in highly regulated industries	Easier to manage compliance in regulated environments
Scalability	May hit limits as data volume grows	Scales with your data warehouse capabilities

These distinctions highlight why composable CDPs enable real-time, flexible customer data activation. Next, we'll explore the practical advantages marketers can expect when they adopt a composable model.

5.2.3 *The composable CDP advantage*

Now that you've seen how composable CDPs came about, let's look at what they do in practice. By connecting directly to your CRM, website logs, social feeds, and other channels, composable CDPs do the following:

- Unify data access
  - Instead of juggling multiple rigid pipelines, the composable CDP dynamically queries or streams data from your primary customer data feeds—like CRMs, social platforms, or call center logs—as needed.
  - Marketing teams get a holistic view of customer interactions without manually merging spreadsheets.
- Enable advanced personalization
  - With a real-time feed of user behaviors, you can quickly spot customers who performed key actions (e.g., abandoned a cart yesterday) and trigger targeted offers.

  - You can create dynamic segments (e.g., "high-value users who logged in twice this week") and instantly sync them to email or ad platforms.
- Improve data governance
  - Because you're not replicating data into a proprietary silo, your existing security settings and compliance rules still apply.
  - It's easier to enforce privacy policies like the General Data Protection Regulation (GDPR) or the California Consumer Privacy Act (CCPA) across all channels.
- Offer modular scalability
  - If you want to introduce a new customer support channel or switch your email service provider, you can plug in that component without rebuilding your entire CDP.

Composable CDP implementation considerations

While composable CDPs excel at real-time data activation, teams should note the added complexity of continuous data pipelines. Unlike a batch-based approach, real-time streaming requires robust infrastructure (e.g., Kafka or Kinesis) and vigilant monitoring to ensure data quality and compliance. Marketing and data engineering teams must collaborate on schema evolution, performance tuning, and governance to avoid bottlenecks or compliance risks, especially if personal data is involved.

5.2.4 Tying it back to the lakehouse

Much of a composable CDP's power comes from its ability to tap into a single source of truth, often a data lakehouse. Think of the lakehouse as the foundation where all customer data resides in one place, while the composable CDP is the activation layer that

- Segments users based on real-time activity
- Pushes targeted campaigns to email, social ads, or other channels
- Processes inbound events (like website clicks) to update customer profiles instantly

Figure 5.2 shows a simplified view of how a composable CDP layers on top of a lakehouse.

By connecting to the lakehouse, the composable CDP avoids the need to replicate large volumes of data. Instead, it just queries or streams relevant fields—like "users who abandoned carts in the last hour" or "VIP customers with high lifetime value"—right when it needs them.

5.2.5 Streamlined and future-ready

Together, the composable CDP model does the following:

- *Cuts costs*—You're not paying for duplicative storage in a separate CDP.

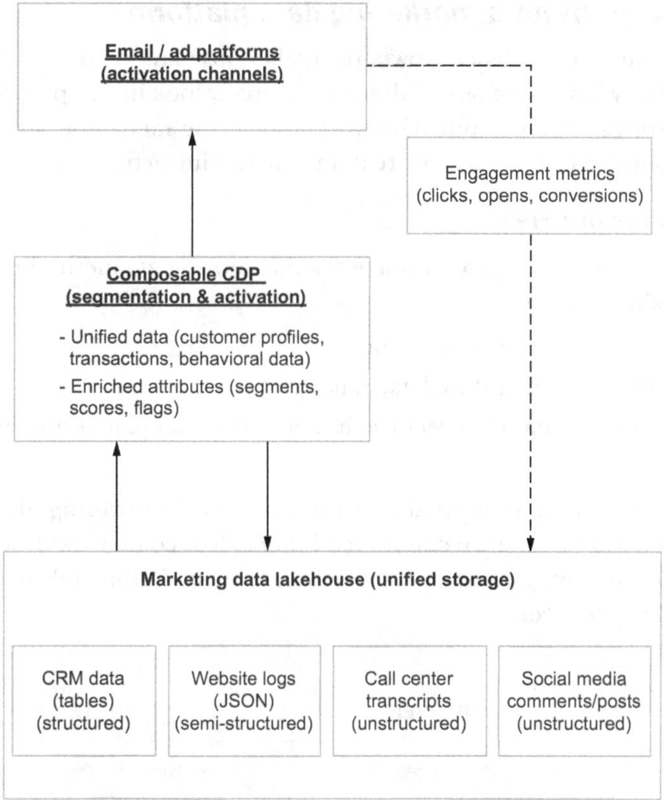

Figure 5.2 A simplified view of a marketing-focused lakehouse

- *Shortens deployment times*—Connecting existing sources is often faster than migrating everything into a new platform.
- *Provides real-time insights*—As soon as data hits your lakehouse (or any connected system), the composable CDP can use it for segmentation and personalization.

And because each module (ingestion, analytics, campaign orchestration) is loosely coupled, your marketing tech stack is more future-proof. If your team decides to adopt a new social channel, or if you want to experiment with an advanced AI personalization engine, you can integrate it without dismantling your entire infrastructure.

A composable CDP shifts the focus from "copying data into a new silo" to "activating data wherever it already lives." By integrating smoothly with a lakehouse (and other systems), you gain the agility to personalize campaigns in real time, scale to new channels, and maintain rigorous governance—all without overhauling your existing marketing stack.

Now that you've seen how composable CDPs complement a data lakehouse in unifying and activating customer data, let's explore practical patterns for integrating the two in your organization.

5.3 Architectural blueprint for a marketing data platform

In the previous sections, we discussed how a data lakehouse and a composable CDP can work together. But what does this collaboration actually look like in practice? One effective pattern involves aligning your data workflows to the medallion architecture and layering a composable CDP on top for real-time marketing activation.

5.3.1 Medallion architecture overview

The medallion architecture is a layered framework that moves data methodically from raw inputs to high-value insights:

- *Bronze layer*—Stores raw, unrefined data
- *Silver layer*—Cleanses and unifies data, making it analytics-ready
- *Gold layer*—Prepares data for direct use in marketing campaigns and advanced analytics

Figure 5.3 illustrates this layered approach in the context of recovering abandoned carts, a common scenario for many e-commerce brands. Notice how the raw interactions flow in at the bronze layer, transform at the silver layer, and ultimately power real-time campaigns at the gold layer.

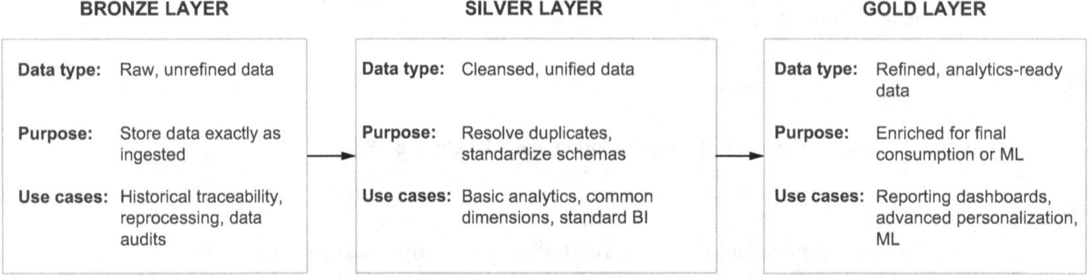

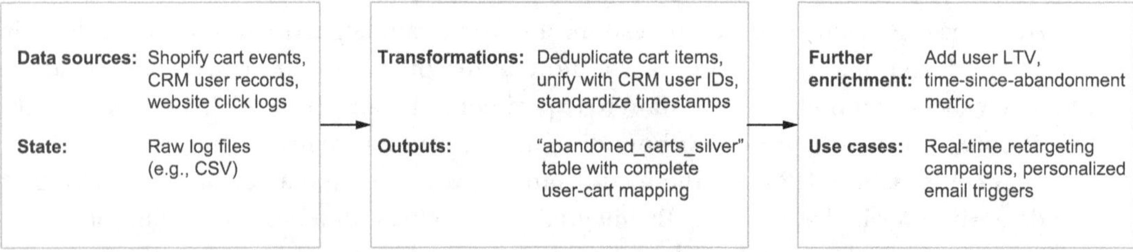

Figure 5.3 Medallion architecture for abandoned cart recovery

By marrying a composable CDP with a lakehouse that follows this layered design, you gain real-time agility and robust data governance. In the sections that follow, we'll break down each layer, highlighting how it contributes to a seamless marketing data pipeline.

5.3.2 Bronze layer

The bronze layer is where all your raw data arrives, exactly as it's generated, from CRM logs to website clicks—no filters, no transformations. This unaltered approach captures the maximum fidelity of each event, ensuring you can always revisit the data if new questions or analyses arise.

Beyond merely storing the raw data, the bronze layer also preserves critical metadata—not just timestamps and source or process IDs but also schema definitions and lineage details. This metadata is essential for governance and troubleshooting, letting you track exactly where each record originated, how the schema has changed over time, and which upstream processes contributed to the dataset. As shown in figure 5.4, the abandoned cart scenario brings together raw e-commerce events, CRM details, and email engagement metrics in a single repository, with the metadata ensuring you can maintain full visibility and consistency as these streams evolve.

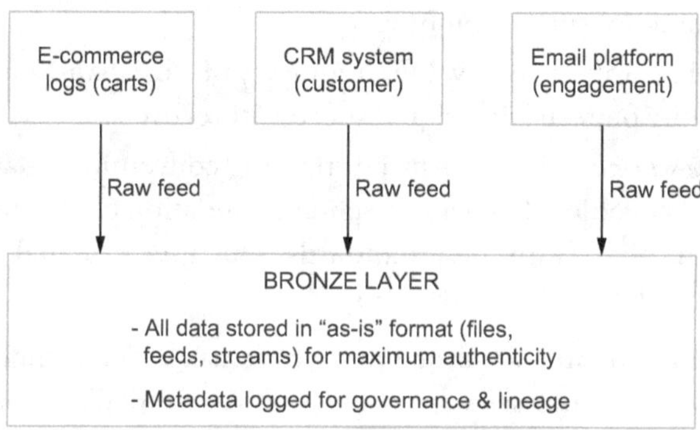

Figure 5.4 Bronze layer data flow for abandoned cart recovery

Why it matters:

- *Authenticity*—You're not losing details through early filtering.
- *Flexibility*—Future marketing questions (e.g., "Which promo codes did they see?") can be addressed without re-ingesting data.
- *Foundation*—This layer sets the stage for the silver and gold transformations.

Here's how you can turn abandoned carts into conversions:

- *Collect abandoned cart data.* For instance, Shopify logs every cart event with timestamps and cart values.

- *Enrich with CRM insights.* Capture user attributes (demographics, purchase history) in parallel.
- *Integrate email engagement.* Track opens and clicks to see if shoppers responded to a cart-reminder email.

All of these raw feeds merge in the bronze layer, forming the basis for deeper transformations.

5.3.3 Silver layer

In the silver layer, the raw data undergoes targeted transformations such as cleansing, merging, and standardizing. The goal is to produce a reliable, consistent view of your key business entities—customers, products, carts—free of duplicates or missing values.

This step often uses an extract, load, transform (ELT) strategy: load the raw data first (in the bronze layer), and then transform it here. By the time data reaches the silver layer, it's ready for analytics, reporting, or machine learning. Marketing, data science, and analytics teams all rely on these curated tables to derive meaningful insights.

To complete the abandoned-cart conversion workflow, follow these additional steps:

1. *Ensure data quality.* Remove incomplete cart data (e.g., missing IDs), eliminate duplicates, and confirm that each record meets required formats or standards.
2. *Merge and enrich.* Link abandoned cart events with CRM profiles. Add email engagement metrics for a holistic customer view.
3. *Aggregate metrics.* Calculate average cart value, frequency of cart abandonment, or time-to-purchase. Identify patterns that signal successful recoveries.
4. *Standardize and validate schema.* Adopt consistent naming conventions, data types, and date formats across all tables. Then apply schema validation checks to ensure that new or updated data aligns with these standards. This approach makes it simpler for analysts to query data without confusion.

By applying these transformations in the silver layer, you ensure clean, high-quality data that can feed into advanced analyses or can even power immediate marketing campaigns.

> **NOTE** In the silver layer, we transform raw data by removing duplicates, standardizing schemas, and resolving missing values. While we may generate some metadata in the process (like timestamps, job IDs, or data lineage), the chief output is clean, high-quality datasets, not just metadata. These refined tables are full-fledged customer records (e.g., unified cart events, consolidated CRM attributes) ready for analytics and machine learning.

5.3.4 Gold layer

The gold layer represents the culmination of your data pipeline, where the silver layer's curated datasets become analytics-ready for marketing initiatives. Here, data might be denormalized to reduce complex joins, boosting performance for everything from business intelligence (BI) dashboards to real-time personalization.

In many organizations, dedicated databases exist within the gold layer, each mapped to a specific function (e.g., "Customer Analytics" or "Segmentation"). This structure helps teams quickly locate relevant data without sifting through every table in the lakehouse.

Because the gold layer offers clean, high-quality datasets, your composable CDP can plug in directly and sync up-to-date audience segments. Rather than replicating data again, the CDP queries or streams what it needs, enabling instant campaign launches.

Here are the final steps to turn abandoned carts into conversions:

1. *Dynamic segmentation*—Marketing analysts define segments, such as "customers who abandoned carts in the past 7 days but made at least one purchase before." These segments come straight from the gold layer's customer_segment or abandoned_cart tables.
2. *Campaign activation*—The composable CDP picks up these segments for retargeting ads or personalized emails. Each user's behavior data (from the silver layer) and demographic data (from the CRM) combine seamlessly for hyper-targeted outreach.
3. *Performance monitoring and iteration*—As conversions roll in, metrics (open rates, click-throughs, purchases) flow back into the lakehouse, closing the loop for continuous optimization.

By building the bronze-to-gold pipeline and integrating a composable CDP, you achieve a sustainable, agile marketing data framework—one that can handle anything from routine cart recoveries to advanced predictive modeling.

5.3.5 Bringing it all together

Figure 5.5 summarizes how the bronze, silver, and gold layers deliver a unified foundation for activation via a composable CDP. Each layer serves a distinct purpose:

- *Bronze*—Captures raw data in full fidelity
- *Silver*—Transforms and unifies data for consistency
- *Gold*—Prepares ready-to-use datasets for campaigns and advanced analytics

When combined, they future-proof your marketing efforts by ensuring data is always accurate, accessible, and actionable.

The medallion architecture isn't just theoretical: it maps directly to real-world marketing scenarios, like abandoned cart recovery, where a composable CDP plus lakehouse approach provides the speed, flexibility, and governance you need to drive better campaigns. Now let's examine the key considerations for implementing a marketing data lakehouse, ensuring your data pipeline remains secure, compliant, and aligned with your broader business objectives.

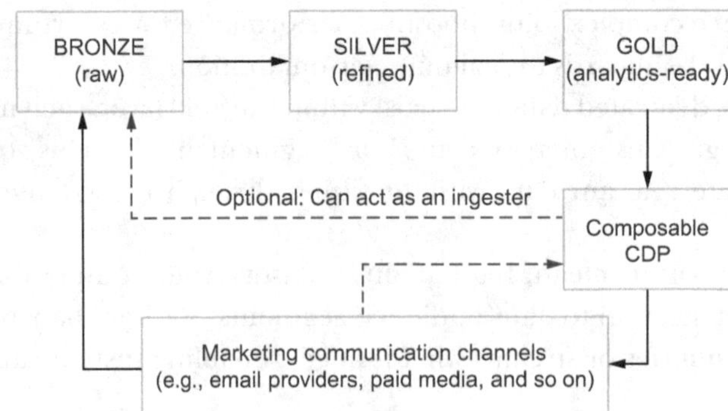

Figure 5.5 From bronze to gold, fueling a composable CDP

5.4 Key considerations for implementing a marketing data lakehouse

Throughout this chapter, we've shown how data lakehouses and composable CDPs can unify and activate marketing data, offering real-time insights and more personalized campaigns. Yet anyone who has tackled a data transformation knows there's often a gap between theory and real-world practice. In this section, we'll map out a practical approach to moving from messy, siloed systems to a modern marketing data lakehouse—highlighting how timelines, complexity, and stakeholder priorities can shift along the way.

5.4.1 Laying the groundwork: Scope, estimates, and planning

Before diving into implementation, you'll need a solid handle on the project's scope, resource allocation, and timeframe. Marketing leaders often ask critical questions: "How long until we see ROI?" "Which data should we unify first?" "What if we add AI-driven features next year?" The answers hinge on whether you're upgrading a legacy platform (a brownfield) or building from scratch (a greenfield).

These two alternatives help to categorize your project:

- *Brownfield (modernizing an existing system)*—If you already have a data warehouse or data lake, transitioning it to a lakehouse will likely involve parallel runs, where old and new systems operate side by side until the lakehouse is fully validated. This adds overhead—think double storage and potentially reworking older scripts—until you're confident enough to retire the legacy setup.
- *Greenfield (starting fresh)*—If you rely heavily on SaaS tools (like CRMs or email marketing platforms) without a central data store, you'll avoid heavy migrations from an older warehouse. However, you must plan carefully so your lakehouse can scale as more data sources come online. Otherwise, you risk recreating data silos—just in a new environment.

In the following subsections, we'll illustrate each approach with two realistic examples: a mid-sized e-commerce retailer upgrading a legacy warehouse and a fast-growing SaaS startup building a brand-new data platform.

BROWNFIELD E-COMMERCE EXAMPLE

Imagine a mid-sized apparel retailer running a legacy on-premises data warehouse for historical sales, plus a separate SaaS platform for email marketing. Their marketing team now wants real-time segmentation and plans to adopt AI-based product recommendations next year. Here's how they might break down the project:

- *Months 1 to 2*—The data architect inventories existing feeds (Shopify orders, warehouse logs, email activity) and finalizes a cloud-based lakehouse approach, including cost estimates for parallel runs.
- *Months 3 to 6*—The team migrates a portion of historical sales data into the lakehouse and pilots new campaigns with fresh Shopify data, focusing on dynamic retargeting or cart abandonment.
- *Months 7 to 9*—A composable CDP is attached for activation only, reading from the lakehouse in near real time. Meanwhile, they run parallel validation—comparing old warehouse metrics to new lakehouse outputs—ensuring data quality before switching everything over.

NOTE Parallel validation can be tricky if new data sources feed only into the lakehouse, creating discrepancies. One workaround is to freeze the same time window or a subset of data in both environments for apples-to-apples comparisons. You can also compare aggregates (e.g., daily total orders) at consistent cutoffs, rather than expecting real-time metrics to match across systems with different ingestion schedules.

- *Months 10 to 12*—If the results align, the project team addresses advanced governance (e.g., anonymizing PII) and prepares for AI readiness. However, if the leadership demands accelerated AI mid-project, the overall timeline can stretch beyond a year.

NOTE Actual timelines for anonymizing PII may be dictated by regulations like GDPR or CCPA. In many cases, personal data must be encrypted or obfuscated immediately upon ingestion. The 10 to 12 month window here refers to advanced governance measures—like implementing automated data lineage, advanced masking policies, or extended compliance frameworks. Organizations should ensure basic privacy requirements are in place from day one.

A glimpse of stakeholder conversations might look like this:

- *Chief Marketing Officer (CMO)*—"We're leaving money on the table without personalizing our campaigns. Our customer data sits in Shopify, Mailchimp, and Google Analytics. How do we unify it into one view?"
- *Chief Data Officer (CDO)*—"From an enterprise-wide perspective, we need a governed and compliant environment—especially to handle PII. I propose we adopt a data lakehouse to streamline these data feeds and maintain full audit trails. But

to ensure accuracy, we may need two or three months of parallel runs with our legacy warehouse to detect inconsistencies before we retire it."

- *Data Architect*—"Exactly. Technically, integrating CRM data, email metrics, and site analytics into a single lakehouse is feasible, but we'll have to rework some old scripts and handle any schema mismatches. While we run parallel systems, we'll compare key metrics (like total orders or CTR) in both environments."
- *Chief Financial Officer (CFO)*—"Let's watch costs. While both systems run, we pay for double storage. When can we cut over fully?"
- *Chief Data Officer (CDO)*—"Once we confirm data quality and validate the new environment meets compliance standards, we'll decommission the legacy system. That should be near the end of the parallel run window, assuming no major surprises."

Ultimately, they adopt a phased approach: migrate the most crucial data first (e.g., last year's sales records and current Shopify orders), prove success, and then gradually incorporate older archives and advanced governance. But if the company suddenly fast-tracks AI-based product recommendations, the timeline can stretch further.

For a brownfield migration, key challenges include the following:

- *Undocumented legacy scripts*—Many of the SQL procedures your marketing team depends on aren't documented, so you'll have to reverse-engineer or rebuild that logic in your new lakehouse pipeline.
- *Timeline risk from AI feature creep*—If leadership pushes for accelerated AI-driven features mid-project, you'll need extra data modeling and compute resources—efforts that can stretch your schedule beyond the original twelve-month window.

While a brownfield approach must juggle legacy systems, parallel operations, and older scripts, a greenfield project starts from scratch. That can accelerate the initial rollout but poses different risks, especially around scaling and preventing new silos. Let's see how this plays out in a fast-moving SaaS environment.

GREENFIELD SAAS EXAMPLE

On the other end of the spectrum, a SaaS startup might have no central warehouse at all—just a handful of SaaS tools (CRM, email logs, user analytics). They want to unify these feeds into a lakehouse for quick segmentation and then use that single source of truth to run basic AI models, such as churn-prediction algorithms.

- *Weeks 1 to 4*—The marketing leader meets with a newly hired data engineer. Together, they list core data sources (CRM, email engagement, user analytics), define naming conventions, and choose an open table format (e.g., Parquet) to keep the system flexible.
- *Weeks 5 to 8*—They spin up a cloud-based lakehouse, ingest initial datasets, and run spot checks for data quality—no parallel runs are needed because there's no old warehouse to retire.

- *Weeks 9 to 12*—A composable CDP is connected to run near real-time campaigns (e.g., "new users who haven't logged in for 7 days"). They refine governance for personal data compliance (email addresses, usage history).
- *Months 4 to 6*—If user growth spikes, they bring in more SaaS tools or consider adding a simple AI pilot for churn analysis, provided the data is robust enough for modeling.

Internal conversations could unfold like this:

- *CMO*—"Finally, one source of truth! No more juggling three or four different dashboards."
- *CEO*—"We must keep costs lean but ensure we can handle surging sign-ups next quarter."
- *Data Engineer*—"Since we're building fresh, we can design for scale from day one. Our ingestion framework should keep consistent schemas to avoid new silos."

For a greenfield implementation, potential challenges include the following:

- Greenfield projects may have fewer historical records for long-term trend analysis, so verifying new segments often relies on shorter data windows.
- If leadership decides mid-project to launch AI-based recommendations, the effort can suffer from scope creep, requiring deeper data modeling and additional compute resources.

To keep a greenfield implementation on track, identify key tasks up front and assign realistic schedules. Your team's expertise, data volume, and chosen tech stack all influence how quickly you can move to production. Training on new tools (like orchestration frameworks or open table formats) may add weeks. Surprises can also reshape your timeline, such as undiscovered silos or leadership demanding AI personalization. A smaller greenfield effort, focusing on core data sources, might see results in a few months. A large brownfield modernization, handling terabytes of historical data or advanced personalization, could stretch beyond a year.

Whether you're juggling an older warehouse or forging a new path, once you have the scope, estimates, and broad approach established, it's time to design a resilient lakehouse architecture that fits your marketing objectives.

5.4.2 Designing a resilient architecture for marketing data

Once you've defined the project scope and timeline, the next step is to design an architecture that can handle diverse data—everything from structured CRM records to unstructured social media logs—while navigating real-world constraints like budget, partial migrations, or legacy dependencies. Next we'll explore how each approach (brownfield versus greenfield) shapes these decisions.

Analyzing your current systems (brownfield only)

Brownfield often calls for running the new lakehouse in parallel with the legacy system for weeks or months. This side-by-side comparison helps you confirm that key metrics (like total orders or campaign ROI) match across both environments so teams can gradually shift to the lakehouse without jeopardizing daily marketing activities. For instance, in our e-commerce example from section 5.4.1, you might uncover undocumented SQL scripts used by marketing for specialized campaign reports, which will need extra effort to migrate or rebuild within your new data pipeline.

Greenfield has no legacy system to retire, which can accelerate your rollout. However, you risk creating new silos if you simply connect each SaaS tool (CRM, email logs, user analytics) directly without a coherent ingestion strategy. A fast-growing SaaS startup, for instance, might move quickly to set up a lakehouse on a cloud platform like Google Cloud Platform (GCP) + Snowflake, only to realize they must define consistent naming conventions and schema evolution policies early on. Otherwise, they'll have a "messy" data lake just a few months later.

CHOOSING THE RIGHT DATA MODEL

Marketing and analytics teams usually crave fast, straightforward queries in the "silver" or "gold" layers of the lakehouse—especially for segmentation and campaign analysis. You have a few common modeling choices:

- *Entity-relationship (ER) modeling*—ER modeling is familiar to teams who've used relational databases.

NOTE While ER models are ideal for structured datasets, many lakehouse environments also store unstructured data (like call center transcripts or social media text). In these cases, you might rely on metadata tagging, search indexes, or machine learning tools to organize and derive insights from unstructured sources. Thus, your data model may blend relational schemas (for structured data) with less rigid storage and indexing approaches for unstructured or semi-structured content.

- *Dimensional modeling (star or snowflake schema)*—This approach is often simpler for dashboards and targeting specific user cohorts, though star schemas are typically easier to query, whereas snowflake schemas can reduce redundancy at the cost of more joins.
- *Data vault modeling*—This methodology is well suited for large, complex, and rapidly evolving data environments. Its granular structure (hubs, links, and satellites) supports auditing and versioning, which can aid in security and compliance. However, you still need separate access controls, encryption, and governance measures. Because data vault modeling can be intricate, specialized expertise is often required.

TIP Involve marketing ops, analytics leads, and product managers early. If your model doesn't reflect real campaign needs (like "target lapsed buyers" or "segment by email click behavior"), you'll build a technically sound system that marketers find cumbersome to query.

SELECTING A TECHNOLOGY STACK

Your technology choice depends on both short-term constraints (budget, existing contracts) and long-term goals (real-time personalization, AI expansions, multicloud, etc.). Generally, you can pick from two main categories or even combine them:

- *Cloud-native services*—These are offerings from AWS, Azure, or GCP that integrate seamlessly with other managed services (storage, serverless functions, ML tooling). They're often cost-effective if you're already in one ecosystem, and they can simplify governance by using a single vendor's security model.
- *Third-party platforms*—These are solutions like Snowflake, Databricks, or Dremio. They can streamline certain aspects of lakehouse adoption (e.g., built-in performance optimization, near-limitless scaling), but they come with licensing costs or vendor-specific features. They may also support multicloud scenarios more readily than a single cloud provider. Table 5.2 highlights the key differences between cloud-native services and third-party platforms.

Table 5.2 Cloud-native versus third-party: key differences

Aspect	Cloud-native (AWS/Azure/GCP)	Third-party (Snowflake, Databricks, etc.)
Integration	Deeply integrated with the respective cloud ecosystem (IAM, managed storage, serverless, etc.)	Often supports multiple clouds, providing more flexibility if your company operates on several platforms
Licensing and cost model	Pay-as-you-go for cloud services; typically straightforward if you already have a contract	May offer specialized pricing or advanced features at additional cost; licensing can be more complex
Feature scope	Varies by cloud provider; some advanced features (like real-time ML) can lag or differ between services	Often ships with cutting-edge analytics, ML integrations, and performance optimizations out of the box
Lock-in	Generally tied to one cloud, which can be fine if you're deeply invested in that ecosystem already	Potentially more portable if you later decide to operate in a multicloud or hybrid environment, but still subject to that vendor's ecosystem
Use cases	Ideal for teams that want to keep everything under one cloud vendor or avoid complexity in multicloud	Suited to orgs requiring best-of-breed analytics, multicloud, or specialized features (e.g., advanced ML orchestration or robust collaboration tools)

Blended or hybrid approaches are possible. A large enterprise might run most workflows on a single cloud yet adopt a third-party lakehouse tool for advanced analytics or multicloud support, so you only pay for the specialized functionality you genuinely need.

Avoid over-engineering. For example, adopting a multicloud strategy might sound appealing, but it can inflate costs and complicate governance if you don't truly need it.

If your SaaS startup (greenfield) is purely on GCP for everything else, sticking to GCP-based lakehouse solutions might keep deployment simpler and cheaper.

> **NOTE** Use what you have. If you already have strong GCP skills or a Snowflake contract, use those. Don't adopt advanced features (like real-time streaming analytics or multicloud replication) unless they directly serve your marketing objectives, like delivering real-time personalized offers or ensuring compliance across multiple regions.

In short, designing a resilient architecture means balancing technical possibilities with real-world priorities. Brownfield teams need robust parallel run strategies (and may need to re-engineer old scripts), while greenfield teams must be careful not to accidentally create new silos as they rapidly connect SaaS tools. Once you've hammered out these architectural details, you'll be ready to implement and test your lakehouse in production, where data ingestion pipelines, validation checks, and ongoing governance become the day-to-day reality.

5.4.3 Implementation and testing in real environments

Once you've designed your lakehouse architecture and mapped out how data will migrate, the real work of implementation begins. This phase typically includes setting up ingestion pipelines, running parallel systems (in brownfield cases), and ensuring that security and data quality measures are ready for prime time. The exact timeline often depends on the implementation's scope and complexity. A simpler greenfield project might stabilize within a few months, whereas a large brownfield overhaul could take more than a year, especially one involving advanced AI or strict compliance.

MANAGING DATA MIGRATION AND PARALLEL RUNS

When planning data migration, you must weigh two common scenarios:

- *Brownfield*—If you're modernizing an existing warehouse, you'll likely need multiple passes to migrate historical records. Teams often maintain old and new systems side by side, comparing key metrics (e.g., total orders, average cart value) for validation. For instance, in our e-commerce example, the data architect might run parallel queries on both the old warehouse and the new lakehouse for several weeks or months, ensuring consistency before fully switching the marketing team to the new system.

> **NOTE** Because brownfield migrations require running two environments in parallel—along with potential re-engineering of legacy scripts—the associated costs can climb quickly. To avoid runaway expenses, it's critical to define clear goals, timelines, and exit criteria for phasing out the old warehouse.

- *Greenfield*—A SaaS startup, on the other hand, may skip parallel runs because there's no legacy environment to compare. Instead, they focus on cleanly ingesting data from CRM, email, and user analytics, validating that each SaaS feed maps correctly into the lakehouse's silver and gold layers. This can speed up the timeline, but it also demands vigilance to avoid creating new silos if more data sources come online mid-project.

ADDRESSING DATA QUALITY AND PRIVACY

Because marketing data often includes sensitive attributes, such as email addresses, purchase history, or location, it's crucial to plan early for anonymization, encryption, or both:

- *Data classification*—Identify which fields are personal identifiers or are regulated (e.g., under GDPR).
- *Validation scripts*—Automate checks for completeness and consistency. A marketing ops lead might run daily spot checks, comparing user accounts in the lakehouse to the composable CDP.
- *Governance oversight*—If your organization has a compliance officer or privacy specialist, loop them in now. It's easier to implement encryption or role-based access before the data volumes explode.

REVERSE-ENGINEERING SCRIPTS AND AI EXPANSIONS

No matter your approach, you may discover undocumented scripts or custom logic that marketing depends on, like specialized SQL queries for segmenting high-value shoppers. Reverse-engineering these can add weeks to your schedule, as someone must translate the logic into your new environment.

> **NOTE** When rebuilding your lakehouse logic, document each transformation and segment definition in a version-controlled repository (for example, Git) or a centralized data catalog so future teams won't need to reverse-engineer your work. Assign clear owners to each workflow, and establish a review process to ensure the logic remains transparent and easy to maintain over time.

Depending on whether you're in a brownfield or greenfield scenario, you'll encounter distinct challenges:

- *Brownfield*—Undocumented or custom scripts might live in a legacy warehouse, requiring thorough testing to ensure the lakehouse replicates the same outputs. If an on-premises database includes stored procedures, those need to be refactored or replaced in your lakehouse pipeline.
- *Greenfield*—Even without a legacy warehouse, you may still face embedded scripts or "hidden logic" inside your SaaS tools. For example, an email platform might include internal segmentation scripts that never lived in a central repo. You'll need to extract and re-implement those scripts in your lakehouse for consistent, centralized governance.

If leadership decides to pilot AI-driven campaigns, like recommendation engines or churn prediction, be prepared for additional data modeling layers, specialized compute, or data science input. A marketing leader might say, "We're seeing an uptick in cart abandonments; can we do a predictive model?" Setting up these AI features can further extend your timeline, especially if you need to add feature stores or advanced ML frameworks.

By coordinating these tasks—data migration, parallel validation, security checks, and potential AI expansions—marketing leaders can ensure a smooth transition from legacy environments or ad hoc SaaS setups to a reliable, scalable lakehouse foundation. Once these core implementation steps are in place, the focus often shifts to long-term governance and maintenance. This ensures the lakehouse stays up-to-date, compliant, and resilient for the next wave of marketing innovations.

5.4.4 Ensuring long-term success and governance

Even after your lakehouse is up and running, robust support, maintenance, and contingency measures are vital, especially if real-time, personalized campaigns are at the heart of your marketing strategy. By embedding governance and disaster recovery (DR) early, you'll preserve the quality, availability, and cost-effectiveness of your data operations for the long haul.

Auditing and rollback

Every data pipeline inevitably faces hiccups: a batch load might include incorrect mappings, or a marketing ops user might load outdated files by mistake. To handle these situations gracefully, try these strategies:

- *Comprehensive audit trails*—Capture fields like `load_timestamp` and `job_id` each time data is ingested or updated. This helps you to pinpoint which load triggered an anomaly (e.g., a sudden dip in conversions) and to quickly undo or fix the problem.
- *Versioning and rollback*—Depending on your lakehouse tools, you may have the option to revert tables to an earlier version. For instance, if you store data in an open table format (like Delta or Iceberg), you can "time travel" to a prior snapshot. This can be a lifesaver if a flawed script corrupts user segments needed for a critical campaign.

Brownfield teams continue running legacy jobs alongside the new lakehouse. To validate each record, have the lakehouse record every migration step—including timestamps, job IDs, and affected table names—in detailed logs. Those logs let you match new-environment outputs against your old reports, ensuring parity before cut-over.

Greenfield startups, by contrast, can build audit and rollback processes from day one, embedding change-event logs and versioning into every pipeline, so there's no need to reverse-engineer missing context later.

Disaster recovery considerations

Your approach to DR depends on your budget, your marketing SLAs, and the effect of downtime on revenue or brand reputation:

- *Active-active*—If near-zero downtime is crucial (e.g., an online retailer pushing real-time offers), you might maintain duplicate environments. Although pricier, this approach cuts failover time to minutes—or even seconds.
- *Active-passive*—This approach is cheaper to operate but allows for some downtime. For example, a SaaS startup might accept an hour or two of reduced capabilities if a secondary region needs to spin up.
- *Trade-offs*—The CFO might balk at higher monthly bills for active-active. The CMO might argue that even a short outage disrupts campaign metrics. Aligning these perspectives ensures you pick a DR approach that meets core business needs without overspending.

For brownfield organizations, you might initially rely on existing DR arrangements while you roll out a new plan for the lakehouse. Greenfield teams can build cloud-based backups or multiregion replication from the start, potentially saving rework later.

PHASING OUT LEGACY SYSTEMS

For brownfield migrations, your old warehouse or lake infrastructure won't vanish overnight. A practical off-ramp plan looks like this:

- *Parallel runs*—Operate both environments while you confirm that critical metrics match (e.g., total daily orders, email click-through counts).
- *Reconciliation*—Conduct in-depth comparisons or aggregations, ensuring the lakehouse meets performance targets and data accuracy.
- *Gradual decommission*—Once the new environment is stable, you can systematically retire legacy hardware or deprovision old cloud services, thus reducing duplicated costs.

For a greenfield scenario, this step might be minimal or nonexistent. There's no legacy system to retire, but you'll still want a roadmap for adding new data sources or tools without creating fresh silos.

Once these governance and DR strategies are in place, you have laid the groundwork for a sustainable, future-proof lakehouse—one that can adapt to evolving marketing goals, from adding new CRM feeds to rolling out AI-driven campaigns. In the following section, we'll bring together essential project deliverables and reference architectures that will help your lakehouse thrive in the long run.

5.4.5 Putting it all together: Deliverables and reference architectures

By the time you reach this stage, you've tackled scope decisions, architected a lakehouse that fits your marketing needs, and implemented the core pipelines. Now you must formalize the lakehouse for daily operations, which involves the following steps:

- *Comprehensive documentation*—Include architecture diagrams, data modeling guides, and governance policies. If your marketers or analysts ever question how a particular data feed flows into the lakehouse, a clear diagram or reference can help them (and your data engineers) troubleshoot or adapt quickly.

- *Team training and onboarding*—Marketing ops, data analysts, and even product managers should learn how to query or activate data in the lakehouse (and composable CDP). Without adequate training, your investment may sit underused, with teams reverting to outdated spreadsheets or siloed reports.
- *Reference architectures*—Whether you have a cloud-native (AWS, Azure, GCP) or third-party solution (Snowflake, Databricks, Dremio, etc.), adopting proven blueprints can speed up deployment and reduce misconfiguration. Tailor these blueprints to your brownfield or greenfield context, avoiding over-engineering while still allowing for future AI expansions or more advanced analytics.

At this point, marketing ops can create real-time segments within the composable CDP—pulling fresh data directly from the lakehouse—and trust it as the single source of truth for personalization, retargeting, or new campaign experiments.

Here are the five key lessons marketing leaders should keep front-of-mind:

- *Scope influences complexity.* A brownfield modernization often involves parallel runs and re-engineering, while greenfield implementations can move faster but might produce new silos without careful planning.
- *Timelines vary widely.* A smaller greenfield rollout might stabilize in 3 to 6 months, whereas a major brownfield overhaul could exceed a year if AI or complex data sources appear mid-stream.
- *Composable CDP is for activation.* Keep the lakehouse as your single source of truth; the CDP reads from it to build real-time segments, rather than storing large volumes of data itself.
- *Governance is critical.* Marketing data is often sensitive, demanding robust compliance, auditing, and possibly advanced security (like encryption or anonymization) from day one.
- *Incremental pilots help.* Prove value quickly with a pilot (e.g., a cart abandonment retargeting campaign) before tackling a full-scale migration. Early wins build stakeholder confidence and create momentum for bigger leaps.

By balancing theory (scope definition, design patterns, governance frameworks) with practical realities (parallel runs, hidden legacy scripts, cost constraints, evolving AI needs), you can steer your organization—whether brownfield or greenfield—toward a future-ready lakehouse. The result is a data-driven marketing operation that delivers real-time segmentation, personalized user experiences, and the agility to adapt as business demands evolve.

5.4.6 Visualizing your project and measuring ROI

Even with a clear plan for scope, architecture, and governance, visualizing your project timeline can help stakeholders see how each phase unfolds. Measuring ROI ensures you can articulate the business value of your lakehouse initiative.

BROWNFIELD VS. GREENFIELD: A HIGH-LEVEL TIMELINE

Figure 5.6 outlines a typical sequence of phases for both brownfield (migrating legacy systems) and greenfield (building net-new). While exact timelines differ by organization, seeing them side by side can clarify when tasks like data ingestion, parallel runs, composable CDP integration, and AI readiness usually occur.

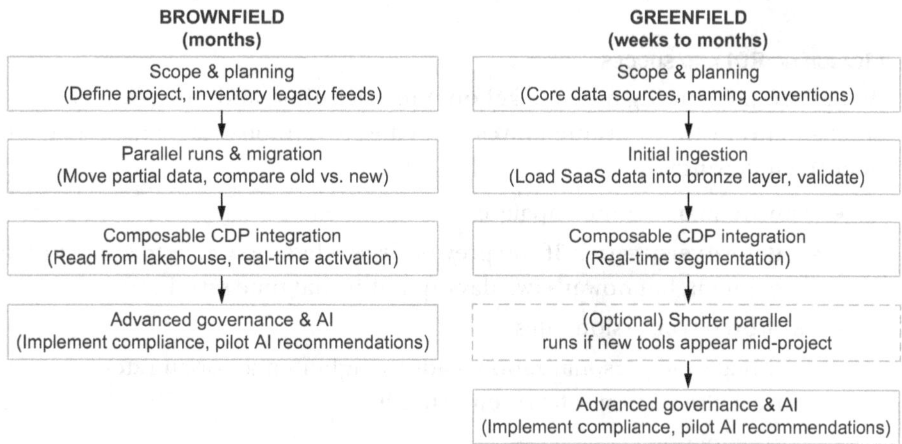

Figure 5.6 Implementation sequence: brownfield vs. greenfield

Implementation timelines vary depending on whether you choose a brownfield or greenfield approach:

- Brownfield implementations typically run for several months (or more) to accommodate parallel runs, legacy script re-engineering, and incremental cutovers.
- Greenfield implementations often accelerate early ingestion but must guard against new silos if multiple SaaS tools come online mid-project.

In either case, the composable CDP is usually introduced once the core lakehouse layers are stable, providing near real-time activation without duplicating data.

Now that we've seen the sequence visually, let's summarize the key challenges in table 5.3.

Table 5.3 Summarizing key challenges

Aspect	Brownfield	Greenfield
Parallel runs	Often crucial to compare new versus old metrics; doubles costs temporarily	Usually not required unless you're connecting multiple SaaS tools at once
Legacy scripts	Must be reverse-engineered or retired	Minimal or no legacy code, but risk of hidden logic in SaaS tools

Table 5.3 Summarizing key challenges (*continued*)

Aspect	Brownfield	Greenfield
Scalability	Must migrate data gradually to avoid disruption	Can scale from day one, but must define naming conventions early
AI readiness	Potentially delayed if old system can't handle large ML demands	Easier to integrate AI if the architecture is planned for it

MEASURING ROI AND SUCCESS

Because implementing a data lakehouse involves time and budget, measuring ROI is crucial to justify the continued investment and to demonstrate tangible benefits. Consider the following:

- Time-to-market for campaigns
  - Before versus after: If you previously needed two weeks to build and test a new segment, but now it's two days, quantify that time saved.
- Improved conversion rates
  - If real-time personalization leads to higher email open rates or cart recovery, track the incremental revenue uplift.
- Cost reduction
  - Decommissioning a legacy warehouse or cutting redundant storage saves money. Calculate monthly or annual cost differences to show operational savings.
- Data team productivity
  - Fewer hours spent merging spreadsheets or manually cleaning data can be redirected toward advanced analytics or creative strategy.

A simple ROI formula could look like this:

$$\text{ROI \%} = \frac{(\text{Financial benefits} + \text{Cost savings}) - (\text{Project costs})}{\text{Project costs}} \times 100$$

You can refine what goes into "financial benefits" depending on your marketing KPIs, such as increased sales from personalized campaigns or reduced churn via AI-driven retention programs.

With a clear project timeline, explicit challenge summaries, and a basic ROI measurement approach, you and your stakeholders can better plan for each phase of a lakehouse implementation. You'll ensure the outcome isn't just a theoretical upgrade but a transformative step forward for marketing.

Summary

- Data lakehouses provide a holistic framework for unifying and managing fragmented marketing data, reducing silos, and creating a single source of truth.
- Composable CDPs serve as the real-time activation layer, tapping directly into your lakehouse so you can transform raw customer data into targeted segments for immediate campaigns.
- The medallion architecture (bronze, silver, gold) guides data from raw forms to analytics-ready states, ensuring consistent quality at each stage.
- Together, these components help marketers build personalized, scalable, and effective interactions, leading to better business outcomes.
- Start with realistic planning by assessing brownfield versus greenfield scenarios, anticipating parallel runs or changing needs, and setting feasible timelines.
- Prioritize governance and data quality with robust security, compliance, and data modeling, especially as your marketing stack grows.
- Adopt the lakehouse approach incrementally—migrate historical data in phases, reconcile old and new outputs, and retire legacy systems only when you're confident in the new environment.
- Balance performance with cost by weighing advanced capabilities (like active-active DR) against your marketing ROI.
- Collaborate across teams—involve marketing ops, data engineering, and analytics stakeholders early to align on goals, avoid siloed efforts, and accelerate problem-solving.
- Visualize each project phase and track ROI continuously so stakeholders can see tangible gains, ensuring sustained support for your marketing lakehouse initiative.

6 Identity resolution and enrichment: Building a complete customer profile

This chapter covers

- Understanding identity resolution's importance for marketers
- Common identity resolution recommendations and algorithms
- The role of third-party enrichment in marketing technologies

Before identity resolution can happen, one has to ensure that accurate data from first-party data sources—apps, websites, or smart devices—is collected and made available where the identity resolution algorithm runs. The process is non-trivial and requires a deep understanding of the customer journey.

—Arpit Choudhury, Founder of Databeats

First-party data can come from many different sources, often creating a fragmented view of each customer by data source. We covered the marketing data architecture in chapter 5, so now let's dive deeper into how we can harmonize those fragmented data sources into a single customer profile. Identity resolution refers to the way your organization chooses to match these various fragments into a unified profile of each customer.

Solving identity resolution is absolutely essential and often the most challenging piece to solve in your team's first-party data strategy. It is also one of the highest leverage points your team has to drive value and reach. As a marketer, it affects the way you target and personalize your campaigns across every channel. If it's done well, it extends your marketing team's reach to new contact methods (assuming opt-ins are obtained) and increases the effectiveness of your campaigns. If it's done poorly, it leads to poor customer experience, churn, and, in some cases, regulatory penalties.

Few topics in the first-party data space cause as much confusion as identity resolution, and for good reason. The topic refers to a variety of different solutions that may include first-party data, third-party "identity spines," analytics engineering, a variety of matching algorithms, or several combinations thereof. Even well-intentioned experts in first-party data struggle to collaborate on identity resolution projects due to their complexity.

In this chapter, we will demystify identity resolution by breaking it down into its building blocks so you and your team can understand the fundamentals of identity resolution (and entity resolution in general) and why it's a critical part of your first-party data strategy. With that foundation, we'll provide recommendations for the core of your identity resolution in the context of other common approaches. After reading this chapter, your team will have a common framework and language to discuss identity resolution and make the right decisions for your organization.

6.1 Getting started with identity resolution

We define *identity resolution* as the process by which your organization identifies and matches prospect and customer activity to create a unified record of that prospect or customer. In other words, how does your team link the right activity to the right person?

Consider a modern shopper named Brittany Hamilton. Brittany has been a long-time Target shopper who regularly goes to her local store, uses the Target Android application, and has a Target Circle account (a part of their loyalty program). Yes, it seems Brittany is quite a fan of Target! Through all these engagements, Brittany leaves a digital footprint of herself in various systems and channels. Some of these interactions may include an email address, a mailing address, a browser cookie, an IP address, a phone number, a device ID, a credit card, and Brittany's name.

Like many shoppers, Brittany may create records that confuse Target with actions like the following:

- Shopping while staying at her parent's house over the holidays (linking a new IP address and browser)
- Mailing packages to her friend's house for an out-of-state birthday party (linking a new mailing address)
- Buying in-store without her Target Circle account because she was in a rush (no loyalty program link)

- Borrowing her friend's credit card while shopping in-store because she left her wallet in the car (linking a new credit card)
- Moving to a new apartment because she needed more space (linking a new permanent mailing address)

The goal of identity resolution is to discern the best way to unify all of Brittany's activity and contact information without risking false matches (often called *false positives*). We picture Brittany's activity from her point of view and how it intersects Target's systems in figure 6.1. This helps Target run the most effective and personalized campaigns to increase its customer lifetime value.

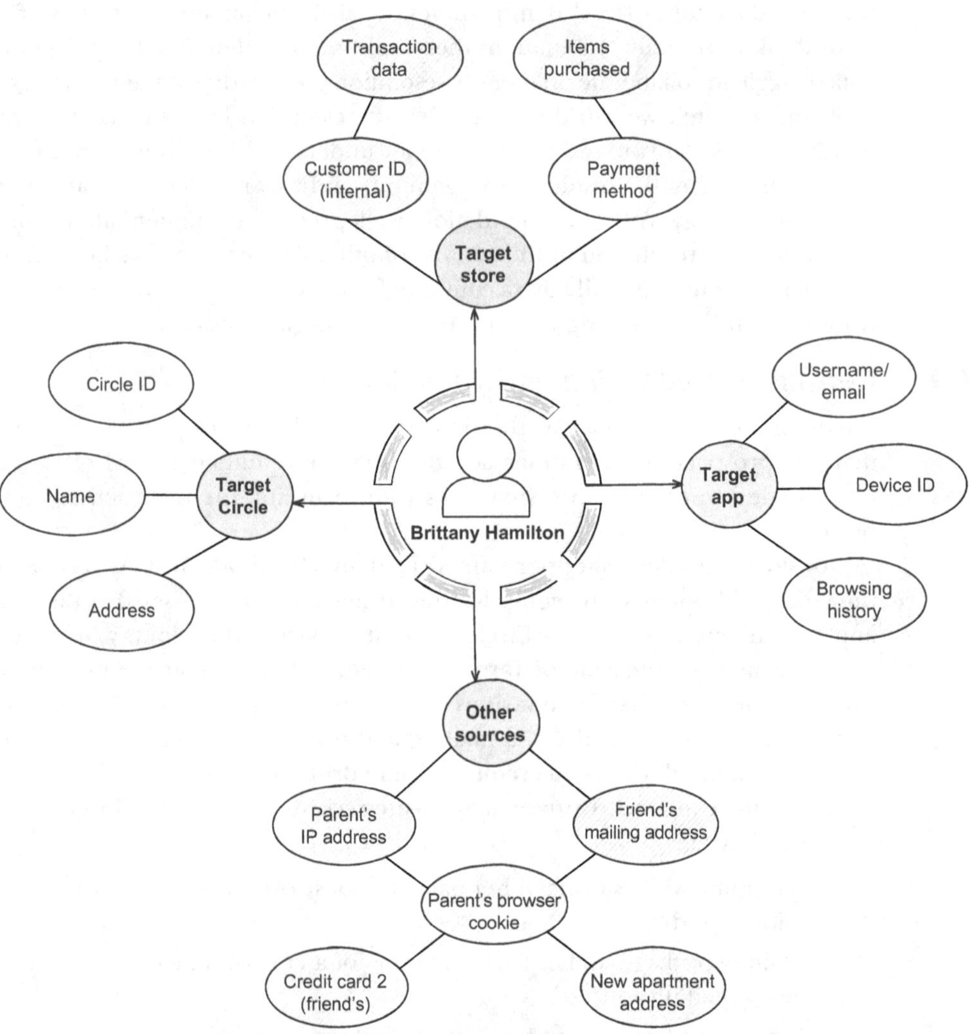

Figure 6.1 One customer, many data points: the quest for a unified view

What happens if Target's marketing team gets it wrong? For example, what if they assume that all the shopping activity at the IP address for Brittany's parent's house is made by Brittany? They may recommend products to Brittany that are better suited for her parents, which results in ineffective campaigns at best and potentially churn or worse. Or what if the Target marketing team misses key information about Brittany (*false negative* matches)? In this case, they may miss an opportunity during an upcoming life event, such as moving apartments, that others like Walmart may use to convert Brittany to their own retail experience.

It's common to show the results of identity resolution sampling tests in a two-by-two confusion matrix, which is a simple way of organizing the share of true positive matches alongside the false positive and negative matches. Figure 6.2 shows the label for each cell along with a quick description of some consequences of each outcome. This should provide your team with a common framework and language to use when discussing identity resolution risks and results. By understanding the confusion matrix, teams can make informed decisions about identity resolution thresholds and strategies to minimize false positives and false negatives.

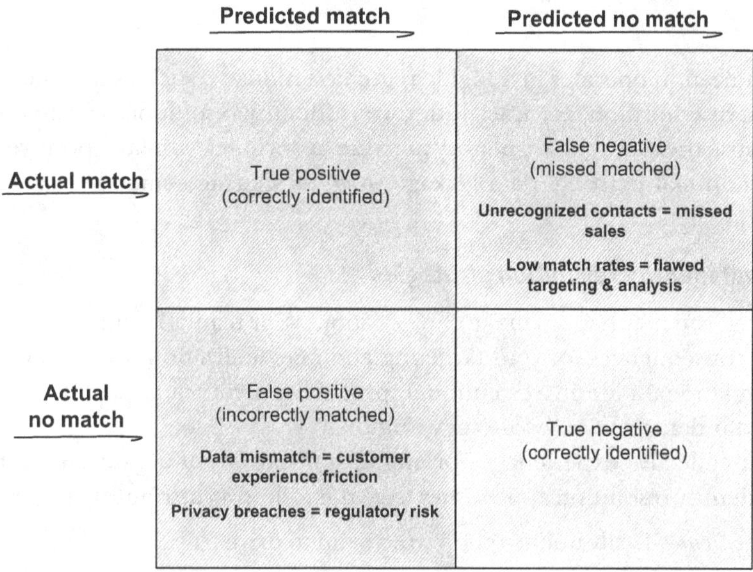

Figure 6.2 Identify resolution confusion matrix

The confusion matrix in figure 6.2 shows what each quadrant represents:

- *True positive*—The system correctly identifies two records as belonging to the same individual. This is the desired outcome.

- *False negative*—The system fails to identify two records as belonging to the same individual. This can lead to missed opportunities (e.g., not recognizing a valuable customer) and inaccurate data analysis.
- *False positive*—The system incorrectly identifies two records as belonging to the same individual when they are actually different people. This can lead to a bad customer experience (e.g., sending someone else's information) and even regulatory fines if data privacy regulations are violated.
- *True negative*—The system correctly identifies two records as belonging to different individuals.

A note on data hygiene

Strong data hygiene practices are one of the first and most important steps in achieving successful identity resolution results. If your team has poor data hygiene or integrates unreliable data sources, it may struggle to find successful matches (as the old saying goes, "garbage in, garbage out"). As you reach diminishing returns for your team's efforts, decide how far you will go based on your business or campaign goals.

In case you've skipped ahead, the Medallion architecture we covered in chapter 5 is one recommended approach to ensuring strong data governance.

If your organization operates in a highly regulated industry, such as healthcare, financial services, or education, accuracy within your identity resolution may be even more critical because there may be regulatory penalties associated with false positive matches (e.g., unintentional personal data leakage, such as sharing someone's order history with the wrong person).

6.1.1 Foundational identity resolution strategies

As a marketer, you may have to make choices about your team's identity resolution that have major consequences for your targeting and personalization. In this section, we'll discuss foundational identity resolution approaches so you can make informed decisions with your data team or technology vendors.

From our collective experiences working with hundreds of organizations, the most successful identity resolution approaches have the following attributes:

- *Transparent*—Easily understood by the team to drive trust.
- *Observable*—Easy to monitor with practical checks to enforce reliability.
- *Foundationally linked*—It is built upon a primary source of truth, often your organization's transaction data, that serves as the basis for unified identity resolution on additional sources. We recommend most organizations start by adopting one of the following deterministic (i.e., rules-based) strategies for the foundation of their identity resolution strategy:
  - Single field matching

- Composite key matching
- Deterministic cascade matching

SINGLE FIELD MATCHING

Single field matching is an exact match on a primary key across records for all the data sources that contain that key, such as user ID, mobile number, or email address. Under this simple identity resolution approach, if the email address on two or more records matches, those records are assumed to represent activity for the same person, as shown by example in figure 6.3.

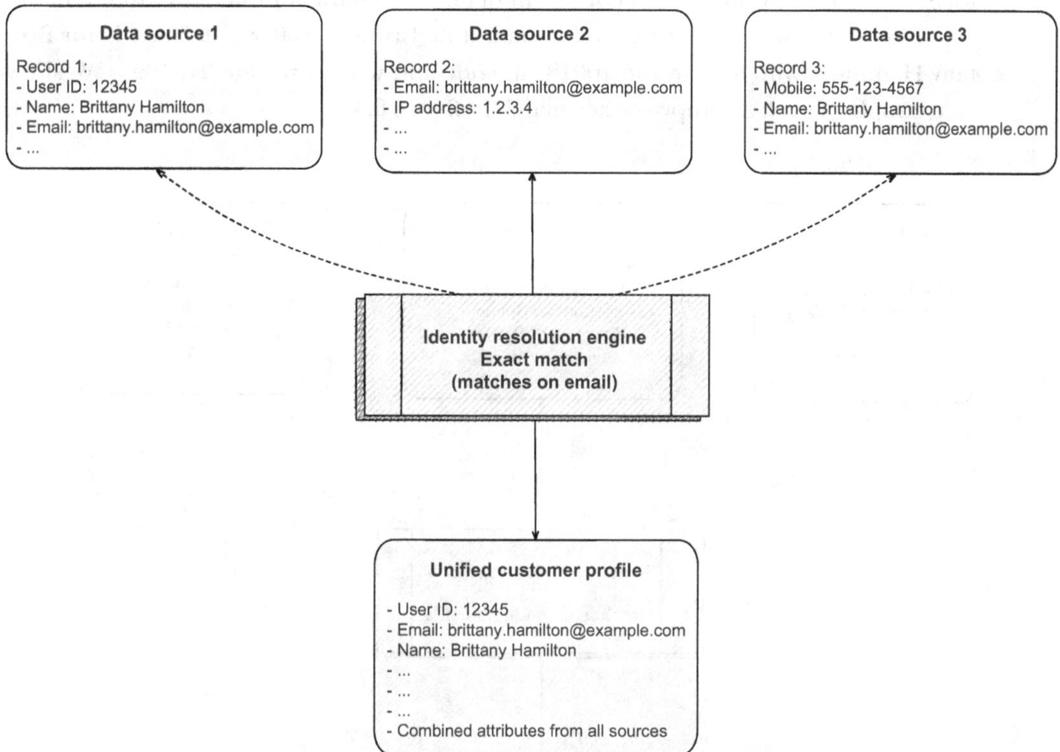

Figure 6.3 Diagram demonstrating single field identity resolution

Since email addresses and user IDs often require customers to authenticate themselves (i.e., to log in), this approach to identity resolution may have the lowest false positive rate of all the approaches. So long as your customers do not "borrow" each other's accounts, your identity resolution would be unlikely to confuse two or more different people for the same person. Also, single field matching is a straightforward approach.

The trade-off with single field matching is its limited scope. Organizations may have plenty of activity data that cannot be tied to a specific email address. For example, patients of healthcare organizations may not sign up for a digital account, which means there is no email address or unique user ID with which to associate activity data. Additionally, acquisition marketing teams may wish to reach further up into the typical conversion funnel to connect activity data before someone has logged in or provided their unique credentials.

COMPOSITE KEY MATCHING

Composite key matching extends a single field match to join records when multiple fields of data match (e.g., last name, first name, zip code, and date of birth). The simplest version of composite key matching can be applied by concatenating the match fields together for each source with a consistent delimiting character that is not found in the match fields themselves; for example, "hamilton_Brittany_10018_1995-06-21" for Brittany Hamilton, who lives in the 10018 zip code and was born June 21, 1995. We show an example of such a composite key match in figure 6.4.

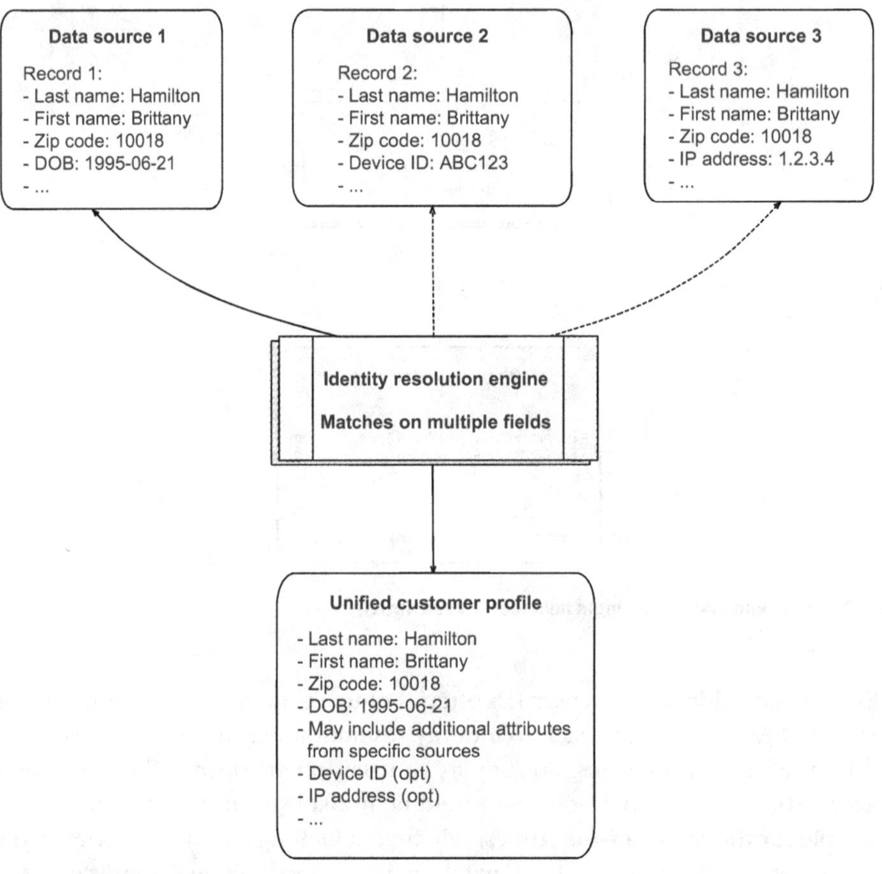

Figure 6.4 Diagram demonstrating composite field identity resolution

This approach is very helpful in non-digital contexts, but non-standardized fields, such as names, that may vary widely for the same person make it challenging to get right in practice, requiring multiple rounds of iteration and testing. Additionally, not all sources will contain all of the matching fields necessary for the composite key match, which often leads teams to explore more complicated rules-based approaches, such as deterministic cascade matching.

Let's explore an example where this may work very well. A video streaming service wishes to make content recommendations to its users, but users often share logins within the same family, making individualized recommendations challenging. What could the company's data science team do in this case? They could create a composite key that includes the email address associated with the subscribing account and add a secondary identifier such as the device ID, IP address, or other differentiating attribute to tell apart different members of the family. The data science team could then apply an item-item recommendation model based on content views for each composite key to make more personalized recommendations than a simple field-matching approach would achieve.

DETERMINISTIC CASCADE MATCHING

Deterministic cascade matching is a sequential, rules-based approach that extends both single field match and composite key match by enforcing a prioritization or precedence of sources and fields to the problem of identity resolution. We know intuitively that some fields, such as email address, are more consistent than first name and last name. We also know that some sources of data, such as transactions, are more reliable than other sources of data.

In deterministic cascade matching, we use this knowledge to apply a set of conditional match rules in a specific sequence to find the best matching approach, as shown in figure 6.5. The term "cascade" refers to the fact that the conditional match rules will be applied to each record sequentially until a match rule applies successfully, at which point the match is made and the next records are evaluated. If no matching rule is found for this particular set of records, the algorithm cascades down the sequential steps to a base case. Most organizations apply a base case that assumes no match, which is often used to create a new record.

> **Advanced identity resolution approaches**
>
> Your team may explore more advanced identity resolution approaches such as probabilistic matching—methods that use statistical likelihoods rather than deterministic rules to decide whether two records belong to the same individual. These approaches assess the similarity of multiple data fields, such as name, email, address, or behavior patterns, and calculate a probability score that the records refer to the same person. Common techniques include fuzzy string matching (e.g., edit distance), phonetic algorithms (e.g., Soundex), and machine learning models trained on labeled datasets. While probabilistic matching can capture matches that deterministic methods miss, it also introduces the risk of false positives due to its less rigid rules.

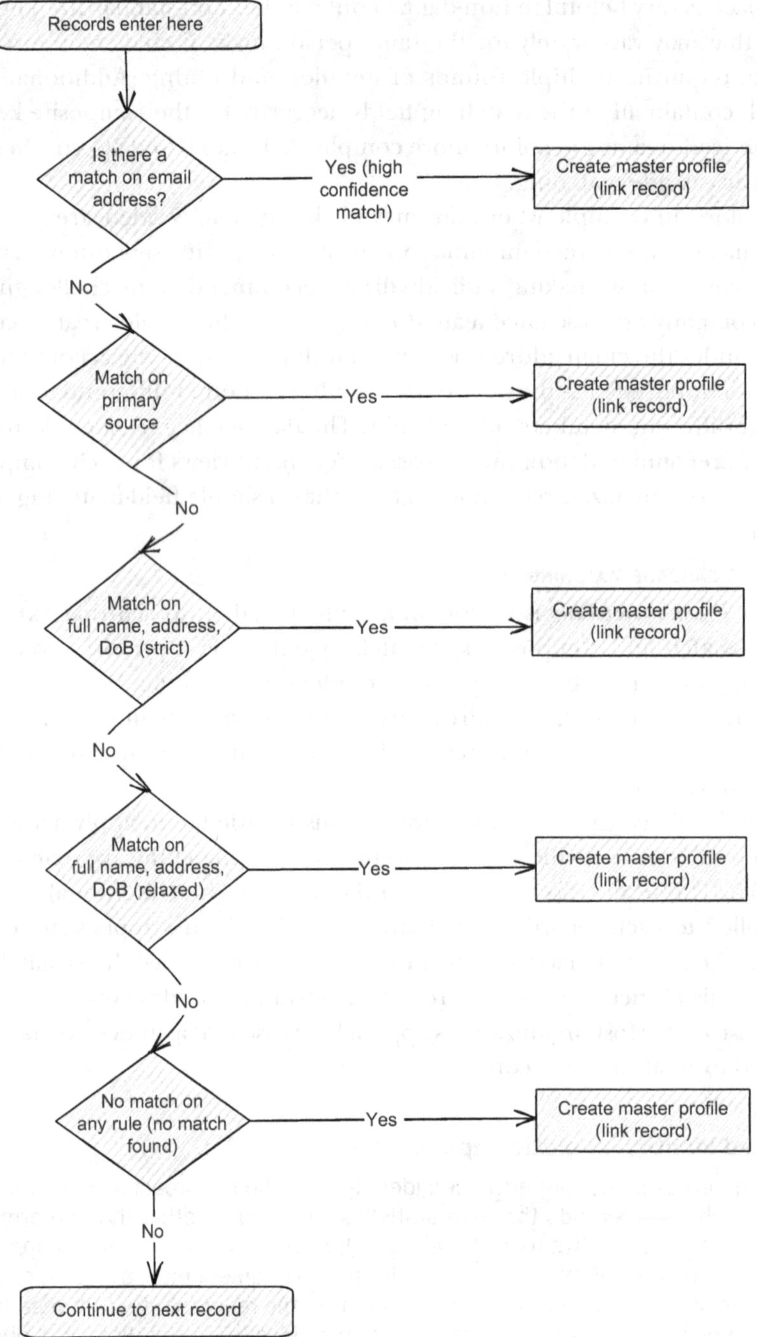

Figure 6.5 Diagram demonstrating deterministic cascade identity resolution

> ***(continued)***
>
> Most modern customer data platforms (CDPs) include probabilistic identity resolution capabilities out of the box, especially for web and mobile traffic where deterministic identifiers are often missing. Because these capabilities are typically embedded in your marketing technology stack and managed by the vendor, we won't go into the mechanics of probabilistic matching in this book. Instead, we recommend using a deterministic approach as the foundation of your customer communications strategy and augmenting it with probabilistic matching where it's available through your CDP—particularly for anonymous-to-known resolution and behavioral linking in digital environments.

CHOOSING AN IDENTITY RESOLUTION APPROACH

Many teams start with single or composite key matching and eventually add new, prioritized rules to reach a form of deterministic cascade matching because it meets all of the criteria we laid out for a successful identity resolution approach:

- *Transparent*—The rules applied in all three approaches are deterministic (i.e., rules-based) and are relatively simple to explain to everyone on the marketing team. This helps ensure a consistent understanding across the organization to engender trust.
- *Observable*—These matching algorithms can be engineered into the data pipeline with a variety of checks that can alert the data team of any anomalies, such as non-unique keys, stale data sources, or conflicting sources. This makes all three approaches ideal for alerts and monitoring to catch problems before they affect any production marketing campaigns or other use cases.
- *Foundationally linked*—Let's break this attribute down by case to see how it could apply to each of the three approaches we've covered in our recommendations:
  - Single field match should be based on a key that is (nearly) universally unique per person, such as email address, mobile number, or a user ID that is often used to authenticate customers or transact with them.
  - Composite key match should start with a primary source of truth, such as orders or transactions, that can be linked to the multiple fields of data used to construct the composite key.
  - Deterministic cascade match effectively combines single and composite key matches in a series of steps, so it should follow a prioritization based on a primary set of data sources.

One of the reasons we recommend these approaches is that they are relatively quick to test, may be implemented on virtually any data platform in SQL, and your team can start with a simple identity resolution algorithm and grow its complexity over time as your team masters new data sources. This makes it a very compelling alternative to other matching approaches.

6.1.2 Identity resolution for company records

Identity resolution for individual people is a subclass of the broader topic of entity resolution. *Entity resolution* includes the reconciliation and unification of records for entities such as businesses (often referred to as "accounts" by sales teams) and households.

In the consumer marketing world, often referred to as B2C (business-to-consumer) or DTC (direct-to-consumer) marketing, identity resolution may be focused on individual people. However, for certain channels like direct mail or in certain industries such as banking, it may be essential to resolve households as well. Using the physical address to resolve multiple people into a single household is an approach that successfully determines households most of the time. Since people may have multiple addresses and complicated familial relationships, it can be very difficult to reduce false positive and false negative error rates further. Some organizations require direct customer input or corrections over time for their household identity resolution models.

In the business marketing world, often referred to as B2B (business-to-business) marketing, accounts and company hierarchies may require a second level of entity resolution. Most companies have several people or contacts associated with them, which makes it very important to unify disparate company records into one. Figure 6.6 shows that

- An account can have many contacts (one-to-many relationships).
- Each contact belongs to one account (identified by the account ID foreign key).

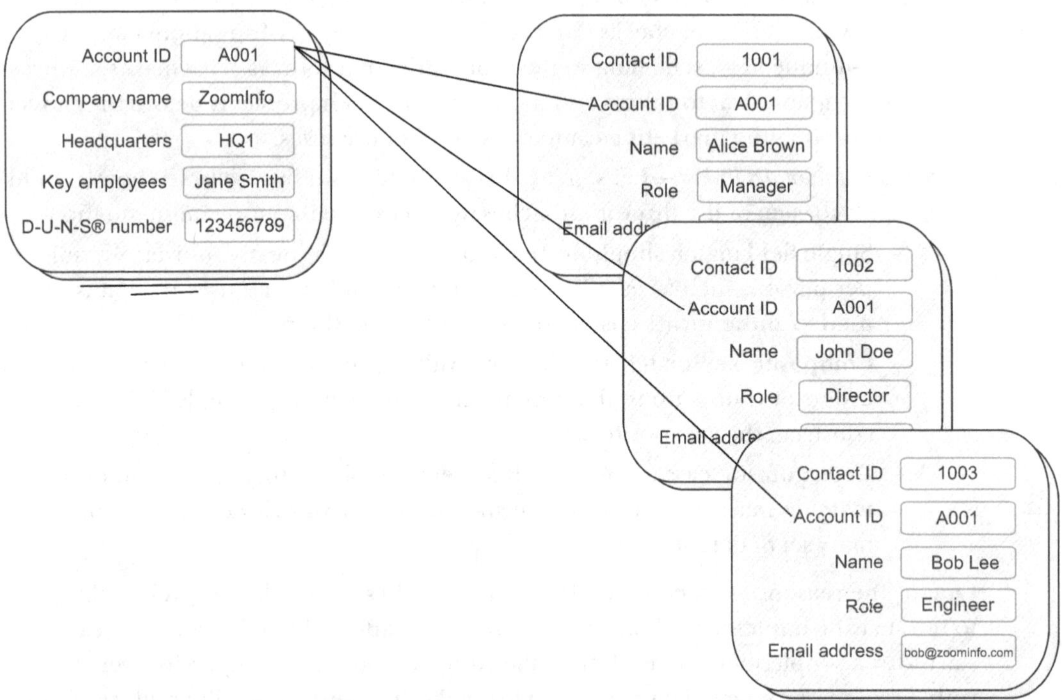

Figure 6.6 Account and contact one-to-many relationships

Let's dive into an example of why getting this right may be critically important. Let's assume your organization has a lead score model that triggers a marketing-qualified lead to be routed to the sales team when multiple contacts at a company show positive engagement (e.g., whitepaper downloads or responses to marketing email sequences). What if two contacts at the same company show positive engagement, but those contacts are erroneously found on separate accounts? Your B2B marketing team might miss the threshold to engage sales at the critical moment when a target company is in a buying cycle for your software.

Since the addressable market for most B2B products is well known, many marketing teams will invest in purchasing a company target list from companies like ZoomInfo or Dun & Bradstreet. They use attributes to select a subset of all the companies in the third-party database to reduce the cost of the purchase and make it much more targeted (or to refresh their data on companies and their contacts). Some go so far as to find industry-specific indicators of buying intent, such as tracking web searches from IP addresses associated with company offices.

Within the context of your day-to-day sales and marketing efforts, your team can approach company-level entity resolution much the same way that you resolve consumer identities using other key facts about the company. These company-level records are often matched using deterministic cascade matching on key data fields such as the following:

- Company name
- Headquarters
- Key employees
- Third-party identifiers such as the Dun & Bradstreet D-U-N-S® Number

However, in contrast to consumer identity resolution, data hygiene upon entry plays a much more important role since it is often the sales team that inputs company information into your sales CRM software. Many companies have a sales operations team member who manually reviews accounts in the CRM and merges duplicate company-level records to ensure all the knowledge about that company can be referenced together. In the context of B2B marketing and sales, this is especially important for lead scoring, where a certain threshold of activity from contacts at a company is needed to trigger certain sales or marketing activity.

6.1.3 Marketing technology solutions

If building your own identity resolution seems daunting to you and your data team, you may want to consider marketing technology solutions that offer identity resolution services built in. How should you approach this search and evaluation? If you search for identity resolution on the web, you will find a multitude of solutions offering everything from customer data platforms (CDPs) to data onboarding services and third-party data providers. This may be very confusing for the uninitiated because identity resolution actually refers to an entire class of services that we'll break down in the following sections.

CDPs and the emerging category of *customer data infrastructure* providers focus on first-party identity resolution. Some will capture identifying activity from your organization's web and mobile surfaces to connect activity across sessions (which can subsequently be associated with logged-in accounts). Most will support unifying a customer profile based on that web and mobile data and any other data sources you can bring to the CDP, often with probabilistic matching that lacks transparency. A new category of composable CDPs, covered in chapter 4, allows your team to take more active control of your identity resolution approach.

For those that adopt a monolithic CDP, you may have no a choice but to use what comes with your platform (in fact, it may be why you chose it). The advantage of these solutions is often that they provide a user interface to assist with identity resolution rules and assumptions. We recommend those for marketing teams that have no data team support.

For companies adopting a composable architecture, we recommend deterministic identity resolution models residing in your marketing data lakehouse or equivalent because it allows your data team to define your team's identity resolution approach transparently via a series of steps (often in SQL). You can also add monitoring and alerts to proactively identify and address any problems before they affect campaigns in production (for example, if the primary key from a data source is unexpectedly not unique). Identity resolution is company-specific and important enough for most organizations to manage it in-house.

Data onboarding services help you use your first-party and third-party data to achieve greater match rates on advertising platforms such as Meta and The Trade Desk by using a third-party identity graph that has prematched fields, such as device ID to email address, to identify individual people on the web and mobile. The model is based on paying per activation and rarely grants your organization access to any of the identity spines in your own data environment.

Third-party data providers can help provide prematched fields and enriched data fields on whatever first-party data your organization has to increase match rates, both internally and externally, with ad platforms. Increasingly, the benefit of these datasets has been made available within CDPs, onboarding services, and even the major cloud platforms themselves, so there are good alternatives to direct licensing.

6.1.4 Risk mitigation approaches

You can mitigate much of the risk of managing personally identifiable information (PII) for identity resolution purposes by proactively designing your solution, policies, and practices in privacy-safe ways.

Privacy-first methodologies help you mitigate risk by design. First, you should ensure that you are collecting customer opt-in information with each piece of PII and that you are carrying that information through each step of your identity resolution algorithm so that it's available in your final matched records. Doing so reduces the chance that someone will use PII for an unauthorized channel or purpose.

Next, you can optionally consider whether you want to hash or encrypt PII as part of your data pipeline if you only need the PII for matching (for example, many ad platforms support SHA-256 encryption for targeting). This reduces the chance that a user's unencrypted information is exposed to anyone—even your own internal team members.

Clear compliance policies that spell out what the final, matched records may be used for by marketing, analytics, and other teams are a must-have to avoid the risk of unauthorized use when you match various data sources together that contain PII.

Automated testing helps identify any errors in your identity resolution algorithm that may compromise results and helps identify incompatible data entries before they corrupt your final, matched results. For example, you may test whether you have malformed email address data before you attempt to match it so you prevent the creation of any false records in your final, matched results.

Regular manual audits are essential because they help you catch "everything else" that could go wrong in your identity resolution. Nothing can replace what a team member applying critical thinking will catch when looking at the results of your identity resolution. We recommend randomized sampling (to get a broad sample) and localized spot sampling (to identify problems and patterns that may not be obvious when reviewing randomized samples across your entire identity dataset).

6.2 Anonymous-to-known identity resolution

There is a special case that's particularly important for acquisition marketing: understanding and engaging with anonymous visitors. Anonymous visitors are those who visit a website or interact with a brand's online presence without providing any identifying information about themselves, such as their name or email address.

Most websites implement cookies (small data or text packets stored on your web browser) to track visitors during the duration of their web session. These may include

- *First-party cookies*—These packets of data are generated, updated, and read by the website domain listed in your address bar (the one you are currently visiting) rather than the domain of another website. Most web browsers place far fewer restrictions on first-party cookies, and most companies are investing in first-party cookie-based tracking.
- *Third-party cookies*—These packets of data are generated, updated, and read by a website other than the one listed in your address bar. Browsers such as Firefox block these by default, but Chrome and other browsers allow them to expire after a maximum of 400 days as of this writing (though the expiry period is often much shorter on other browsers that enable them).

This cookie-based tracking is used for a number of useful purposes, such as remembering what you placed in your shopping cart during your checkout process. In cases where you begin a purchase and sign in again later, these cookies can connect all your prelogin activity to your logged-in account. For example, airlines will often prompt you to sign in to expedite your purchase and then connect all of your prelogin activity, such as the flight you chose, with your account details.

Many websites still use third-party cookies to track consumers as well, though this is an increasingly controversial practice. Anonymous visitors represent a significant portion of lost potential leads and customers, so businesses constantly strive to engage with their website visitors and provide seamless, personalized experiences. However, since most website traffic comes from anonymous users, companies are left in the dark about their preferences, needs, and potential value. This lack of information makes it difficult to personalize the visitor experience or provide customized offers.

Here's why it's important to extend anonymous identity resolution:

- *Unlock valuable insights*—Anonymous visitors generate valuable data through their browsing behavior, product interactions, and content engagement. Marketers can better understand user flows, and identity resolution techniques can help connect this anonymous data to known customer profiles, providing a more holistic view of user behavior and preferences.
- *Personalized marketing*—By potentially identifying or linking anonymous visitors to existing customer segments, you can tailor your marketing messages and recommendations to their interests.
- *Retargeting and remarketing*—Understanding anonymous browsing behavior allows for more effective retargeting campaigns. You can show relevant ads or promotions to those who have expressed interest in specific products or services, even if they haven't identified themselves yet.
- *Improve conversion rates*—By understanding visitor behavior and interests, you can optimize your website and marketing messages to better resonate with potential customers, ultimately leading to higher conversion rates.
- *Reduce customer acquisition costs*—Effective anonymous-to-known identity resolution can improve the efficiency of your marketing efforts by allowing you to target the right audience with the right message, potentially reducing wasted ad spend and increasing return on investment (ROI).

While completely identifying an anonymous visitor might not always be possible, various techniques are used today to achieve a better understanding of web visitors. Here are some approaches to anonymous visitor identification:

- *Session-based cookies*—These tools track user behavior across a website (first-party cookies) or even across different websites (third-party cookies), allowing for the creation of profiles based on browsing habits. Session-based cookies generally have an automatic expiration set by each browser or the user's settings, though first-party cookies have a longer time to live than third-party cookies.
- *IP address analysis*—While this approach is not foolproof due to shared networks and proxy servers, IP addresses can provide a general location and potentially be linked to existing customer data for that region.

- *Device IDs*—A user's unique device identifiers (possible on Android, often blocked on iOS) allow you to track something usually used by a single person.
- *Device fingerprinting*—This technique gathers information about a user's device (browser, operating system, etc.) to create a unique identifier. However, privacy concerns and evolving technologies can limit its effectiveness.
- *Progressive profiling*—By strategically placing opt-in forms throughout the user journey, you can capture some identifying information (e.g., email address) in exchange for valuable content or offers, gradually building a more complete profile of the web visitor.
- *Single-sign on*—You can try to convert the anonymous user to identified by having them sign in or connect via their Google, Apple, Facebook, or another account. This approach lowers the friction of entering details that are already associated with one of those accounts if the anonymous user is willing to share access to their account.

Historically and through the present day, many web-based companies outsource their tracking by embedding third-party marketing technology products such as Adobe Analytics, Google Analytics, or one of the CDPs listed in chapter 4. These products may use third-party data to connect sparse details across web sessions to the same web visitor. Since these products functionally provide similar capabilities, choosing one comes down to your team's prior experience with these platforms, the ease of integration, and whether your team is focused on *understanding* (via analytics solutions like Adobe Analytics or Google Analytics) or is most interested in campaign *activation* (via CDPs). These technologies combine the best of first-party cookie tracking and third-party technology, which we'll describe in more detail next.

6.2.1 Third-party cookie tracking

Policymakers have begun to enact regulations to restrict third-party tracking on the web, and several browsers have begun removing third-party cookie tracking proactively (e.g., Apple Safari since 2020, Mozilla Firefox since 2019, and Microsoft Edge since 2020). If you are starting from scratch, your organization should consider building a more future-proof strategy by investing in providers that help you create your own *first-party tracking* capabilities.

Let's look at the difference between *third-party cookie-based* and *first-party cookie-based* tracking that is still in use today. A company offering infant probiotic formula may believe (or discover via customer surveys) that discerning parents make multiple visits and comparison shop before buying infant probiotics. Thus, staying top of mind for these discerning parents is key, especially as they build enough confidence to make a purchase. The stakes are high because the company knows that parents tend to stick with whatever formula they choose for future purchases.

The company could choose to install The Trade Desk's pixel tracking on their product pages. This pixel is simply a piece of JavaScript code or an HTML image that sends information such as clicks, page views, and a unique user-level cookie identifier back to The Trade Desk's ad servers when a user visits the page with third-party cookie tracking enabled. In simple terms, The Trade Desk then collects all these user-level identifiers to create a list of everyone who visited that product page.

Once that's done, the infant formula company can select the list of people who have recently visited the probiotic infant formula page and show them ads about the formula they viewed on any websites serving digital ads from The Trade Desk. Discerning parents who have been reading pediatrician's blogs commenting on the benefits of infant formula with probiotics may see the ad for the product they viewed a few days ago alongside that pediatrician's content.

While they may not click on the ad or make a purchase at that moment, there is a good chance their ability to recall the product's name will increase. (They may even subconsciously associate the specific probiotic infant formula with the positive and credible reputation of the pediatrician!) This type of advertising is called *retargeting* or *remarketing*, and it can be highly effective.

6.2.2 First-party cookie tracking by third parties

Given all the challenges with third-party cookies, companies like Google and Meta have redesigned their tracking to use first-party cookies for their ads (e.g., Google Ads and Meta Ads) and analytics products (e.g., Google Analytics 4 or GA4).

These companies use JavaScript anyone can install on their web page to collect events (e.g., page views and clicks) and connect them to persistent identifiers (e.g., first-party cookies, device IDs, etc.) stored on your domain rather than on Google's or Meta's domains. The challenge then becomes how to get this data back to Google or Meta so they can help you create anonymous audiences or help you better understand your web analytics.

Let's take GA4 as an example since it is a very mature web analytics platform. (Adobe Analytics is the other most popular web analytics platform, though there are many others.) GA4 allows you to send data back to Google in multiple ways, requiring varying levels of effort, via either client-side tracking or server-side tracking. Note that "client-side" refers to code that is executed on a web visitor's browser as they interact with your web page; "server-side" is code that is executed at the web server as it "serves" web pages to the visitor's browser. Here's a quick breakdown of each:

- *Client-side tracking*—If you'd like to keep things simple, GA4 provides JavaScript you can install on your web pages that will send each visitor's events and identifiers to Google by making a `POST` request to Google's servers from the visitor's browser. Most marketing teams that use this approach do so out of convenience (it is usually easier to install tracking tags and JavaScript code on the client side), and it has the added benefit that the "load" of making all those `POST` requests is delegated to each visitor's browser. The downside is that ad blockers and browser privacy features (e.g., Safari ITP, Firefox ETP) can block these client-side requests to third parties.

- *Server-side tracking*—In response, Google created server-side tracking, which requires both client-side code and additional server-side code to be installed. The benefit is that all tracking data is first sent back to your own company's web server, which is generally allowed by all browsers (though ad blockers may still specifically look to block Google's code whenever they successfully identify it). This means that the `POST` request containing all the tracking parameters about a visitor is made by your company's web servers directly to Google's servers. While setting this up is extra work for your web or engineering team, and it creates extra load for your servers, it is a more resilient tracking method than client-side tracking.

Figure 6.7 shows how various pieces of information can be sent from the client side or server side to build an enhanced customer profile. Note that the two sides may have different information available to be collected.

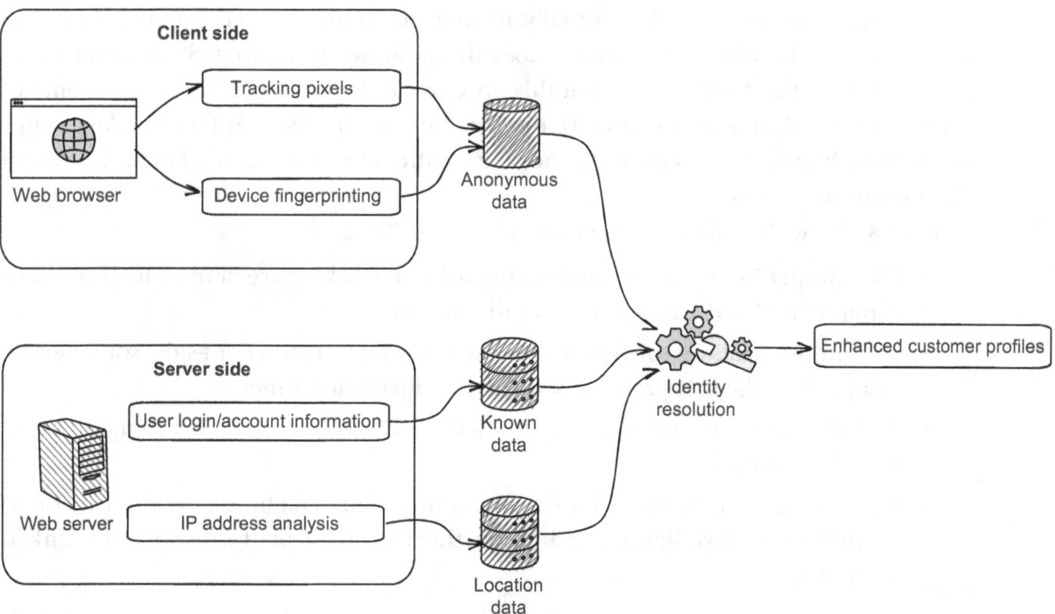

Figure 6.7 Client-side vs. server-side data collection for anonymous-to-known identity resolution

The marketing team can then view summarized reports about these users on GA4 for insights and can create audiences in the Google Ad platform based on user behaviors and demographics to drive conversions. While you can also access much more granular data tables by having GA4 data sync to Google Cloud BigQuery, you will only see a subset of what Google knows about web visitors because Google is using its own identity spine to connect visitor behavior or sessions that may have seemed separate. As you'd expect, the integration between GA4 and Google Ads is great, but the advantage does not carry over to other competing ad platforms. And what if Google's servers are down? Are you willing to risk your own website going down too by relying on them?

6.2.3 Full first-party tracking

With *full first-party* tracking, you implement code on your website that is captured and stored entirely by your company's web infrastructure. This is what some of the largest e-commerce brands, such as The Home Depot Canada, do today because it allows them to access all the data the user provides, increase the duration with which they can use that first-party data, and customize their tracking to suit their needs. First-party tracking also removes the risk that a third-party tracking problem takes down your website.

New companies like MetaRouter have sprung up to provide tracking software that a company can deploy in its own cloud environment to more easily deploy their own first-party tracking. In MetaRouter's case, they combine first-party identifiers with third-party identifiers to maximize match rates before storing all of them together on your company's servers (and, eventually, in your marketing data lakehouse). The step-by-step process by which MetaRouter does this is shown in figure 6.8. The event data tables produced by MetaRouter with this process can be used after the fact by some of the identity resolution techniques we discussed earlier in this chapter to make greater inferences about visitors to your site and activate them to most major ad platforms using third-party identifiers.

Here's a basic description of how it works:

- MetaRouter helps create a first-party cookie to track web sessions, which contains things like IP addresses and device identifiers.
- MetaRouter calls on third parties in various ways (mostly client-side, some server-side) to link the first-party cookie with third-party identifiers.
- MetaRouter stores everything on the server side (backend) rather than the client side (browser).
- Everything is then synced to a marketing data lakehouse or equivalent to be further analyzed and activated on third-party ad platforms with the linked identifiers.

By combining these approaches, businesses can gain a deeper understanding of their anonymous visitors and improve their acquisition marketing strategies. So if third-party cookie tracking is on its way out, what about third-party data?

6.3 Third-party enrichment of identity resolution

Buying third-party lists was traditionally a tactic used by direct mail marketers and B2B marketers looking for firmographic data to kick off their direct marketing efforts. While this practice certainly continues, new ways of using third-party data in conjunction with your organization's first-party data have emerged in recent years to augment targeting, personalization, and reach. This may be worthwhile for your

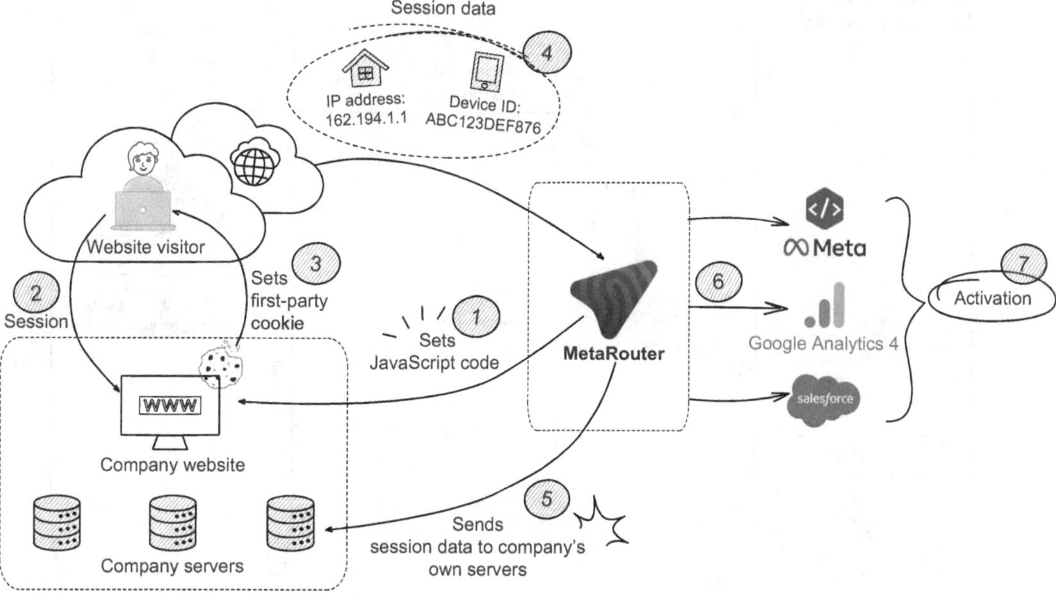

Figure 6.8 The MetaRouter journey: client-side and server-side data linking for enhanced targeting

organization if you are reaching the limits of your first-party data and have some budget you can use to license third-party data.

6.3.1 How third-party enrichment works

Several companies focus on capturing and matching data about consumers or corporate buyers, including identifiers (i.e., who they are), attributes (i.e., what they are), and preferences (i.e., what they are looking for). Since this is not your company's data about prospective customers, we refer to it as "third-party data." We'll get into several ways companies today use third-party data, but let's start by discussing how it works.

Historically, you would need to send your first-party data to the third-party data provider to be enriched (as shown in figure 6.9) or pay a steeper licensing fee for the third-party data provider to send you a subset of third-party data for your team to match itself. While encryption and hashing have improved the security of these approaches, they introduce risk because sensitive (and valuable) data must be sent to another company. As a result, new technology offerings have surfaced to make the matching process easier and more secure.

In response to this risk, *data clean rooms* (DCRs) have emerged. These DCRs allow two or more parties to match information without revealing it to one another by entrusting the match to a shared data environment to which no party has direct access (usually administered by a third-party company that specializes in providing DCR services). The

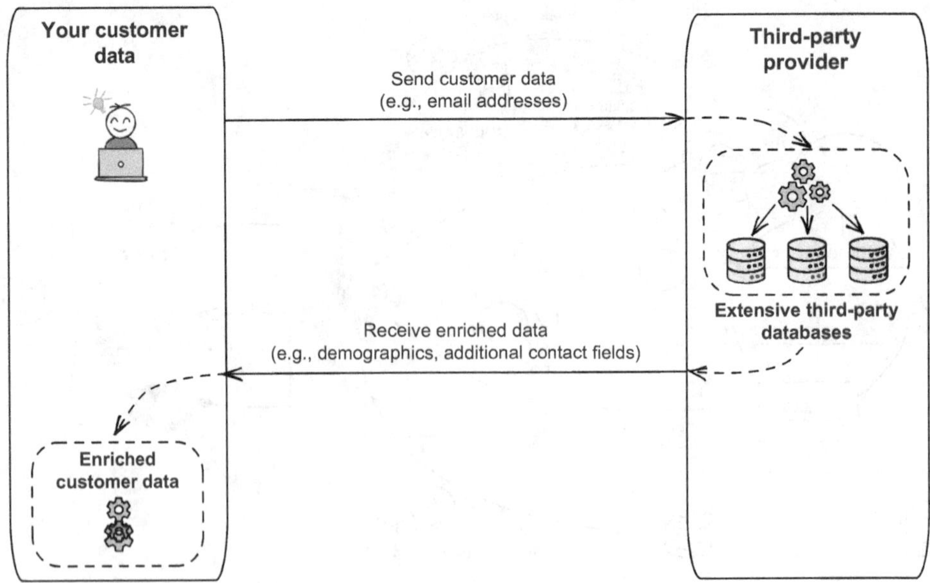

Figure 6.9 Traditional third-party enrichment (sending/receiving data)

matching and sharing rules are built into the DCR environment itself, so the risk of misuse or unauthorized access is very low. We'll share much more on this emerging technology in chapter 8.

In the last two years, Amazon Web Services and Google Cloud have also launched "entity resolution" services by partnering with leading providers, such as LiveRamp and TransUnion. These new services make it possible to stitch together or enrich your first-party data directly in your cloud resources, such as your marketing data lakehouse.

Finally, universal identifiers such as UID 2.0 have replaced vendor-specific identifiers such as RampID, making it much easier for companies to take greater control over their first-to-third-party data matching. Additionally, UID 2.0 is supported by a large (and growing) number of digital ad platforms, which makes it a compelling open alternative to vendor-specific identifiers.

Let's dive into three of the most common use cases for third-party data in a first-party data world:

- *Identity stitching*—Stitching together first-party data using a third-party identity spine to link records
- *Contact expansion*—Expanding identifiers and contact information to reach additional channels or enhance match rates on paid media
- *Profile enrichment*—Enriching prospect or customer profiles with additional attributes such as demographics

We'll look at each in turn.

6.3.2 Identity stitching

Identity stitching consists of using identifiers (e.g., device ID) sourced by third parties to match a prospect's activity (e.g., web sessions) that would otherwise be impossible to match. While your company may not know who the visitor is, a third party may know enough to help you unify independent web sessions under one visitor profile.

Consider the case of a major clothing retailer that sells in-store and online. When you arrive on the website, the marketing team would like to personalize the products displayed to maximize the chance that one will resonate with you. The problem is that you have not signed in, so you are effectively an anonymous visitor. What can the retailer do to personalize your experience?

What if the marketing team is limited to first-party data? Perhaps the website has created a first-party cookie to track your sessions over time, so they know that you looked at women's shoes in your last browser session. That may work well for a subset of cases to link your recent activity on the site, but it will not work if you are joining from a browser on a different device, such as your phone instead of your laptop.

In order to link those sessions, your marketing team may need to use a third-party identity spine (i.e., a prematched dataset managed by a third party that links things such as email addresses to phone numbers and device IDs). Third-party providers embedded in web analytics and CDPs may already know that your laptop's device identifiers and your phone's device identifiers should both be associated with you. This gives the marketing team a competitive advantage and allows it to show you women's shoes instead of a generic screen of products.

6.3.3 Contact expansion

A more common problem is trying to target anonymous visitors after they have left your website. Perhaps you were browsing a specific pair of women's shoes, and an offer for 10% off popped up in exchange for enrolling in an email marketing program. The marketing team may choose to send you a follow-up email about the offer on the shoes, but they may also want to reach you where you spend the most time (for this example, we'll assume that's on social media).

If the marketing team is limited to first-party data, they will be able to use your email address on those social media advertising platforms, but the match rate may be low. For example, let's assume you use a different email address for your social media account than you do for shopping, and those emails are not linked by the social media advertising platform.

In order to achieve a higher match rate, a third-party provider may be able to fill important gaps in your marketing team's data. For example, as shown in figure 6.10, the third-party provider may be able to take each (hashed or encrypted) email address that your marketing team provides and append other contact information, such as home address, different email addresses, and device identifiers that your paid media team can use across many ad platforms to increase match rates to the intended target audience (also known as *enhanced match rates*).

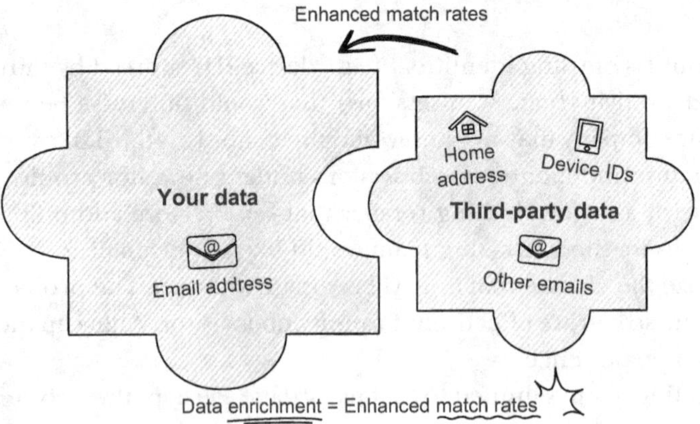

Figure 6.10 Data enrichment for enhanced match rates

If the third-party provider links your home address to the email address you used to enroll in the email marketing program, the retailer may want to start sending you their monthly catalog. This effectively helps the marketing team expand their marketing channels to reach you, from email to social media and direct mail.

6.3.4 *Profile enrichment*

Expanding on our example, what if the anonymous visitor to the retailer's website was actually a husband searching for a gift for his wife's birthday? It may be very helpful to know that he regularly buys sporting goods, and his search for women's shoes may be an isolated instance of a purchase unrelated to sporting goods.

Here are some examples of what third-party data enrichment can add to the profile of the visitor:

- Estimated household income
- Age range
- Marital status
- Credit behavior
- Potential first-time homebuyer
- Highest education achieved
- Renter versus home owner

While the marketing team could target many of these demographics on most digital ad platforms, it is much more helpful to link them to a recent visitor who has already demonstrated interest in the retailer's products.

In addition to enabling more refined targeting on digital ad platforms, such as a display ad targeting the husband for Valentine's Day, the marketing team may choose to personalize their email creative to be more relevant to the web visitor. They could design promotional campaigns around demographic subcategories of their customers or simply better understand their ideal customer profile.

6.3.5 Purchasing third-party data services

There are several leading providers of third-party data, including TransUnion (who bought Neustar), LiveRamp, Acxiom, FullContact, Deep Sync, Dun & Bradstreet, and ZoomInfo. Before you contact them for a purchase, it's worth learning a bit more about them and the rest of the vendor ecosystem. The third-party data use cases we've covered may be performed together, and licensing fees vary based on a number of factors:

- How valuable is the target audience? (A specialized or higher income audience may cost more.)
- How recently has the data been collected or confirmed? How often is it refreshed? (Some data, such as credit utilization, may change often, while other data, such as home ownership, may change infrequently.)
- What is the matching process? How easy is it to integrate the third-party data services into your organization's marketing efforts?
- How much of the data do you have access to (e.g., how many attributes, and do you keep the data persistently)?
- How do you use the data (e.g., for enhanced match on paid media only), and are the provider's collection and your use case in compliance with regulations?

Here are a few of the most popular third-party data providers:

- *TransUnion*—Since the purchase of Neustar, TransUnion now has one of the most comprehensive third-party data resources for the US market. They specialize in credit-specific data, which is most helpful for the financial services, automotive, and telecommunications industries.
- *LiveRamp*—LiveRamp transformed the digital advertising ecosystem by creating one of the largest and most widely used third-party digital and device identity graphs. They specialize in offering onboarding solutions to help digital advertisers maximize their match rate and reach across ad platforms.
- *Acxiom*—Acxiom is one of the largest third-party data providers and offers a unified suite of services and third-party data products.
- *FullContact*—FullContact offers identity resolution on a SaaS basis, and it also powers many marketing technology platforms that provide identity resolution services.
- *Deep Sync*—A more recent entrant into the third-party data ecosystem, Deep Sync has a strong and economical offering for US addresses, which makes it a good partner for direct mail campaigns.
- *Dun & Bradstreet*—Historically, Dun & Bradstreet has been the primary third-party data provider on US businesses, including firmographics such as creditworthiness, size, and industry.

- *ZoomInfo*—For many B2B marketing teams, ZoomInfo is the most cost-effective starting point for company-level data and individual contact information.

If you are a major enterprise customer with bespoke needs, it may make sense to contract with these companies directly. For most organizations, however, you may be able to get much better terms by using third-party data within the marketing technology (and now cloud services) you purchase. These marketing technology vendors, such as MetaRouter, Google Cloud, and GrowthLoop, have often negotiated bulk-rate deals that give you access to more competitive pricing on the most common datasets and use cases.

You now have what you need to design and select consistent, centralized customer experiences. Next, we'll cover the important topic of marketing activation, which is how you can effectively deliver targeted audiences and personalization to your marketing destinations and channels (e.g., email and ads platforms).

Summary

- Identity resolution is a critical aspect of your first-party data strategy because it directly affects who you can target with your marketing.
- Identity resolution is the process of linking various pieces of customer data to create a unified view of each individual. It's crucial for effective targeting, personalization, and customer experience.
- The biggest challenge is the fragmentation of customer data from different sources. This makes it difficult to accurately link all relevant data to the correct individual, risking both false positives and false negatives.
- We recommend starting with deterministic methods like single field matching, composite key matching, or deterministic cascade matching as foundational approaches. These methods are transparent, observable, and reliable, making them suitable as the core of your identity resolution strategy.
- Anonymous-to-known identity resolution is a valuable extension for acquisition marketing. Companies track anonymous website visitors over time and target them on paid media channels. Third-party cookie tracking has given way to first-party cookie tracking supported by third parties, and now, to full first-party tracking.
- Third-party enrichment enhances your first-party data with external data from providers like TransUnion or LiveRamp, which can provide valuable additional information about your customers. This can improve match rates, expand audience segments, and provide a more holistic view of your customer base.

7 First-party data activation: Igniting the marketing engine

This chapter covers

- Activating data for personalized marketing
- Turning insights into actions
- Targeting with first-party data
- Nurturing customers via email and messaging
- Empowering sales with CRM insights

In healthcare, first-party data isn't just a marketing asset—it's a matter of life and insight. The more we understand patients through their own data, the more precisely we can predict, prevent, and personalize care—while respecting their privacy every step of the way.

—Scott Penberthy, Distinguished Engineer,
Google – Applied AI & CTO, AI for Cancer

This chapter focuses on data activation—the critical step that turns the customer insights you've collected and segmented into high-impact marketing initiatives. For marketing leaders, activation isn't just the final technical step; it's the moment when data-driven strategies become tangible results. By transforming raw information into actionable campaigns, activation empowers teams to deliver personalized experiences, improve conversion rates, and outmaneuver the competition.

To illustrate these concepts, we'll highlight GrowthLoop, a platform designed to streamline the activation process. GrowthLoop's features make it simpler to connect your data sources (whether a lakehouse, warehouse, or other repository) to various marketing channels, allowing you to deploy personalized messaging quickly and at scale. While GrowthLoop serves as our key example, the principles we cover apply across multiple platforms, including paid media tools, email service providers, CRMs, and support systems. Whether you use GrowthLoop or another solution, the goal remains the same: to use first-party data, orchestrate multichannel campaigns, and ultimately drive measurable growth.

7.1 Understanding data activation: From insights to effect

Data activation transforms the vast potential of customer data into tangible results. It's about taking raw information, like browsing behavior, purchase history, preferences, and interactions, and turning it into actionable insights that drive personalized experiences across marketing channels. With data activation, marketers can move beyond simply understanding their customers to delivering the right message at the right time through the most effective channels.

For example, a marketer at an e-commerce brand could use data activation to tailor highly personalized experiences. Instead of generic outreach, they could send targeted campaigns relevant to each customer's interests based on real-time data. This precision increases engagement and builds stronger relationships between brands and customers.

However, the real effect of data activation comes when insights are integrated into actionable strategies. Modern platforms and tools empower marketing, sales, and customer support teams to work from the same dataset, transforming how they interact with customers at every touchpoint:

- *Marketing*—Data activation enables marketers to run highly focused campaigns that resonate with specific audience segments, improving conversions and building brand loyalty. These segments can be uploaded directly to advertising platforms, ensuring that messages reach the right people with precision and timing.
- *Sales*—For sales teams, personalization is critical. A sales rep equipped with real-time insights—such as a prospect's recent browsing activity—can have more relevant conversations, suggesting products or solutions that address immediate needs.
- *Customer support*—Data activation extends to support teams as well. Armed with predictive models and customer data, they can prioritize high-risk cases and respond faster, improving the customer experience while reducing churn.

Ultimately, data activation fosters real-time, data-driven decision-making across the entire organization. This collaborative approach allows every department to understand the customer journey more deeply, enabling proactive, informed interactions that strengthen relationships, enhance loyalty, and drive growth.

7.2 Precision targeting with paid media

First-party data transforms paid media from generic advertising into highly personalized, data-driven experiences that resonate with your audience. By using this data, marketers gain precision targeting, more compelling creative, and more effective bidding strategies. Paid media platforms give marketers an essential way to extend their reach beyond organic efforts, allowing for precise audience targeting. By tapping into first-party data, you can unlock the full potential of these platforms. For instance, Search Ads (like Google Ads) can use customer purchase history and website behavior to generate targeted keyword lists and ad copy tailored to specific customer segments. Social media ads, such as those on Facebook and Instagram, can use first-party data to create custom audiences based on demographics, interests, and site visitors, enabling hyper-targeted campaigns that are far more effective than generic advertising.

These paid media channels are indispensable for building brand awareness and expanding your customer base. A particularly powerful tactic is lookalike audience targeting. Suppose you've identified a segment of your most valuable customers. By uploading anonymized data to a social media advertising platform and activating lookalike targeting, you can use algorithms to find similar individuals likely to engage with your brand.

Beyond lookalike targeting, paid media offers several other high-impact strategies:

- *Retargeting*—This approach reconnects with site visitors who haven't yet converted. By serving personalized ads based on their browsing behavior—like abandoned carts or recently viewed products—you can re-engage them and encourage conversions.
- *Campaign optimization*—First-party data enables you to track website conversions, analyze user behavior post-click, and continually refine your campaigns for maximum ROI.
- *Dynamic product ads*—These ads automatically generate personalized content featuring products a user has previously shown interest in, increasing the chances of conversion.

At every stage of your paid media strategy, first-party data is the foundation for making smarter decisions:

- *Precision targeting*—First-party data allows you to use demographics, interests, and past behavior to reach the right audience, driving higher click-through rates (CTR) and conversions.
- *Compelling creative*—Insights from first-party data help craft ad copy and visuals that resonate with your target audience, capturing attention with relevant and personalized messages.

- *Data-driven bidding*—By identifying high-value audiences, you can allocate your ad spend more efficiently, bidding strategically for the most valuable clicks.

In our work with clients, we've often seen success in combining multiple channels for activation. For example, if your goal is to reduce churn and retain high-value customers who haven't engaged with recent marketing emails, paid media platforms like Google Ads and Meta Ads are ideal for use. Let's say you've identified these high-value customers based on their purchase history, but they've stopped responding to traditional email marketing efforts. The challenge lies in reaching them precisely through other channels, like social media.

By combining email with paid media, we addressed this audience's declining engagement in several ways:

- *Refreshed the creative*—Rather than recycling the same email offers, we developed targeted ads in Meta Ads featuring a personalized discount code or spotlighting a product they'd shown interest in previously.
- *Segmented and retargeted*—We built a custom audience from first-party data (those who hadn't opened an email in 60 days) to serve them specialized ads on social platforms.
- *Tested multiple offers*—We ran short A/B tests (e.g., 10% off versus free shipping) to see which incentive resonated most with lapsed customers.
- *Measured incremental lift*—Over four weeks, these combined efforts re-engaged nearly 25% of the previously dormant audience, leading to a measurable increase in repeat purchases.

This example demonstrates how a coordinated multichannel approach can recapture the attention of valuable customers who might otherwise slip away. By using first-party data for precise targeting and testing different incentives, you can refine your messaging until you find the sweet spot that drives conversions.

While paid media is a critical channel for activation, it's only one part of a broader ecosystem of platforms and tools. For instance, GrowthLoop is a data activation platform that helps unify first-party data and streamline audience segmentation and targeting across multiple channels. In section 7.6, we'll explore a detailed use case with GrowthLoop to show how these principles play out in real-world applications.

7.3 Nurturing relationships through personalized communication

Email and messaging platforms remain the backbone of personalized communication throughout the customer journey. By activating first-party data, you can deliver tailored messages at every stage, from acquisition to nurturing long-term loyalty.

Here's how data-driven communication transforms the customer journey:

- *Acquisition*—Greet new customers with personalized emails based on signup information or browsing behavior. Trigger automated sequences depending on the source of acquisition, whether from a social media ad or a referral, to offer relevant content and deals.

- *Activation*—Use purchase history and browsing data to recommend complementary products or provide tutorials, guiding new customers through product onboarding and driving early engagement.
- *Nurturing and retention*—Segment your email list using customer demographics, purchase history, and past interactions to send personalized content like product recommendations, loyalty updates, or winback campaigns for dormant customers.
- *Advocacy*—Identify high-value customers and encourage them to become brand advocates. Personalized email campaigns can prompt them to leave product reviews or engage with your brand on social media.
- *Showing ongoing value*—Continuously highlight the benefits of your product or service through personalized emails or in-app messages. Reminding customers how your product solves their problems or meets their needs, especially before a subscription renewal, reduces doubts or hesitation about continuing the relationship.

Beyond traditional email newsletters, messaging platforms broaden the scope for personalized communication:

- *SMS marketing*—Use first-party data for targeted SMS campaigns, sending appointment reminders, shipping updates, or flash sale alerts based on customer behavior.
- *Push notifications*—Trigger personalized notifications using in-app browsing or purchase history, such as abandoned cart reminders or exclusive app-only offers.

For example, let's say you run an e-commerce store selling outdoor gear and want to drive repeat purchases. First-party data allows you to send highly targeted email campaigns. If a customer recently purchased hiking boots, you could follow up with a personalized email featuring complementary products like hiking socks or backpacks, hiking trail guides, or gear maintenance tips. Similarly, if a customer has been browsing camping tents but hasn't made a purchase, you could send an email showcasing best-selling tents, customer reviews, and a limited-time discount code.

You can also alert these customers to an upcoming sale event or the arrival of new inventory that matches their interests. For instance, if you know a flash sale on camping gear is around the corner, an automated email highlighting relevant deals can rekindle interest and drive them back to your site. By combining purchase history, browsing data, and timely promotional announcements, your campaigns can deliver relevant, valuable content that resonates with your audience.

Incorporating first-party data into your email and messaging strategies creates a seamless, personalized experience. From the moment a customer joins your email list or engages with your app, you can tailor you communication to their needs and preferences. This approach not only enhances engagement but also fosters long-term loyalty. As you refine your strategies with ongoing data insights, you'll ensure that every interaction with your brand is timely, relevant, and valuable.

7.4 Empowering sales teams with data through CRM and sales outreach

Customer relationship management (CRM) systems and sales outreach tools become powerful engines for personalization when fueled by first-party data. When sales teams can access rich, real-time customer insights, they can transform generic interactions into meaningful conversations that resonate with individual prospects.

Here's how first-party data empowers sales teams:

- *Customer insights*—CRMs consolidate valuable information such as website behavior, purchase history, and past interactions, giving sales reps a unified view of each customer. This allows them to tailor outreach based on specific needs and preferences, leading to more relevant and engaging conversations.
- *Lead scoring and qualification*—First-party data powers predictive models that score leads based on factors like website activity, demographics, and engagement with marketing campaigns. This enables sales teams to prioritize high-potential prospects, focusing the team's efforts on leads with the greatest likelihood of conversion.
- *Targeted nurturing campaigns*—By segmenting leads based on behavior and engagement, sales teams can create personalized nurturing campaigns within the CRM. These campaigns trigger automated email sequences or custom outreach efforts, keeping leads engaged and moving them through the sales funnel.
- *Post-campaign analysis*—After launching targeted outreach campaigns, sales teams can analyze which messages, offers, or touchpoints led to the highest conversion rates. This feedback loop allows them to refine their lead-scoring models, outreach cadence, and messaging for improved results in subsequent campaigns.

When first-party data is fully integrated, CRM and sales outreach tools evolve from basic contact management systems to dynamic platforms that drive personalized sales interactions, improve lead qualification, and increase conversion rates.

A standout example of this approach can be seen in the collaboration between GrowthLoop and the Boston Red Sox. Using advanced data analytics with BigQuery and GrowthLoop, the Red Sox transformed their marketing efforts by building audience segments based on deeper insights. For instance, they identified single-game ticket buyers with a high propensity to upgrade to season tickets. An AI model scored these fans, and when a high-scoring fan purchased a ticket to a homestand game, Salesforce notified a sales rep immediately. The rep could then offer a VIP tour before the game, creating a personalized opportunity to upsell season ticket packages. This use of first-party data not only enhanced sales interactions but also delivered a highly personalized customer experience.

Integrating first-party data into CRM and sales strategies fundamentally changes how sales teams engage with prospects and customers. With rich customer insights at their fingertips, sales reps can have personalized conversations that directly address each individual's unique needs and pain points. This data-driven approach streamlines the sales process, enabling teams to prioritize their efforts and focus on the most promising leads. As sales teams continue to use and refine first-party data strategies, they can adapt to shifting customer behaviors and deliver consistently high-value interactions. By embracing these insights, organizations can build stronger customer relationships, boost sales performance, and drive sustainable business growth.

7.5 From reactive to proactive with customer engagement and support data

Customer engagement and support are vital in building lasting relationships and fostering brand loyalty. First-party data empowers support teams to move beyond reactive problem-solving, enabling them to create proactive, personalized experiences that build trust and strengthen customer connections.

Here's how first-party data transforms the customer support experience:

- *Customer history and context*—First-party data consolidates purchase history, past interactions, and support tickets, giving support reps full context with each customer inquiry. This eliminates the need for repetitive explanations and allows problems to be addressed more efficiently, leading to faster resolution times.
- *Predictive ticketing and routing*—By analyzing past support data, teams can predict customer needs and prioritize tickets based on factors like customer value or problem complexity. This ensures high-priority tickets are resolved quickly, improving the overall customer experience.
- *Self-service knowledge base*—First-party data helps identify common support inquiries and pain points, enabling companies to personalize their self-service resources with targeted FAQs, articles, and troubleshooting guides that address frequent customer problems.

But first-party data doesn't just improve problem resolution—it offers insights that can elevate your entire customer experience (see table 7.1):

- *Customer feedback analysis*—Data from surveys, reviews, and support interactions can be analyzed to identify recurring customer frustrations and areas for improvement. These insights allow businesses to prioritize product development and address core problems that matter most to their customers.
- *Sentiment analysis*—Using sentiment analysis tools, companies can monitor customer satisfaction across various channels such as email, social media, or support tickets. By identifying negative sentiment early, teams can proactively address concerns before they escalate, which protects brand reputation and improves ROI by reducing churn and costly escalations.

Table 7.1 Benefits of real-time insights in support

Benefit	Description	Result
Faster problem resolution	Immediate visibility into past problems and customer history	Quicker response times and higher satisfaction
Personalized service	Access to data on preferences, purchases, or usage patterns	Stronger customer trust and loyalty
Predictive ticket prioritization	Uses AI to rank tickets based on potential effect or urgency	Ensures high-value or critical problems are addressed first
Proactive engagement	Identifies potential problems or negative sentiment before it surfaces	Prevents escalations and reduces churn
Data-driven product feedback	Aggregates recurring problems to inform product development and improvements	Continuously enhances the customer experience

Here are some best practices for integrating customer feedback into product development:

- *Establish a feedback loop.* Ensure that your support platform automatically tags and routes recurring complaints or feature requests to the product team.
- *Prioritize based on effect.* Use lead or impact scoring to determine which feedback items offer the highest potential ROI if addressed.
- *Close the loop with customers.* When a requested feature is released or a known problem is resolved, proactively notify the customers who initially raised the concern. This reinforces a sense of partnership and transparency.

Integrating first-party data into customer engagement and support strategies enables businesses to provide personalized and proactive support, anticipating problems and tailoring responses to individual customer needs. Support teams gain valuable insights into each customer's preferences and pain points, allowing them to offer customized solutions that exceed expectations.

By using customer feedback and sentiment analysis, businesses can also make data-driven decisions that continuously improve their products and overall customer experience. As organizations deepen their use of first-party data, they can foster a culture of continuous improvement, adapt to evolving customer needs, and stay ahead of the competition. As a result, organizations are better positioned to anticipate customer needs, innovate based on real feedback, improve ROI, and maintain a competitive edge.

7.6 Use case with GrowthLoop

Before diving into this use case, it's essential to understand what GrowthLoop is and why we're using it as an example. GrowthLoop is a data activation platform designed to help marketing teams use their first-party data—website interactions, purchase history, and email engagement—without relying heavily on technical resources. It enables marketers to create and activate audience segments across multiple channels (email, paid media, and more) through a self-serve interface. This reduces the friction often associated with audience targeting and allows marketing leaders to respond more quickly to changing customer behaviors.

It's important to note that GrowthLoop is just one of many solutions available. Marketing leaders may already use platforms like Segment, mParticle, or custom-built data pipelines. Each solution has its own pricing model, integration requirements, and feature sets. Evaluating these options in terms of cost, compatibility with your existing data lakehouse, and the level of technical expertise required is crucial. GrowthLoop integrates with modern data warehouses and offers out-of-the-box connections to popular marketing channels, making it a compelling choice for teams looking to streamline their activation efforts.

7.6.1 Problem and effect

In our use case, an e-commerce company faces a clear challenge: a once-engaged customer segment no longer responds to email promotions, signaling a risk of churn and lost revenue. For marketing leaders, this scenario underscores why first-party data—and the right activation platform—matter: by tapping into purchase frequency, recent browsing history, and past email engagement, teams can deploy highly targeted, multichannel campaigns that recapture attention, optimize spend on proven segments, and sustain long-term loyalty.

7.6.2 Selecting engagement channels

To address the problem, the team chooses two primary channels for the campaign. The first is email, aimed at re-engaging high-intent customers with personalized offers and recommendations. The second is paid media on Facebook, targeting individuals who didn't respond to the email outreach. The company can deliver cohesive messaging and measure engagement at multiple touchpoints by activating first-party data across these two channels.

Before we break down the pipeline, illustrated in figure 7.1, let's highlight the key data sources feeding into it:

- *GA4 (Google Analytics 4)*—Captures website and app interactions—pageviews, event completions, and session data—providing visibility into customer behavior on owned properties.
- *Klaviyo*—An email and SMS marketing platform that records who opened and clicked on your emails, how they interacted with your campaigns, and whether they converted from those efforts.
- *Adobe Analytics (if used)*—Tracks on-site activities, content consumption, and user flows, helping identify which pages or products resonate most with customers.
- *Google Ads*—Collects data on which ads users see, click, and convert from, informing how well different paid campaigns perform and which audiences respond best.

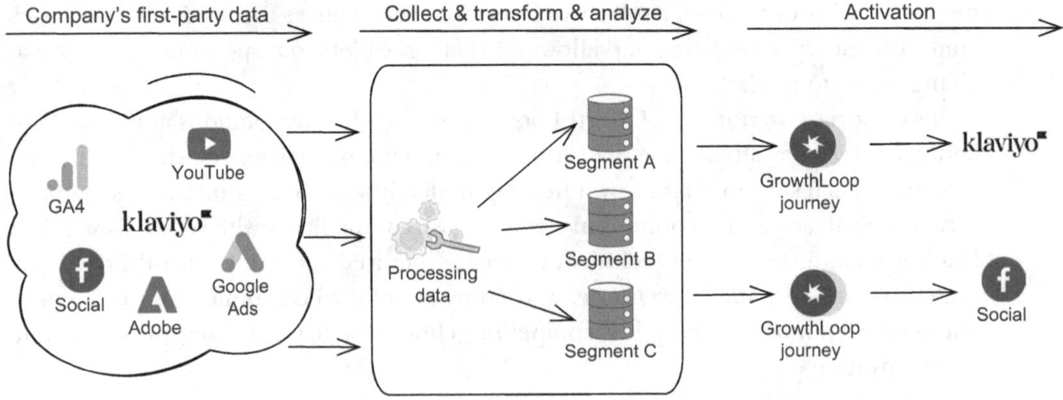

Figure 7.1 Marketing data pipeline

This first-party data ecosystem feeds into your company's data lakehouse, which can be unified and analyzed for insights.

7.6.3 *Breaking down the pipeline*

The marketing technologist integrates these first-party data sources into the data lakehouse, as discussed in chapter 5. The marketing analyst refines raw data into actionable insights by using a medallion architecture (with bronze, silver, and gold layers). For example, the analyst doesn't just pull attributes; they create actual audience segments, like "high-value customers who haven't engaged with emails in 30 days," to guide marketing strategies.

Setting up these workflows and preparing data for activation traditionally required technical support. However, with a platform like GrowthLoop, marketers can do much of this work themselves. Once the segments are defined, the marketing technologist or marketer can sync these segments with various marketing platforms, such as Klaviyo for email and Facebook Ads for paid media.

Initially, the Facebook audience is empty. After the email campaigns run, marketers can analyze who opened or clicked the emails and who remained inactive. Armed with this insight, they can retarget the non-engagers on Facebook with tailored ads—perhaps offering a unique discount code or highlighting a product that aligns with their browsing history.

7.6.4 *Empowering marketers with GrowthLoop*

GrowthLoop's self-serve segmentation capabilities reduce marketers' reliance on technical teams. Marketers can directly manage which segments to activate, which channels to target, and how often to update the data. This agility means marketing leaders can pivot quickly, test new approaches, and continuously optimize campaigns based on performance data. GrowthLoop supports various destination integrations and can provide custom solutions, ensuring marketers can adapt to evolving toolsets (www.growthloop.com/destinations).

By activating email and paid media channels in tandem, the company can strengthen its messaging across multiple touchpoints, increasing engagement and conversions. First-party data is the foundation here, making personalized, relevant experiences possible.

By unifying first-party data in a platform like GrowthLoop and applying it across channels, marketers can move beyond guesswork and generic messaging, crafting data-driven campaigns that truly resonate. This approach reduces operational friction, empowers teams to act quickly, and helps marketing leaders allocate spend where it's most effective. At the same time, marketers on the ground gain more control and flexibility, enabling rapid testing and iteration. Although we've highlighted GrowthLoop as an example, the principles apply to various tools and technologies. If you're interested in the technical "how-to" steps, detailed instructions can be found in the appendices, ensuring that every team member—from strategic decision-makers to hands-on practitioners—has the guidance they need to execute on these insights.

Marketers can create truly personalized, effective campaigns by mastering first-party data activation and using platforms like GrowthLoop. However, effective data usage doesn't stop at activation. The next critical step is measuring the results of your efforts, ensuring that every dollar spent and every campaign launched delivers tangible ROI.

7.7 Proving the effect of data activation

At its core, data activation promises to transform marketing from guesswork to data-driven precision. But how do you know if your activation efforts are truly paying off? How do you demonstrate the value of your investment in first-party data and the platforms that activate it? The answer lies in robust measurement and analytics.

In this section, we'll outline a practical framework for evaluating the effect of your data activation strategies. By adopting a multifaceted approach to measurement—spanning conversions, customer lifetime value, and engagement metrics—you can move beyond hoping for better results to proving and improving the tangible returns on your personalized marketing initiatives.

Whether you're re-engaging dormant customers in a multichannel campaign or upselling loyal fans to a premium package, establishing the right KPIs and analytics process allows you to iterate on what works and to scale those strategies across channels. As Greg Kihlström (principal at The Agile Brand, bestselling author, and advisor to F1000 brands) has said, "The first step in creating great experiences is the intent to do so, but unless you're able to measure it, you won't know how or where it needs improvement."

7.7.1 The three essential categories of marketing measurement for data activation

To understand how effectively your data activation efforts are performing, it helps to break down your measurement strategy into three essential categories. Each category provides a distinct perspective and addresses different—but equally important—questions:

- *Campaign counts and rates (tracking basic performance)*—This category focuses on the fundamental metrics that indicate how well your data-activated campaigns are doing at a surface level. Are you seeing improvements in conversion rates, engagement, or cost per acquisition (CPA)? By monitoring these key performance indicators (KPIs), you gain a quick snapshot of whether your tactics—such as personalized email offers or retargeted social ads—yield positive results. Tracking these counts and rates is often the first step in identifying where to optimize and invest further.
- *Experiments (proving causal effect)*—While performance metrics show correlation, experiments allow you to establish causation. Through techniques like A/B testing or holdout groups, you can rigorously prove that your data activation strategies drive incremental improvements in customer behavior and business outcomes. For example, test a personalized email campaign (group A) against a more generic version (group B) to see if personalization directly boosts click-through rates or conversions. This experimentation process ensures that your optimization efforts are guided by clear, data-backed evidence.
- *Multichannel models (guiding investment decisions)*—In the multifaceted marketing world, it's crucial to understand how different channels and tactics work together. Multi-touch attribution (MTA) and media mix modeling (MMM) are powerful tools for uncovering the relative effect of each channel on overall marketing effectiveness. MTA tracks user-level interactions to see which touchpoints contributed to a conversion. At the same time, MMM offers a more holistic perspective, identifying how various channels (paid media, email, social, etc.) collectively influence revenue. These models provide a high-level roadmap for where and how to allocate budgets most effectively.

You obtain a complete view of your data activation's effect by deploying all three essential categories—tracking campaign performance, running experiments, and modeling multichannel interactions. From granular campaign metrics to broader investment decisions, this framework helps you consistently prove and improve the ROI of your first-party data strategies.

7.7.2 Essential category 1: Campaign counts and rates (tracking basic performance)

Having introduced the three essential categories of marketing measurement, let's begin with the most immediate indicators of success: campaign counts and rates. These metrics are the foundational building blocks of marketing measurement, giving you a quick snapshot of how your data-activated strategies perform in practice.

Here are the primary metrics to watch:

- *Conversion counts and rates*—Track conversions (purchases, sign-ups, form submissions) directly attributed to data-activated campaigns. Conversion rates (conversion count ÷ total audience reached) give a normalized view of efficiency, allowing you to see whether personalized outreach drives better results than one-size-fits-all efforts.

- *Engagement metrics*—Monitor engagement metrics relevant to your channels, such as email open rates, click-through rates (CTR), page views, or social media interactions (likes, shares, comments). Segment these by activated audiences to gauge how well your messaging resonates with each group.
- *Cost per acquisition (CPA)*—Calculate the cost to acquire a new customer or lead through your data-activated efforts. CPA is crucial for understanding ROI and determining which audience segments deliver the highest return on spend.
- *Sales and revenue metrics*—Track revenue directly attributed to data-activated campaigns. For many marketers, total sales is the ultimate measure of effect. An uptick in revenue among your targeted segments often signals effective personalization.

Why these metrics matter:

- *Easy to implement and understand*—These metrics are typically available in most marketing platforms, making them immediately accessible for team-wide discussions. Their straightforward nature also means that non-technical stakeholders can quickly grasp how campaigns perform.
- *Baseline performance*—These metrics provide initial benchmarks to compare data-activated campaigns against broad-reaching or generic approaches. This comparison reveals whether personalization yields a noticeable uplift or if existing methods still hold merit.
- *Trend analysis*—As you observe changes in these metrics over time, you can identify whether personalization and segmentation consistently lift results or if further optimization is needed. Tracking these trends provides early indicators for campaign adjustments and future testing strategies.

For example, imagine you've launched a personalized email campaign targeting customers based on past purchase history. You could track how these segmented emails compare to generic email blasts regarding open rates, CTR, and conversions. You might also monitor CPA for lookalike audiences on Facebook to see if they outperform broad demographic-based targeting. These metrics offer a baseline understanding of your data-activated initiatives' short-term effectiveness. While these foundational numbers give you quick insight, they suffer from two main drawbacks:

- *Correlation, not causation*—Counts and rates show only that performance improved; they don't necessarily prove why. External factors, such as seasonality, competitor promotions, or industry trends, can also influence results.
- *Limited in multichannel contexts*—Focusing solely on these immediate metrics can oversimplify how various channels interact in complex multi-touch journeys. A user might see your brand on social media before finally converting in response to an email. This category alone won't tell you the full story.

Regularly monitoring these basic metrics gives you vital insights into how well your data activation strategies are resonating. While these counts and rates can't fully reveal why a campaign succeeds or fails, they form a solid foundation for more advanced analysis, leading naturally into the experimentation and multichannel modeling we'll explore next.

7.7.3 Essential category 2: Experiments (proving causal effect)

We've examined the basic performance metrics in essential category 1, so now let's turn to experiments—your go-to method for establishing causation rather than mere correlation. While campaign counts and rates offer valuable insights, they don't always confirm that your data activation strategies are directly responsible for improved outcomes. Experiments bridge this gap by comparing outcomes from a treatment group—customers who receive your data-activated campaign—to a control group that does not. A control group serves as your baseline, letting you distinguish improvements driven by activation from external factors like seasonal trends or competitor promotions.

Use this structure for your test groups:

- *Treatment group*—A set of customers or leads who receive the data-activated campaign (e.g., a personalized email series or tailored SMS messages)
- *Control group*—A comparable set of customers or leads who do not receive the data-activated version (or receive a generic alternative)

By measuring differences in performance (e.g., conversions, revenue) between these two groups, you can prove that personalization or segmentation tactics truly drive the uplift.

Once you've defined those groups, you can choose from three common experiment types:

- *A/B tests on personalized messaging*—Compare a personalized email subject line referencing a recipient's recent browsing history to a generic subject line. Track open rates, click-through rates (CTR), and conversions to see if personalization drives measurable gains.
- *Audience segmentation experiments*—Compare paid media performance when targeting lookalike segments (activated with first-party data) versus broader, non-segmented audiences. This reveals whether the added effort of precise segmentation provides a real uplift in ROI or cost per acquisition (CPA).
- *Channel-specific experiments*—Add an SMS sequence to your existing email sequence (a series of automated, targeted messages) for the treatment group. If you find higher conversions or revenue than the control group (which only receives email), you've identified the incremental effect of SMS.

When it comes to measuring those experiments, focus on three key metrics:

- *Incremental conversion rate* measures the difference in conversion rate between treatment and control, showing how much lift comes directly from your campaign.
- *Incremental revenue lift* measures the additional revenue generated by the treatment group compared to the control, providing clear financial evidence of success.
- *Customer lifetime value (CLTV) uplift* measures the extra value (average purchase value × purchase frequency × customer lifespan) that the treatment group delivers over time, revealing whether your activation drives lasting ROI.

As an example, you might test a personalized landing page that greets users by name and suggests relevant products, while the control group sees a generic page. Tracking how much extra revenue (incremental revenue lift) or higher CLTV emerges in the personalized group proves whether personalization drives the improvement or is simply a coincidence.

Experiments deliver three key advantages:

- *Proving causality*—They remove guesswork by isolating your treatment from external factors, so you know that your tactics (not seasonality or competitor activity) drive results.
- *Quantifying incremental effect*—You measure the exact lift in conversions, revenue, or CLTV that your personalization and segmentation efforts produce.
- *Optimizing tactics*—Targeted A/B tests let you pinpoint which campaign elements—creative, timing, channel mix—move the needle most.

Beyond one-off tests, you can track treatment and control groups over weeks or months to measure sustained effect. This longitudinal approach differs from short-term A/B tests in three ways:

- *Sustained effect versus one-off gains*—While a short-term A/B test might show an immediate revenue bump, a longitudinal approach helps you see if that advantage persists or fades over time.
- *Capturing true CLTV*—If your product or service relies on repeat purchases or subscription renewals, measuring incremental lift in CLTV requires observing customer behavior across multiple purchase cycles. A longer observation window ensures you capture these repurchases, upgrades, or churn events.
- *Refining retention and engagement strategies*—By comparing retention rates, churn, or reactivation behaviors in the treatment group versus the control group, you can identify if your data activation efforts create deeper customer loyalty, not just a short-lived boost.

For instance, a streaming service could serve personalized content recommendations to one group and generic "top-rated" suggestions to another and then follow both groups across three billing cycles. If the personalized group shows fewer cancellations and higher lifetime revenue, you've proven sustained ROI.

Experiments, especially when extended longitudinally, provide the clearest possible evidence that your data activation efforts drive meaningful, sustained results. Once you know which tactics produce consistent gains, you'll be ready to tackle the broader question of how different channels interact—a subject we'll explore in the next essential category.

7.7.4 Essential category 3: Multichannel models (guiding investment decisions)

As marketing grows increasingly complex, customers engage with brands across multiple touchpoints—email, social media, SMS, display ads, and beyond—before purchasing or signing up. Multichannel models offer a holistic perspective on how these channels contribute to conversions and revenue. While they don't provide the granular proof of causation that experiments do, multichannel models do deliver valuable directional guidance on where to focus your budget and resources.

To assess how each channel contributes and to guide your investment decisions, consider the following approaches:

- *Multi-touch attribution (MTA)*—Multi-touch attribution assigns credit for a conversion across multiple touchpoints in the customer journey. These are some common approaches:
  - *Linear*—Distributes credit equally among all touchpoints
  - *Time-decay*—Gives more credit to recent interactions
  - *Position-based*—Emphasizes the first and last touchpoints while distributing partial credit to the middle interactions

  By evaluating how each channel (e.g., email, paid media, SMS) contributes to conversions, MTA reveals the relative performance of your data-activated campaigns across touchpoints.
- *Media mix modeling (MMM)*—Media mix modeling is a statistical technique that analyzes historical marketing spend and sales data, often covering online and offline channels. For data activation, MMM helps you see the macro-level ROI of different channels in your overall strategy. By assessing how spending changes across channels (e.g., email versus paid social) correlate with sales outcomes, you gain a high-level roadmap for budget allocation.

By aggregating metrics across email, social media, paid search, and other touchpoints, you gain a comprehensive view of how each channel contributes to your goals, and you can allocate budget where it drives the greatest effect. For instance, you might discover that customers who click a personalized email and then see a targeted social ad convert at twice the rate of those who only received one touchpoint—this insight shows you precisely where to invest next.

Despite their strategic value, multichannel models have three key limitations:

- *Correlation, not causation (at scale)*—While they're advanced, these models often rely on correlational analysis, making it difficult to prove causation at a granular level.

- *Channel interdependencies*—Highly integrated campaigns may have overlapping channels (e.g., a consumer clicking an email link and then seeing a social retargeting ad) that affect one another's performance. Multichannel models can underrepresent these interdependencies.
- *Directional guidance*—MTA and MMM are best at offering broad, directional insights for budget allocation and channel strategy. They won't provide the same individual-level detail or incremental "lift" clarity that an A/B test or control group experiment delivers.

You can build a robust measurement ecosystem by combining multichannel models (for strategic, portfolio-level guidance) with experiments (for precise causal insights). That way, you'll understand both how channels work together at scale and which tactics drive incremental lift—guidance that powers everything from daily optimizations to major budget decisions.

7.7.5 Data collection for effective data activation measurement

Comprehensive measurement across all three essential categories—basic performance metrics, experiments, and multichannel models—depends on having robust, reliable data. Without the right data collection processes, even the best-designed campaigns and analyses can fail to deliver meaningful insights. Let's look at some key recommendations for establishing a data foundation that supports effective data activation measurement:

1. Collect campaign-level metrics segmented by activated audiences.

   Why it matters—This segmentation lets you directly compare how different audience groups respond to your data-activated campaigns.

   Practical tip—Make sure your marketing platforms record metrics such as conversions, budget spent, and campaign dates by specific audience segments. This lets you see, for example, whether your lookalike audience outperforms a broad demographic audience.
2. Track customer-level touchpoints across all activation channels.

   Why it matters—Multi-touch attribution (MTA) and advanced customer journey analyses rely on granular event data—every email click, paid media impression, SMS interaction, and website visit.

   Practical tip—Implement consistent UTM tagging or internal tracking IDs to unify these touchpoints at the customer level. This ensures you can follow an individual's journey from first interaction to eventual conversion.
3. Integrate transaction data with audience and campaign data.

   Why it matters—Tying revenue and order details back to specific audiences and campaigns lets you calculate actual ROI rather than stopping at vanity metrics such as clicks or opens.

   Practical tip—Create a link between your transaction database and marketing campaign data, such as a unique customer ID or hashed email address. This linkage allows you to measure how much sales revenue each activation campaign generates and helps determine customer lifetime value (CLTV) in controlled experiments.

4 Use a data lakehouse (or unified data infrastructure, as covered in chapter 5).

   Why it matters—A centralized environment for storing and analyzing data ensures each essential measurement category has access to the same reliable, comprehensive source of truth.

   Practical tip—Ingest raw data from platforms like email service providers, ad networks, and CRM systems into a single data lakehouse or similarly unified infrastructure. You can perform data cleaning, transformation, and modeling to support MTA, MMM, and experiments in one place.

By following these data collection practices, you'll create a solid foundation that supports accurate, actionable insights across every stage of data activation measurement. Whether you're comparing conversion rates across audience segments (essential category 1), validating lift via experiments (essential category 2), or looking at cross-channel synergies (essential category 3), a unified data strategy is the key to making each analysis both reliable and meaningful.

7.7.6 Turning measurement into actionable targeting: The measurement–activation feedback loop

Measuring the performance of your data activation efforts isn't just about generating reports—it's about applying what you learn to create more effective campaigns. By establishing a continuous feedback loop, you can use insights gained from your essential measurement categories to refine your targeting, content, and channel strategy, ultimately improving ROI over time:

1. *Analyze measurement data regularly.* Periodically review your campaign counts and rates (essential category 1), experimental results (category 2), and multichannel model outputs (category 3). Look for patterns in conversions, customer engagement, and overall channel performance.
2. *Identify insights and optimization opportunities.* Determine which channels are exceeding or underperforming expectations, which audience segments respond best, and which messaging tactics resonate. The objective is to uncover actionable insights, not just generate static reports.
3. *Refine audience segments and personalization.* Feed these insights back into your segmentation strategy. Are certain customer segments showing stronger lift? Is a specific product category driving more engagement than others? Use this data to adjust your personalization tactics and channel selection for future campaigns.
4. *Iterate and experiment continuously.* Treat measurement as an ongoing process. Don't be afraid to launch new experiments, whether you're testing fresh creative, pivoting to a different channel, or fine-tuning your lookalike audiences. Each

measurement cycle informs the next campaign, creating a closed-loop system of continuous improvement.

To illustrate, consider this closed-loop analytics example from a specialty retailer: the retailer created audience segments based on purchase history and browsing behavior and then activated those segments via targeted email and paid-social campaigns. Rather than relying on surface metrics alone, they ran an incrementality test using control groups and uncovered two key insights:

- *Key finding*—Customers receiving personalized product recommendations saw a 32% higher revenue than the control group.
- *Deeper insight*—Certain product categories performed significantly better with personalization than others.

Armed with these results, the retailer refined its segmentation strategy to prioritize high-performing product categories and tailor messaging even more precisely. Because they consistently fed each new insight back into campaign planning, their results kept improving over time, making this a prime example of how a measurement–activation feedback loop drives sustained growth.

Integrating these learnings into your day-to-day marketing workflow transforms metrics into meaningful action. The combination of continual analysis, experimental validation, and strategic adjustments empowers your data activation strategies to evolve along with your customers, driving stronger engagement, higher conversion rates, and long-term growth.

7.7.7 Visualization and reporting

Collecting great data is only half the battle. How you present and share those insights can make or break your ability to drive meaningful change. Clear visualization and reporting ensure stakeholders across the organization understand the effect of your first-party data activation efforts and can make informed decisions.

To communicate the effect of your data-activation efforts, use four key visualization and reporting tactics:

- *Real-time dashboards*—Establish live dashboards that track critical metrics (conversions, revenue, engagement) for each data-activated campaign. This helps teams monitor performance and quickly spot any trends or anomalies.
- *Regular performance reports*—Summarize the effect of first-party data activation in periodic (e.g., weekly or monthly) reports, highlighting which segments and channels outperform expectations.
- *Experiment summaries*—Clearly communicate results from control-group experiments or A/B tests, especially incremental lift and statistical significance, so everyone understands what's driving improvements.
- *ROI analyses*—Demonstrate the overall business value of your data activation initiatives by showing how shifts in channel spend or personalization tactics translate into concrete revenue gains or cost savings.

Throughout this section, we've emphasized a multifaceted approach to measuring the effect of data activation:

- Campaign counts and rates (essential category 1)
- Rigorous experiments (essential category 2)
- Multichannel models (essential category 3)

By combining these essential categories, you can gain a well-rounded, actionable understanding of how data-driven personalization efforts truly perform.

This robust measurement framework does more than just prove the value of data activation; it fuels continuous improvement. As you refine your segmentation, messaging, and channel mix, you can optimize marketing spending and build long-term, profitable customer relationships. Ultimately, a data-driven, measurement-focused mindset is key to unlocking the full potential of first-party data activation, helping you thrive in today's complex marketing landscape.

In the next chapter, we'll explore data clean rooms, a secure environment that allows you to combine your first-party data with external data sources without compromising privacy. This next step will help you further refine your data strategy and uncover new growth opportunities.

Summary

- Data activation takes raw information, like browsing behavior, purchase history, preferences, and interactions, and turns it into actionable insights that drive personalized experiences across marketing channels.
- Modern platforms and tools empower marketing, sales, and customer support teams to work from the same dataset, transforming how they interact with customers at every touchpoint.
- GrowthLoop is a data activation platform designed to help marketing teams use their first-party data—website interactions, purchase history, and email engagement—without relying heavily on technical resources.
- First-party data drives personalized marketing strategies.
- Precision targeting and personalized communication increase engagement.
- Sales and support teams benefit from data-driven insights.
- Platforms like GrowthLoop enable seamless multichannel activation for improved conversions.
- A comprehensive measurement framework—combining campaign counts and rates, experiments, and multichannel models—provides a well-rounded view of your data activation performance and ROI.

Part 3

New and upcoming technology opportunities

The marketing technology landscape is evolving rapidly, with new tools emerging to address privacy-first data collaboration and AI-powered automation. Businesses embracing these innovations can refine targeting, improve measurement, and increase efficiency while ensuring compliance with privacy regulations.

Chapter 8 explores data clean rooms and secure environments that allow businesses to collaborate on insights without exposing sensitive customer data. With third-party cookies being phased out by major browsers and privacy regulations, clean rooms enable privacy-safe audience targeting, campaign measurement, and fraud suppression. The chapter also discusses how industries beyond marketing, such as financial services, use clean rooms to prevent fraud and ensure regulatory compliance. Chapter 9 shifts the focus to generative AI in marketing, examining how AI-powered tools revolutionize content creation, audience segmentation, and campaign execution. While these advancements offer unprecedented efficiency and personalization, they also present new governance challenges that marketers must navigate.

By the end of this section, you'll understand how emerging technologies like clean rooms and generative AI are shaping the future of first-party data marketing and how you can integrate them into your strategy to stay ahead.

8 Data clean rooms

This chapter covers

- Privacy-first data sharing with data clean rooms
- Navigating privacy regulations in a cookieless future
- Clean room benefits: security, compliance, and multiparty insights
- Types of clean rooms: walled gardens and neutral hubs
- Secure collaboration, flexible application integration, and adherence to industry standards

We're just scratching the surface of what's possible with data collaboration in Snowflake. As more organizations embrace the cloud and data sharing, we'll see an explosion of new ideas and applications that we can't even imagine today.

—Sridhar Ramaswamy, CEO of Snowflake

As privacy regulations tighten and third-party cookies lose their prominence, businesses must adapt to new methods of collecting, analyzing, and activating data. Data clean rooms—secure, privacy-first environments—offer a viable approach, enabling meaningful collaboration without compromising sensitive information. This chapter introduces the foundational concepts behind data clean rooms, examines their role in fostering effective partnerships, and highlights the privacy-enhancing techniques that preserve confidentiality. It also considers core use cases, from audience targeting and refined measurement to advanced machine learning.

We'll open with the concept of a clean room and the market forces driving its adoption. We'll then compare the two primary models—walled gardens and neutral third-party providers—explaining how each balances security, flexibility, and interoperability. We'll also examine key applications, illustrating how clean rooms facilitate effective targeting, comprehensive measurement, and secure model training. Finally, we'll address the evolving ecosystem, ongoing standardization efforts, and potential for data clean rooms to expand into other sectors. By the end, it should be clear why data clean rooms matter, how they align with a privacy-first landscape, and how they can be used for valuable insights while maintaining trust and compliance.

8.1 Introduction to clean rooms

As regulations grow stricter and third-party cookies lose their relevance, businesses are encountering new challenges in sharing data while safeguarding consumer information. Data clean rooms have emerged as a privacy-first solution, enabling organizations to collaborate and derive valuable insights without exposing sensitive details.

Consider an online retailer seeking to deliver relevant advertisements. Access to partner data is needed, yet privacy rules prohibit openly sharing raw information across platforms. A clean room addresses this problem by providing a secure, controlled environment in which to combine first-party data with that of trusted partners. Within this environment, insights such as audience overlaps or campaign performance become accessible while the underlying consumer data remains protected.

This approach is reshaping the advertising landscape. As third-party cookies vanish, marketers must rely on privacy-compliant methods that preserve personalization. Clean rooms support these efforts by aligning with regulations like GDPR and CCPA, enabling collaboration among partners for more effective targeting and accurate campaign analysis.

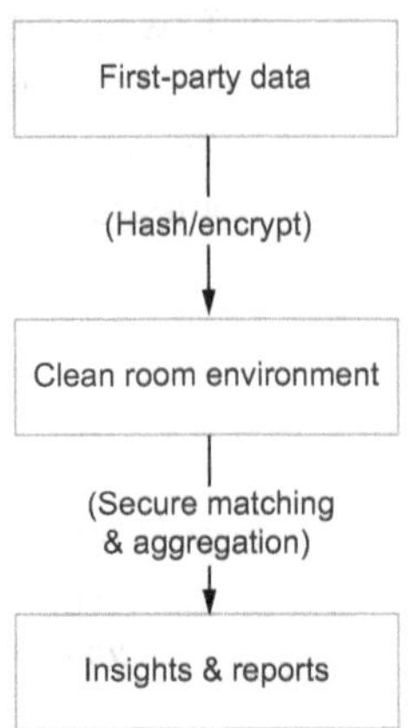

Figure 8.1 Data ingestion, secure matching, and reporting in the clean room environment

Figure 8.1 shows a high-level flow of how data typically moves in a clean room environment:

1 *Hash/encrypt and ingest data*—Each partner applies hashing or encryption to personal identifiers (for example, email addresses) and uploads the resulting dataset to the clean room environment.

2 *Secure matching and aggregation*—Within the clean room, hashed identifiers are matched, and records are aggregated, enabling analysis without ever exposing raw data.
3 *Insights and reports*—Aggregated outputs (such as audience segments or performance metrics) are delivered to partners in anonymized form.

NOTE In some jurisdictions, organizations must conduct a data protection impact assessment (DPIA) before sharing personal data in a clean room. DPIAs help identify and mitigate privacy risks, ensuring that data sharing upholds regulatory and security standards. While DPIAs can be an involved process, they underscore a privacy-by-design mindset that keeps user trust at the forefront.

Two types of clean room solutions have emerged: those offered by walled gardens (such as Google, Meta, Amazon, TikTok, and so on) and those provided by neutral third-party vendors. Walled gardens constrain data collaboration to their own ecosystems, while third-party solutions encourage cross-platform cooperation. Distinguishing between these approaches allows businesses to find a balance that meets both security and flexibility requirements.

Data clean rooms address three primary needs:

- *Targeting*—Securely identifying shared customer segments, leading to more precise ad targeting
- *Measurement*—Gaining comprehensive campaign performance metrics (e.g., impressions, conversions) in a privacy-preserving manner
- *Model training (machine learning)*—Training models on combined datasets without disclosing personal data, enabling robust predictive insights

These core use cases illustrate the versatility of clean rooms, even in an era of reduced data-sharing freedom. Although data clean room solutions are still in their early stages, major platforms offer ecosystem-specific solutions, and independent third-party providers are rolling out more broadly compatible offerings. As the ecosystem evolves, organizations must weigh the focused capabilities of walled gardens against the flexibility of third-party options.

8.1.1 Data clean rooms of walled gardens

In the digital advertising ecosystem, data clean room technologies have taken root within closed environments known as "walled gardens." As shown in figure 8.2, these walled gardens, such as Google Ads Data Hub, Amazon Marketing Cloud, or Meta's data solutions, restrict data sharing to their ecosystems, enabling secure collaboration between advertisers, publishers, and the platform itself.

As discussed in chapter 7, activating data across various advertising platforms is a central strategy for marketers. However, the concept of a "walled garden" is more specific, referring to the restricted and closed ecosystem controlled by a single platform,

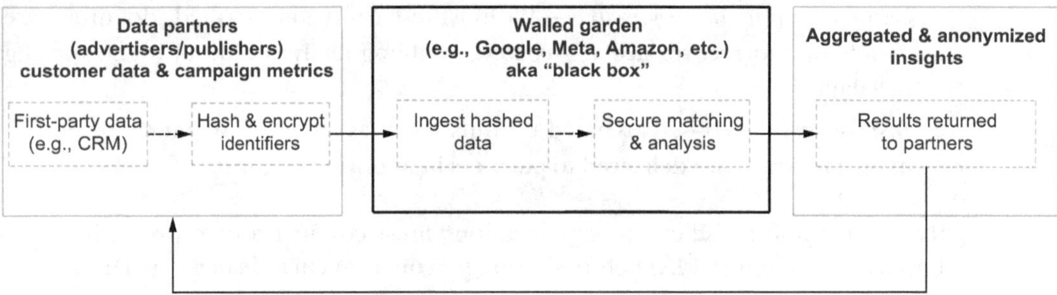

Figure 8.2 Walled garden clean room—hashed data from advertisers and publishers is ingested into a single-platform environment for secure matching and analysis, yielding aggregated, anonymized insights

limiting access to external parties while enabling secure data sharing between advertisers and the platform.

In a typical walled garden clean room setup, raw data is exchanged directly between the clean room provider (such as Google or Amazon) and each participating business partner (referred to as a "data partner"). This raw data, often containing CRM information like email addresses, phone numbers, or customer IDs, is typically shared in a standardized format such as CSV or JSON. A key distinction in walled gardens is that the data exchange occurs exclusively between the platform and the individual data partner. There is no cross-sharing of data between different partners, preserving data boundaries and minimizing exposure risks.

Privacy and security in these environments are maintained through the use of common identification keys or variables, often hashed to protect the underlying data. Hashing is a process where raw data is transformed into unreadable, fixed-length strings, ensuring that sensitive information is kept secure. This process ensures the data remains protected even during exchanges.

Let's consider Google Ads Data Hub as an example. It functions through an API connection that links two BigQuery projects: one owned by the data partner, containing their marketing data, and the other containing Google's vast log data. Google offers two methods for securely handling the raw data:

- The data partner can hash their raw data using a secure hash algorithm (SHA-256) and upload these hashed values directly to their Google Ads account.
- Alternatively, Google can handle the hashing process on its own servers, applying the SHA-256 algorithm to ensure no raw data is exposed within the data partner's environment.

After the data matching process, the clean room generates target group insights that can be fed back into the platform's advertising systems for further use. Table 8.1 summarizes the key advantages and drawbacks of walled garden clean rooms.

Table 8.1 Benefits and limitations of walled garden clean rooms

Aspect	Benefits	Limitations
Data and tools	Access to rich, platform-specific datasets and native analytics	Data stays locked within the platform; limited use outside the ecosystem
Integration	Seamless activation of insights (e.g., running ads directly)	Potential overreliance on one provider's infrastructure and tooling
Security	Platform-managed security and compliance controls	Must trust the platform's handling of hashed but still raw-ish data
Control and ownership	Efficient workflow if you are already a major advertiser on that platform	Data partners may have less visibility into how matching is done
Interoperability	Straightforward if campaigns live primarily on one platform	Challenging to combine data or insights across multiple platforms
Scalability	Often large scale due to the platform's global reach	Additional scale means deeper lock-in and less cross-platform freedom

Interoperability challenges merit particular attention. Because these clean rooms are tightly bound to a single provider's environment, combining or analyzing data across multiple platforms can be difficult or, in some cases, impossible. Advertisers that run campaigns on several ad networks or want a holistic customer profile frequently find the lack of cross-platform synergy a major downside. If data is fragmented across separate walled garden ecosystems, this constraint can inhibit broader data strategies, reduce visibility into overall customer journeys, and complicate compliance.

Walled garden clean rooms offer significant value by offering secure data collaboration and detailed analytics, especially if a business is heavily invested in a single platform's advertising or marketing ecosystem. However, organizations seeking more flexible data sharing (including cross-platform insights) must carefully weigh the tradeoffs, particularly around interoperability, data control, and the potential dependency on a single provider.

While walled garden clean rooms offer significant benefits—such as access to rich datasets and tight integration with the platform's advertising tools—there are critical factors to consider. The raw data, though pseudonymized through hashing, is still shared directly with the clean room provider, meaning companies must trust the platform's security infrastructure. This reliance on a single provider introduces potential concerns around data protection liability and transparency. Moreover, the closed nature of these ecosystems increases dependency on the platform, as data cannot be easily shared or used outside the walled garden for independent analysis.

8.1.2 Data clean rooms of AdTech providers as intermediaries

In contrast to walled gardens, which confine data sharing within a single platform's ecosystem (e.g., Google Ads or Amazon Ads), neutral data clean rooms are offered by independent advertising technology (AdTech) providers and cloud platforms. These neutral environments allow businesses to collaborate securely without being restricted to one vendor's infrastructure. Acting as an impartial intermediary, the clean room provider ensures that partners can analyze their combined datasets without revealing raw data, enabling flexible and cross-platform data collaboration (see figure 8.3). Acting as an impartial intermediary, the clean room provider ensures that partners can analyze their combined datasets without revealing raw data.

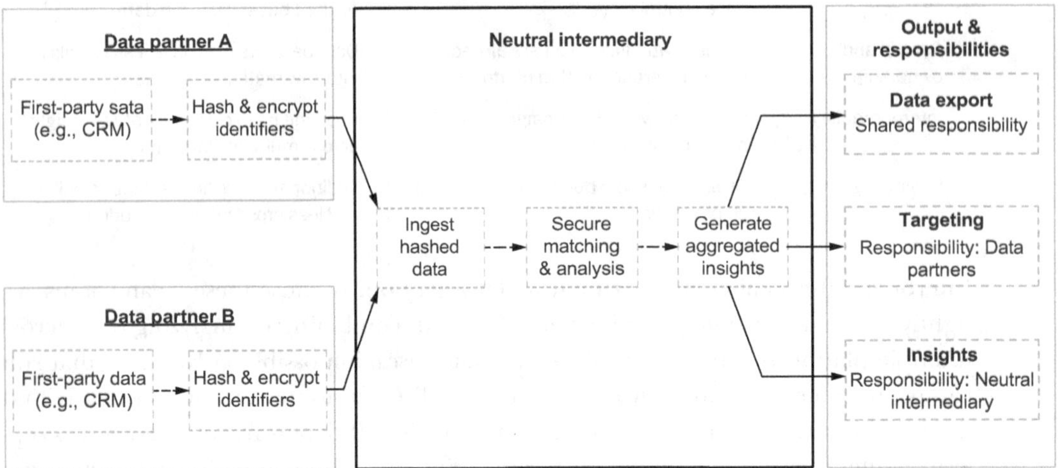

Figure 8.3 Neutral intermediary clean room—hashed data from multiple advertisers and publishers is routed through an independent AdTech environment for secure cross-platform matching, analysis, and delivery of aggregated insights

From a marketer's perspective, neutral clean rooms offer a crucial advantage: the freedom to integrate multiple data sources and work with various advertising platforms. While such solutions may involve additional costs, the ability to collaborate across ecosystems, unhindered by the limitations of a single platform, enhances strategic decision-making and maximizes the value of shared insights.

The neutral position of these independent clean rooms builds trust, addresses data privacy and security concerns, and supports regulatory compliance. As the importance of secure data collaboration extends beyond advertising to industries like media, healthcare, retail, and financial services, neutral clean rooms are increasingly valuable tools for maintaining compliance and delivering actionable insights.

To better understand the landscape, here are some examples of leading data collaboration and cloud providers offering data clean room solutions:

- *LiveRamp safe haven*—Following its acquisition of Habu, LiveRamp's Safe Haven has established itself as a key player in the data collaboration space (https://docs.liveramp.com/safe-haven/en/understanding-safe-haven.html). It enables secure data analysis and activation across multiple platforms, supporting a variety of marketing use cases.

- *Databricks clean rooms*—Databricks offers a scalable solution designed for complex data workloads, including machine learning (ML) and artificial intelligence (AI) (www.databricks.com/product/collaboration/clean-rooms). Its Delta Sharing technology allows secure, cross-cloud collaboration without replicating data, making it particularly well-suited for industries like retail and finance.
- *Google Cloud BigQuery clean rooms*—Google Cloud's BigQuery Analytics Hub provides clean room functionality that enables secure data sharing without the need to move or copy data (https://cloud.google.com/use-cases/data-clean-rooms). It's especially beneficial for industries such as healthcare and financial services, where strict governance and compliance are critical.
- *AWS clean rooms*—AWS offers a solution focused on cross-cloud data collaboration and privacy protection (https://aws.amazon.com/clean-rooms). Its clean room services are used in a wide range of industries, from finance to healthcare, where secure data sharing is vital.
- *Snowflake data clean rooms*—Snowflake provides a highly customizable clean room solution that supports advanced analytics and secure collaboration across industries (www.snowflake.com/en/data-cloud/workloads/collaboration/data-clean-rooms). Its ability to integrate with multiple platforms makes it an attractive option for companies that need flexibility and scalability in their data-sharing initiatives.

Neutral data clean rooms offered by independent marketing technology and cloud providers are becoming critical tools for organizations (including marketers) seeking to securely collaborate on data across multiple platforms. Unlike walled gardens that restrict collaboration to a single ecosystem, these solutions provide greater flexibility, allowing businesses to maintain more control over their data while benefiting from advanced analytics and compliance with privacy regulations.

However, companies adopting neutral clean rooms should also consider the potential trade-offs. Costs for platform licenses, infrastructure setup, and specialized expertise can be higher than relying on walled garden solutions. Additional complexity may arise from managing integrations across multiple data sources and ensuring consistent governance and security protocols. Despite these challenges, for many organizations, the cross-platform collaboration and data control benefits outweigh the higher investment and resource demands. The best approach ultimately depends on each organization's goals, budget, and privacy requirements.

As data collaboration grows in importance across industries—ranging from media to healthcare and financial services—marketers must evaluate the offerings from leading providers like LiveRamp, Databricks, Google Cloud, AWS, and Snowflake. Each solution brings unique strengths, from cross-cloud integration to ML capabilities, empowering businesses to securely derive insights and drive more effective marketing strategies.

8.2 Clean rooms for matching and activation

Marketing data is often fragmented across various platforms—website databases, loyalty programs, and offline purchase records. While each dataset contains valuable insights, its separation limits effective, targeted marketing campaigns. Data clean rooms address this problem by offering a secure and neutral environment where businesses can combine and analyze their data while ensuring user privacy remains intact.

A data clean room allows businesses to integrate data from various sources while safeguarding consumer privacy. All personally identifiable information (PII), such as email addresses or loyalty program IDs, undergoes hashing or other masking techniques before being matched on predefined criteria, ensuring that raw data is never exposed. For example, an email address can be hashed to preserve user privacy throughout the process. By securely matching and combining datasets in this manner, businesses can create more complete customer profiles without compromising privacy.

To ensure data security and privacy during the matching process, clean rooms use several techniques:

- *Data anonymization*—Converts sensitive data, like email addresses, into hashed values. This ensures secure matching without exposing personal details.
- *Homomorphic encryption*—Allows encrypted data to be analyzed without decryption, ensuring that no sensitive information is exposed during analysis.
- *Differential privacy*—Adds controlled "noise" to datasets, making it impossible to identify individuals while still generating useful insights.

To illustrate how secure matching unfolds in a data clean room, figure 8.4 shows a high-level workflow from the initial hashing of sensitive data to the final delivery of aggregated insights:

1. *Hashing/masking*—Both the brand and publisher anonymize sensitive fields (e.g., email addresses and loyalty IDs) before uploading them. This step prevents exposure of raw personal data in the clean room.
2. *Secure upload*—Each party transfers the hashed or encrypted data into the clean room environment via a secure connection.
3. *Secure matching and aggregation*—Within the clean room, matched records are identified using the anonymized keys. Any outputs, such as audience segments or analytics, are aggregated to preserve privacy.
4. *Insights delivery*—Participants receive matched reports, audience segments, or analytics that inform their marketing strategies without revealing personal information. Armed with these aggregated insights, organizations can refine their approaches and drive more effective campaigns.

However, to fully realize these benefits and maintain compliance with privacy regulations, it's essential to follow a set of best practices for integrating and activating data in a clean room.

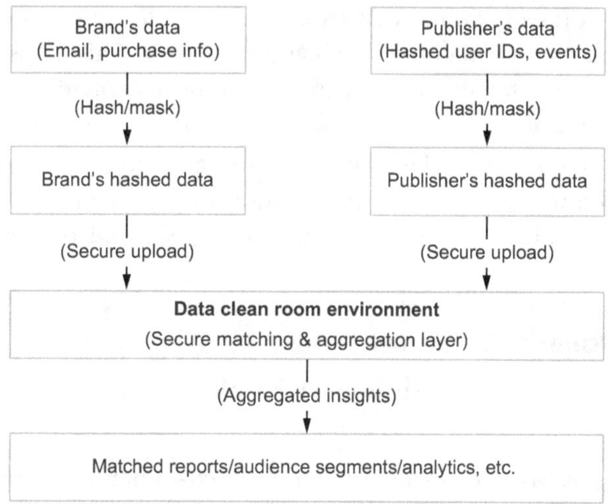

Figure 8.4 A high-level secure matching process in a data clean room

The following checklist outlines key considerations to ensure a secure and successful deployment:

- *Consistent hashing algorithms*—Ensure all parties agree on a standard hashing or encryption approach (e.g., SHA-256) so data matches accurately in the clean room.
- *Role-based access control (RBAC)*—Assign user permissions based on their roles. Restrict who can upload, match, or download data insights to maintain rigorous privacy safeguards.
- *Encryption in transit and at rest*—Data moving to and from the clean room should be protected via TLS/SSL, and it should be stored encrypted using strong encryption keys.
- *Periodic audits*—Regularly audit the clean room environment for compliance, ensuring logs are reviewed and access patterns are monitored.
- *Consent management*—Verify that data used for matching is collected with proper user consent and that it adheres to relevant privacy regulations (GDPR, CCPA, etc.).
- *Limit data retention*—Configure the clean room to automatically delete or de-identify data after a specified retention period, minimizing potential exposure.

Once data matching is completed, clean rooms enable several marketing strategies:

- *Retargeting*—A clothing retailer can use a clean room to match hashed website visitor data with its customer database. This allows the retailer to retarget users who previously browsed specific products, showing them personalized ads across social media or other platforms.

- *Lookalike audiences*—A travel company can analyze high-value customer data in a clean room and match it with a publisher's audience data. This helps identify new users who share characteristics with existing customers, expanding the company's marketing reach.
- *Personalization*—An e-commerce platform can combine purchase history data with a publisher's website behavior data in a clean room. This enables the platform to deliver personalized product recommendations based on users' past browsing behavior.

8.2.1 Example: Brand and publisher collaboration

Here's an example of how clean rooms create value for both parties:

1. Secure uploads
   - *Brand X (sporting goods)*—Uploads anonymized customer data, including hashed email addresses and purchase history, into the clean room.
   - *Publisher Y (fitness website)*—Shares anonymized visitor data, including hashed email addresses and browsing behavior, also in the clean room.
2. Matching and analysis
   - The clean room matches data based on hashed email addresses without exposing individual user information.
3. Targeted campaign
   - Brand X runs a targeted advertising campaign on publisher Y's website, displaying ads for fitness trackers to users most likely to be interested. Table 8.2 summarizes the key benefits for both advertisers and publishers in this scenario.

Table 8.2 Summary of benefits for advertisers and publishers

Stakeholder	Key benefits
Advertiser (brand X)	■ More precise targeting (hashed overlaps yield relevant audiences) ■ Improved campaign performance and ROI ■ Preserved user privacy reduces compliance risks
Publisher (publisher Y)	■ Enriched audience insights (understanding user overlap with brand data) ■ Higher-quality ad inventory leads to better yields ■ Stronger advertiser relationships by offering privacy-compliant collaboration

By enabling secure, privacy-preserving data integration and advanced matching techniques, clean rooms open up new avenues for more effective and personalized marketing. Advertisers can better understand their target audiences, while publishers can enrich their inventory with valuable insights. Together, these capabilities help businesses overcome fragmentation and elevate the quality of their campaigns, ultimately driving stronger results and more meaningful customer experiences.

8.3 Clean rooms for compliance and fraud prevention applications

While much of the discussion around data clean rooms focuses on marketing use cases, these secure environments also play a crucial role in compliance, fraud prevention, and risk management. By enabling organizations to share and analyze data without revealing personally identifiable information (PII), clean rooms help institutions meet regulatory obligations, detect suspicious activity, and prevent fraudulent individuals from being included in marketing or promotional efforts.

8.3.1 Suppressing fraudulent customers

Financial institutions, for example, often need to ensure that individuals flagged as fraudulent are excluded from promotional campaigns. A clean room allows a bank to safely match a list of fraudsters—hashed or anonymized—against a marketing database from another department or institution. Those identified as fraudulent are automatically omitted from the marketing list without revealing their identities or exchanging raw data.

How it works:

1. A bank uploads a list of customers flagged for fraudulent activity, with all PII hashed or anonymized, into the clean room.
2. Another department or external partner provides its marketing list, also anonymized, into the clean room.
3. The clean room identifies overlapping records (fraudsters) and ensures they are excluded from targeted offers (credit cards, loan ads, etc.) without ever exposing sensitive data.

Figure 8.5 presents a high-level workflow for fraud suppression in a clean room environment, from uploading anonymized fraud lists to excluding flagged individuals from marketing campaigns, to illustrate how this process unfolds.

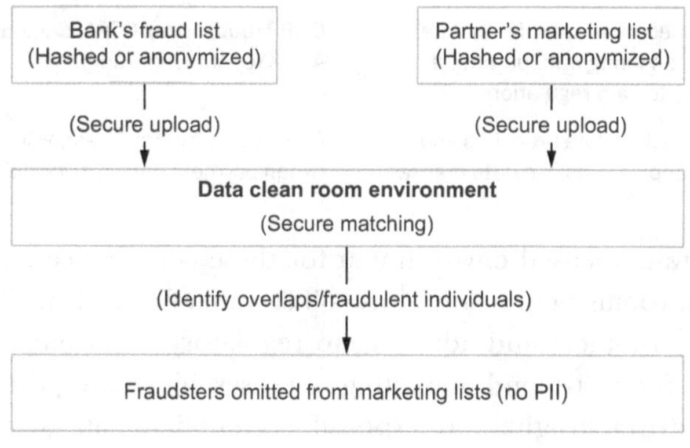

Figure 8.5 A high-level workflow for fraud suppression in a clean room

By matching hashed IDs within the clean room, the bank can suppress fraudsters from marketing outreach without disclosing raw personal information to any external party.

8.3.2 Supporting anti-money laundering (AML) compliance

In addition to suppressing fraudulent customers, clean rooms facilitate collaboration on anti-money laundering (AML) efforts. Multiple financial institutions can securely share anonymized data and suspicious activity patterns, allowing them to detect behavior indicative of money laundering without exposing proprietary information or violating privacy laws like GDPR, CCPA, or the Bank Secrecy Act.

How clean rooms support AML:

- *Secure data sharing*—Multiple banks securely contribute anonymized data on potentially suspicious activity (e.g., unusual transaction patterns).
- *Collaborative detection*—Patterns of illicit behavior, such as multiple accounts under different names, are identified within the clean room environment.
- *Privacy preservation*—The underlying data remains protected, ensuring that no personal details or unique detection methods are revealed.

Table 8.3 summarizes the key benefits of using clean rooms for compliance and fraud prevention, along with the major regulations they help address.

Table 8.3 Compliance and fraud prevention benefits

Benefit	Description	Relevant regulations
Fraud suppression	Automatically exclude known fraudsters from marketing lists or promotional offers.	Varies by jurisdiction; often tied to consumer protection laws
AML collaboration	Share suspicious activity patterns across institutions without exposing raw data or detection methods.	Bank Secrecy Act (USA), 6AMLD (EU), FATF Guidelines, etc.
Data privacy and minimization	Limit unnecessary exposure of personal data by hashing, anonymizing, or encrypting sensitive fields.	GDPR (EU), CCPA (California), PIPEDA (Canada), etc.
Regulatory compliance and audit trails	Provide a secure record of how data is shared, ensuring transparency and adherence to data regulations.	GDPR (audit logs), CCPA, Bank Secrecy Act (KYC/AML reporting).
Reduced liability	Lower the risk of data breaches and fines by keeping sensitive data masked.	GDPR (fines for breaches), PCI DSS (when payment data is involved)

By providing a secure, privacy-focused environment for these compliance and fraud prevention activities, clean rooms help institutions collaborate effectively while maintaining the trust of their customers and adhering to regulatory requirements. This extends the value of clean rooms beyond marketing use cases, illustrating their versatility as tools for both data-driven insights and responsible, compliant data governance.

8.4 Clean rooms for measurement

As third-party cookies are gradually being phased out, measuring ad performance has become one of the biggest challenges in digital advertising. Marketers struggle to track user activity across platforms, resulting in fragmented views of campaign effectiveness. Data clean rooms provide a solution, offering a secure, privacy-compliant environment that allows marketers to measure ad effectiveness across channels in this new, cookieless reality.

Without persistent identifiers like cookies, standard attribution models struggle to connect user interactions across web, mobile, and connected TV (CTV) channels. Consequently, marketers must rely on aggregated signals or partner data integrations, making it more difficult to pinpoint the true influence of each channel on customer behavior. Clean rooms address this challenge by offering a controlled space for advertisers, publishers, and measurement partners to collaborate on data analysis. By securely sharing anonymized data (such as hashed email addresses or device identifiers), marketers can unify website visit data, mobile app engagement, and other relevant events, resulting in a more complete view of the customer journey.

Clean rooms also empower data-driven decision-making. By analyzing combined, cross-channel data, marketers can identify which platforms drive the most conversions and engagement, optimize their budgets, and focus on the most effective channels. They can also gain a more precise understanding of how various touchpoints—web, mobile, or CTV—contribute to conversions, enabling more accurate attribution and ROI calculation. This level of analysis informs where future advertising efforts should be directed.

To illustrate the benefits of cross-channel measurement in a clean room, consider a shoe retailer running a multichannel campaign. The retailer combines data from its website, mobile app, and CTV ads within a clean room:

- *Website data*—Tracks users browsing specific shoe categories. If visitors log in or sign up with an email address, the retailer hashes that email to maintain privacy.
- *Mobile app data*—The app captures product views and cart activity. It may also collect a device ID or hashed user account identifier for matching.
- *CTV ad data*—This shows which users viewed the retailer's ads. CTV platforms may provide an IP address or a household-level device ID. The retailer anonymizes or encrypts these identifiers before sharing them with the clean room.

Within the clean room, these hashed identifiers are matched using privacy-preserving techniques such as deterministic (e.g., hashed email) or probabilistic (e.g., IP + device attributes) matching. As a result, the retailer can map the customer journey:

1. *CTV ad exposure*—A user sees a new shoe promotion on a streaming service.
2. *Website interest*—Later, that user visits the retailer's website, exploring similar shoe categories.
3. *App purchase*—Finally, the user opens the retailer's mobile app, adds shoes to the cart, and completes the purchase.

By analyzing this anonymized, combined data in the clean room, the retailer obtains a holistic view of how each channel contributed to the purchase decision. This insight helps them refine campaign strategies, such as adjusting CTV spending or personalizing follow-up messaging, for more effective future campaigns.

Table 8.4 provides a clear overview and highlights the key benefits that clean rooms bring to measurement in a cookieless landscape. Table 8.5 outlines some important limitations to keep in mind.

Table 8.4 Key benefits that clean rooms bring to measurement

Key benefits	Explanation
Cross-channel attribution	Unifies data across web, mobile, and CTV for a holistic view of the user journey
Actionable ROI measurement	More accurate attribution of conversions to each channel, informing budget optimization
Data enrichment and ML training	Enables collaborative modeling (e.g., purchase propensity) using anonymized data
Privacy compliance	Restricts sharing to hashed/aggregated data, aligning with regulations like GDPR or CCPA

Table 8.5 Key limitations that clean rooms present for measurement

Key limitations	Explanation
Restricted external data	Platforms like Google Ads and Facebook often limit impression-level data for privacy.
Technical complexity	Requires hashing, encryption, and sometimes advanced match logic (deterministic/probabilistic).
Integration overhead	Setting up secure data pipelines and ensuring consistent identifiers can be resource-intensive.

Clean rooms thus offer a crucial solution to the measurement challenges posed by a cookieless world. By enabling a more complete, privacy-safe view of campaign performance, they empower marketers to make smarter, data-driven decisions about ad spend and strategy. As digital advertising continues to evolve, these secure environments will remain essential to measuring, optimizing, and refining campaigns, helping businesses navigate the fragmentation introduced by declining third-party cookies while respecting user privacy.

8.5 The future of clean rooms

Clean rooms have evolved from a purely marketing-focused tool to a foundational component of industry data ecosystems. As they continue to mature, these environments will address emerging compliance challenges, enable more sophisticated data collaborations, and spur innovation in fields ranging from healthcare to finance. Figure 8.6 provides a high-level timeline of their evolution and where they might head next.

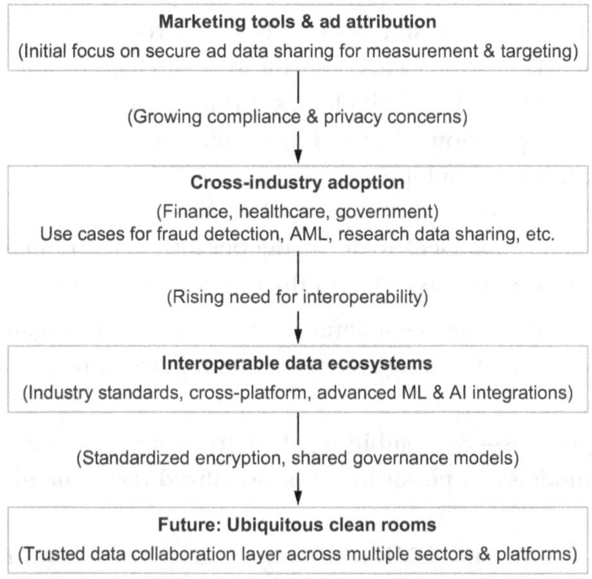

Figure 8.6 The evolution of data clean rooms

Initially developed for advertising and marketing, data clean rooms are now being adopted in healthcare, finance, and government industries. Their ability to facilitate data sharing without compromising privacy enables companies to extract valuable insights while adhering to regulations like GDPR and CCPA. This shift suggests that clean rooms may soon become a standard tool for decision-making and collaboration across numerous sectors.

Despite their expanding popularity, one of the biggest hurdles to widespread clean room adoption remains interoperability. Currently, many clean rooms operate in platform-specific silos, limiting data exchange across different environments. Industry initiatives like the IAB Tech Lab's interoperability guidelines aim to standardize how clean rooms communicate, laying the groundwork for more seamless collaboration with a broader range of partners.

Clean rooms offer transformative potential far beyond their advertising roots:

- *Healthcare*—Hospitals, research institutions, and pharmaceutical companies can use clean rooms to securely share anonymized patient data, fueling medical research and improving diagnostics.

- *Financial services*—Clean rooms are vital for fraud detection, risk management, and customer profiling. Banks can share anonymized transaction data to gain a more holistic view of customer behavior while reducing the exposure of sensitive details.

As data privacy regulations continue to evolve, the demand for privacy-preserving technologies like clean rooms is growing. Businesses use these environments to stay compliant with new and existing data privacy laws, and the role of clean rooms will only expand. Industry bodies like the IAB Tech Lab play a key role in establishing standards and guidelines for clean room operations. These efforts build trust, ensure responsible platform behavior, and foster broader adoption.

A significant part of the future of clean rooms involves AI—particularly generative AI and advanced ML. As organizations seek to derive deeper insights from shared data, models trained within secure clean rooms can offer the following benefits:

- *Improve relevance and effectiveness*—Generative AI can use aggregated, anonymized data to create predictive insights (e.g., content personalization and user segmentation).
- *Enhance customer experiences*—By combining data from multiple sources in a privacy-safe way, AI models can power hyper-personalized recommendations or offers.
- *Streamline collaboration*—Advanced ML techniques, such as federated learning, enable joint model training without revealing raw data, further safeguarding privacy.

As these AI-driven and ML approaches mature, clean rooms will serve as a secure hub for more sophisticated analyses, ensuring that both privacy and performance goals are met. This trend underscores the value of interoperability; AI models become far more powerful when data can flow seamlessly across platforms.

Despite these promising developments, several challenges remain:

- *Data silos*—Many organizations still store data in isolated platforms, creating barriers to broad data collaboration.
- *Complex compliance requirements*—Multiple regulations (GDPR, CCPA, sector-specific laws) can complicate data sharing, especially across regions.
- *Technical overhead*—Implementing standardized protocols, encryption, and advanced AI techniques requires specialized expertise and infrastructure.

These factors highlight the need for continued efforts to standardize interoperability and build organizational readiness to ensure clean rooms can reach their fullest potential. The future of clean rooms is not just about technology. It's about fostering responsible data practices and building trust among all stakeholders. As these environments evolve, they hold the potential to transform data collaboration by providing businesses with the insights they need while keeping privacy at the forefront.

In the next chapter, we'll focus on another transformative technology: generative AI. We'll explore how generative AI tools can enhance marketing strategies, personalize customer experiences, and streamline content creation.

Summary

- Data clean rooms are crucial in enabling privacy-compliant collaboration and helping businesses analyze data securely while adhering to regulations like GDPR and CCPA.
- Clean rooms are widely used for audience targeting, measuring campaign effectiveness, and training machine learning models without exposing sensitive data.
- Clean rooms support cross-industry applications, such as fraud detection in finance and secure data-sharing in healthcare, while ensuring data privacy.
- Walled garden clean rooms focus on platform-specific ecosystems, while third-party providers offer more flexible, cross-platform solutions.
- Interoperability remains a challenge, and efforts toward standardization are essential for widespread adoption.
- As businesses adapt to a future without third-party cookies, clean rooms will be central to how data is securely shared, analyzed, and used for decision-making across industries.

9 Upcoming: Generative AI for marketing

This chapter covers

- What generative marketing is and why it matters
- Examples of current use cases in generative marketing applied to first-party data
- Risks of generative marketing with governance recommendations
- A preview of future capabilities

> *AI will take increasingly more jobs as its sophistication and capabilities increase, from computer use to agents, and the only antidote for people is to skill up on AI.*
>
> —Christopher Penn, Co-Founder and Chief Data Scientist at TrustInsights.ai

Major changes in marketing with first-party data are underway, thanks to the rise of new AI capabilities. The marketing teams that harness these new capabilities in generative AI for marketing stand to gain a strong competitive advantage, but they must be mindful of the prerequisites and risks.

In this chapter, we'll explore the initial opportunities presented by generative marketing, the key risks and questions of governance, and recommendations on how to build your marketing team's strategy as it pertains to AI.

9.1 Introducing generative marketing

Generative artificial intelligence, or generative AI, refers to AI models (including popular large language models, or LLMs) that have learned the underlying patterns and structure of massive amounts of text, images, and videos and use them to create answers to prompts containing text, images, videos, and code. They are the product of advancements in transformer-based architectures that are applied to deep neural networks trained on massive amounts of data. If you don't follow what all that means, don't worry. The key takeaway is that a fundamental change in the world's approach to AI has introduced new capabilities that were made possible only a few short years ago.

What sets generative AI apart from traditional AI is the open-ended nature and quality of the responses the AI models are capable of producing. In effect, the term *generative* in "generative AI" refers to how these new AI models can generate or create outputs such as images or text that are entirely new and distinct from their inputs based on complex instructions. This stands in contrast to what most people would have meant by AI ten years ago when supervised machine learning (ML) models were most popular. While these ML models typically predict a specific outcome based on structured data (for example, a churn prediction score based on product usage history), generative AI can infer patterns across a large range of outcomes based on the patterns it has codified (for example, "what makes a successful customer, qualitatively?").

Generative AI models may be unimodal (e.g., text-to-text, like the original ChatGPT) or, increasingly, multimodal (e.g., image-to-text or document-to-image). They may be generalist in nature or trained on specific types of tasks with a specific, autonomous role (often referred to as "agents"). This makes generative AI models incredibly useful for a variety of applications across business, science, and the arts. Marketing is no exception.

Generative marketing is simply generative AI applied to marketing. At first, many marketers adopted generative AI for marketing just in content production, such as to draft email templates, but more recently, some have adopted it for visual creative development, targeting suggestions, insight generation, sentiment analysis of customer posts, and other use cases. One of our recent favorites is the use of generative AI to test marketing creative and messaging on different marketing personas simulated by AI. Only recently have other applications of generative AI for marketing come to light, some of which have profound implications for the future of marketing.

9.1.1 Why generative marketing matters

Marketers today face a tremendous amount of pressure to drive customer engagement, sales, and customer lifetime value. Smarter and more performant personalization offers the best chance marketers have to deliver on those key business objectives. As new marketing channels emerge, consumer preferences change, and the amount of first-party data grows exponentially, how can a marketer keep up with the thousands or millions of personalization possibilities?

For most of the history of marketing, marketers and their agencies have been responsible for the design of ad creative and for implementing campaigns on each channel. This meant there were relatively low limits to the number of targeted and personalized campaigns an organization could serve, usually numbered in the dozens.

The marketing technologies and solutions covered in prior chapters of this book focus on optimizing marketing operations to help streamline the manual process of personalization. These can help scale marketing personalization from dozens of campaigns to a hundred or more, but they also reach natural limits driven by human teams' ability to understand, generate, and manage the complexity of so many campaigns.

Generative marketing takes a different approach by asking, "What if you could use AI to generate campaigns for *each individual customer*?" Marketing teams outside of large enterprise sales had never asked such a question because it would require an unjustifiably large investment in marketing resources to achieve that extreme level of personalization.

But now, generative marketing offers marketing teams a path to realize that one-to-one personalization. Generative AI-powered tools can take each customer's context into account (i.e., all their first-party and some third-party data) and then generate a persuasive, multichannel experience within guidelines set by the marketing team to achieve reengagement, cross-sell, or any number of other marketing objectives. This leaves marketers with a choice: embrace generative marketing and all it has to offer, despite the uncertainties and challenges, or wait on further developments at the risk of falling behind.

9.1.2 Compound marketing

Beyond that challenge to scaling personalization lies another, more effective opportunity—achieving the exponential growth that comes from compounding results on themselves. Albert Einstein said "Compound interest is the eighth wonder of the world," and the same holds true for compound marketing growth.

How do marketing teams achieve compounded returns? They unlock a virtuous loop between customer lifetime value and investments in marketing, driven by smarter targeting and highly effective engagement. The higher your customer lifetime value becomes, the higher the cost of acquisition your business can support. The higher the cost of acquisition you are able to spend, the greater the reach of your marketing. Traditional segmentation, such as high, medium, and low-value customer onboarding, has helped many marketing teams drive initial results in their virtuous loop, but they eventually reach creative, operational, or other limits to the improvements.

Because generative marketing will be self-improving without these constraints, there is a much greater chance that companies employing it will achieve the compounding effects of that virtuous loop. As those who have studied compounding know, small changes compounded over time can have huge consequences. If generative marketing can drive a 2% self-improvement per week instead of 1% per month, that results in a 13x greater outcome over the course of a year. So if generative marketing is the *how*, then compound marketing is the *why*.

9.2 How to use generative marketing today

We've spoken to dozens of marketing leaders who are under pressure from their leadership to adopt generative AI for marketing as soon as possible. Fears of business model disruption and the promise of intelligent automation with AI have driven CEOs, CMOs, and other executives to push many of their teams, including marketing, for concrete examples of generative AI in action. While generative marketing is an *emerging* technology that has a way to go before it fully matures, marketing teams are finding opportunities to use it day to day.

How can you bring such examples to life for your marketing team? Let's review the current landscape of generative marketing for these opportunities and look at an example before focusing on how to build these into your longer-term AI strategy.

9.2.1 Functional examples of generative marketing

Despite the hype, we are still in the phase of AI *point solutions* that help data teams and marketing teams use AI in very specific aspects of their work but do not design, implement, and measure campaigns in a fully autonomous manner. Here are some of the most useful point solutions.

Business intelligence

Business intelligence includes all the ways that teams uncover insights from their organization's data, often through data visualizations, tabular reports, or simple metrics. It covers all areas of the modern organization, from operations to finance and sales, but it is especially pertinent to marketing.

Recently, several of the leading business intelligence platforms—such as Duet AI in Google Cloud's Looker, Copilot for Microsoft Power BI, and Einstein Copilot in Salesforce's Tableau—began to integrate generative AI features. Some of these features have made it much easier for nontechnical users to access business intelligence capabilities (such as providing answers to questions in natural language or clearly summarizing reports), while other features have augmented the capabilities of power users by looking for anomalies or scalably testing for patterns.

Marketing teams can use business intelligence capabilities with generative AI to find the most important attributes on which to create segmentation models or other customer breakdowns. These segmentation models or breakdowns, in turn, can serve as the basis for targeting individual audiences. Examples of metrics marketers can use to segment their customers include lifetime value, purchase recency, and predictive propensities, among many others.

If your organization has well-structured data, nontechnical marketers can self-serve their business intelligence needs. For example, they can explore and define segment thresholds or gain additional information on what a particular segment is like in personalizing content for that segment.

CREATIVE DEVELOPMENT

Creative development refers to all the text, image, and video content produced by marketing teams and their vendors to be used in marketing campaigns. It includes content created for paid, owned, and earned media across many formats and channels. While creative development for large-scale brand campaigns may not face scalability constraints, many one-to-one or one-to-few channels, such as email, mobile messaging, or digital display ads online, may face creative constraints across all target audiences.

Generative creative solutions are often purpose-built to support marketing teams:

- They can be tuned to incorporate your brand guidelines and brand assets.
- They can be used to artificially incorporate product placements in images and video assets created by agencies or others.
- They can produce assets in predetermined formats useful for marketing, such as common display ad formats and email templates.
- Their user experience design is optimized for marketing workflows, including the production of creative content from marketing briefs or similar documents.

Several startups and more-established marketing software providers have begun to provide creative development solutions augmented by generative AI. Examples include Adobe Express, Jasper, Typeface, and Laetro. For now, these platforms are useful for providing creative drafts that can be sent to creative teams for refinement or long-tail content. At some point in the near future, they may generate creative assets of the caliber needed for a majority of marketing campaigns in production.

AUDIENCE SUGGESTIONS

What if you could bring together everything you know about your organization, its customers, and its marketing channels to propose countless audiences to test? That's what some composable CDPs offer today.

As a reminder, first-party data solutions refer to systems that help your organization capture, manage, and activate first-party data from various sources to target and personalize campaigns via a variety of channels. By definition, they have access to key information for use with generative AI, including

- Customer-level data
- Transactional and engagement data
- Activation channels

If you add your campaign objectives (e.g., customer retention) and business context (such as information about the products or services sold by the business), generative AI models have everything they need to produce useful and compelling audience suggestions at scale.

In 2023, GrowthLoop became the first composable CDP to launch several generative AI features for first-party data management and activation. Other companies in the composable CDP space may follow as marketing technology matures. Here are two examples of the generative marketing capabilities currently available:

- Marketers who do not know SQL are able to use natural language descriptions such as "high-value customers on the West Coast at risk of churn" to create audiences on their first-party data that can be immediately put into production.
- Marketers can provide simple objectives such as "churn winback" to create multiple audience suggestions in a natural language dialogue, incorporating marketers' feedback for any adjustments.

Destination-specific features

Several marketing destinations, such as email providers and ad platforms, have launched generative AI capabilities specific to certain channels. These are limited to the data available to that channel, but they are often purpose-built on large amounts of channel-specific data to provide strong value-added capabilities.

In May 2023, Google Ads announced a series of generative AI features for its search and display ads platform (https://mng.bz/QwWm). These features included

- The creation of search ads that summarize the key offer featured on a landing page
- The creation of image suggestions based on your website
- New ad formats specific to the dialogue-based nature of generative AI-powered search

Klaviyo, a marketing automation platform that primarily serves email and SMS marketing, similarly announced the ability to generate subject line recommendations for marketing emails as well as SMS text message content (https://mng.bz/X7WY).

There is and will continue to be overlap in generative marketing capabilities among all these categories. You should shape your team's strategy so that it combines intelligent context (e.g., first-party data) with actionability (e.g., the ability to scale personalization across or in your marketing channels).

Interpreting and simulating customer responses

Marketing teams have performed *sentiment analysis* on customer feedback, social media, reviews, and other data sources for years using traditional ML models to classify it as positive, negative, or neutral. Generative AI now enables those same marketing teams to create qualitative summaries and deeper insights from the same data sources to learn even more about their customers. This is a key tool in enhancing the understanding of customer opinions, emotions, and attitudes toward a brand, product, marketing message, etc.

Using those insights, some marketing teams have begun to prompt generative AI models (or, in some cases, persistent AI agents) to act as if they are one of a variety of different customer personas. This allows them to test out marketing messaging and creativity with an artificial set of customers for immediate feedback, like having a marketing focus group available 24/7 for questions.

9.2.2 Marketing campaign example

Let's dive into a step-by-step example of how a marketer could use generative marketing to inform, target, and personalize a campaign. We'll start by using AI to create a calculated personalization field using customer data and then use that knowledge to suggest targeting. Finally, we'll produce ad creative specifically for that audience.

For this example, let's imagine we are marketers at REI, an American retail and outdoor recreation services company. It specializes in selling outdoor gear and apparel for activities like hiking, camping, cycling, climbing, and paddling. This includes traditional gear like raincoats and nonperishable food and drink items that are good for camping. Your goal is to win back churned customers who used to be your high-value customers by using data on your best-selling products.

USE NATURAL LANGUAGE TO CREATE A NEW PERSONALIZATION FIELD

First, let's take advantage of the breadth of data found in our marketing data lakehouse to gain some insights about our ideal customer profile. We can ask questions and provide instructions such as these:

- Who are my top-spending customers?
- What are my best-selling products?
- Show me a chart of the products purchased by my top-spending customers.

Figure 9.1 shows a natural language request to determine REI's best-selling products for each customer: "What is our best-selling product by customer?" (Note that we use synthetic data for illustrative purposes.) This query would normally have required a data analyst, but now it's possible for nontechnical marketing team members to pose this question and many others. The result is an SQL statement (providing query visibility to your data team) and a preview of the results of the calculated field of best-selling products for each customer, shown in figure 9.2.

We learn what products we can use to personalize messaging by asking the question, "What is the best-selling product for each customer?" (For example, it is headphones for customer ID 431329 and rain coat for customer ID 312533.) We could use these to personalize our email messaging and to say something like "If you liked <best_selling_product>, you'll love <product_recommendation>."

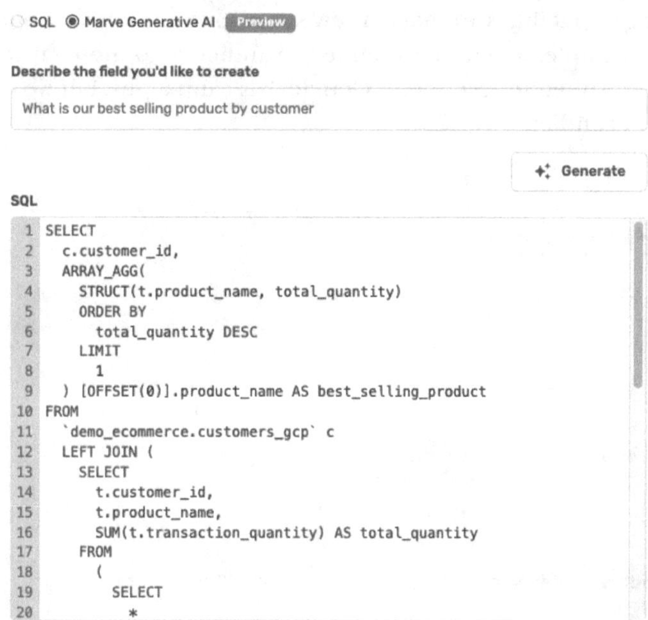

Figure 9.1 Example of AI converting a natural language request to SQL

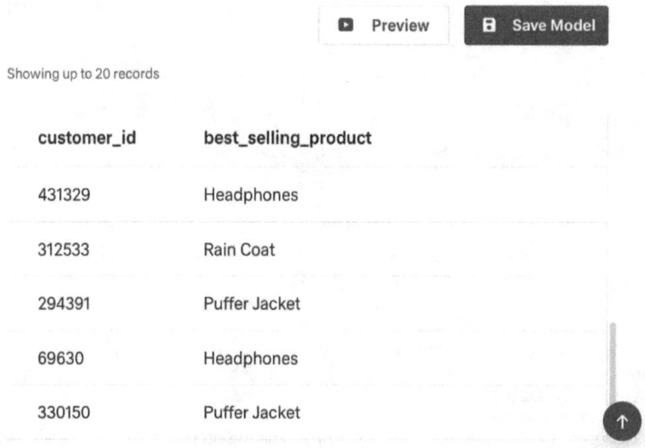

Preview Save Model

Showing up to 20 records

customer_id	best_selling_product
431329	Headphones
312533	Rain Coat
294391	Puffer Jacket
69630	Headphones
330150	Puffer Jacket

Figure 9.2 Data results of the natural language request from figure 9.1

SUGGEST AUDIENCES TO TARGET WITH GROWTHLOOP

Armed with these insights on our best customers and everything else we know from our experience as marketers, we seek targeted audience suggestions from the generative AI models that could perform well. In figure 9.3, notice how it is common for generative marketing capabilities to make a few suggestions at once to open up the possibilities. In this example, we chose to refine the audience to those customers and prospects that are best suited to respond to Google Ads campaigns, but we could have chosen a multichannel audience as well.

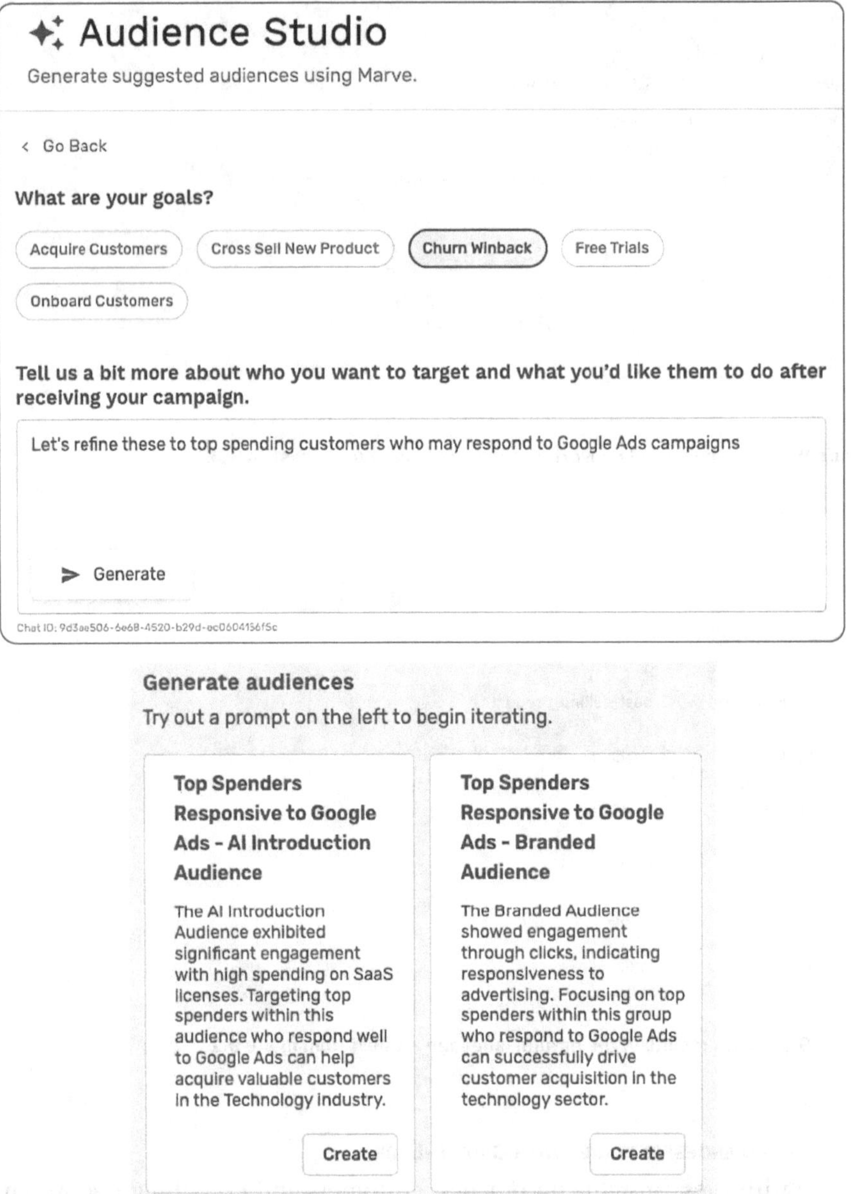

Figure 9.3 Example of audience suggestions provided by GrowthLoop

Most recently, the ability to have a dialogue with the generative marketing agent to refine our selections and request new ideas has emerged. This requires generative marketing tools to keep a persistent representation of each audience throughout the conversation, but it dramatically increases the chance that we'll find useful audience suggestions.

And if we'd like to find out *why* the AI has suggested an audience, we can simply ask for its reasoning. This explainability is a key advantage to generative marketing, which helps build marketers' confidence and understanding as they begin to use AI to drive ideation. It is a welcome departure from some of the opaque ML models of prior years.

Once we find an audience suggestion we like, we simply click it to review it for activation. When we do, the generative marketing platform creates and runs the data query we need automatically. Surprisingly, advanced new generative marketing features often make it easier to use marketing platforms because they speak our language as marketers and can bridge what we mean to the data that lies beneath.

Generate Google Ad creative options for your best-selling products

Finally, with the audience in hand, we'd like to generate some suggested Google Ad creatives to add to our paid media campaign. Generative marketing platforms can take in all your key brand assets and guidelines, along with ad formats, to ensure they generate creative assets that are effective and on brand.

Continuing with our REI example, let's imagine that we've determined that canned organic apple juice is a less expensive purchase that effectively re-engages churned customers. We also provide the generative marketing platform with specific information about this audience, which allows us to automatically personalize the campaign for the kind of customer or prospect in the audience, as shown in figure 9.4.

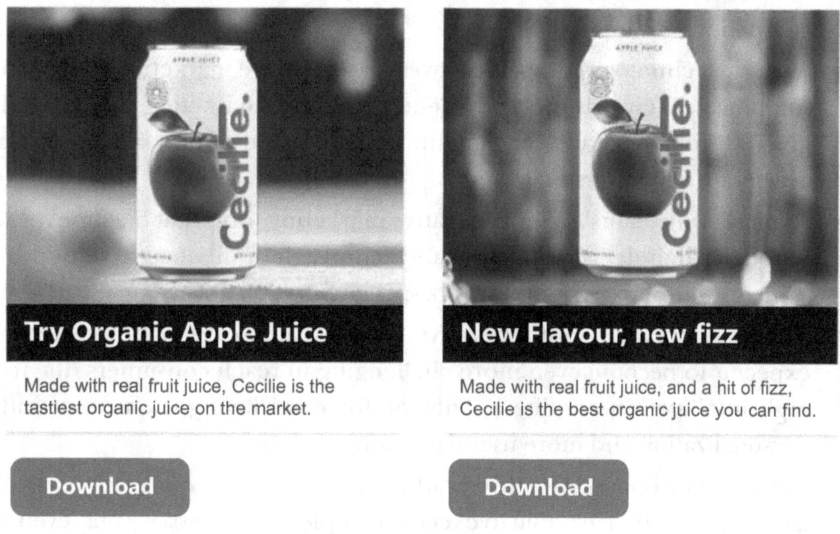

Figure 9.4 AI-generated display ad creative based on an audience

The product placement in each creative has differentiated aesthetics, such as a rustic look in the second image, that may resonate better with certain audiences. The copy below the product image in each creative can also be generated by AI, which opens the door to virtually infinite combinations of ad creative.

We can now upload the target audience and the creative to Google Ads, all of which have been generated by us, as the marketer, in collaboration with the generative AI models. These capabilities are available today and will have a huge effect on the velocity and quality of campaigns that marketers produce in the coming years, helping marketing teams scale from dozens of simultaneous campaigns to thousands of personalized interactions.

Given how early it is in the development of generative marketing, how should you develop your team's strategy to best capture this dynamic opportunity? We'll cover that topic in the next section. But first, let's briefly touch upon some of the major trends that are shaping the future of generative marketing.

9.3 Forming your generative marketing strategy

As you navigate new technology changes, like generative marketing, we recommend starting by informing yourself about the key trends and insights that will help your team make consistent and informed decisions about product purchases, team workflows, and anything else that depends on the new technology.

We summarize a few of these market and technology trends in the following list and encourage you to discuss how these trends could inform your company's strategy in adopting generative AI for marketing:

- As more and more companies adopt generative AI for marketing, their customer-specific knowledge and context will serve as one of the key differentiators or competitive advantages.
- As more technology companies invest in generative marketing innovation, point solutions will give rise to end-to-end generative marketing platforms that integrate customer data management, targeting, activation, and measurement to accelerate hyper-personalization.
- As marketing teams adopt generative marketing tools that become more autonomous in their decision-making and actions, they will need to be mindful of the human-AI user experience, with a special focus on governance and controls.
- As consumers also adopt generative AI at a greater scale, marketing teams should expect it to become even more challenging to reach consumers due to increasingly intelligent spam filters. This will force marketing teams to provide better personalization and more useful communications.
- Even further out, as AI-native platforms expand their integrations with specialized AI agents that are able to execute complex workflows, we may even see traditional, siloed SaaS applications give way to these AI-agentic workflows.

As you consider the specifics of your own company, you should view all the data that your company generates as a strategically important proprietary asset. For example, what do you know about customers, partners, or vendors that other companies do not? Similarly, what customer engagement opportunities does your company have (not just your marketing team) that you could employ to personalize each customer's experience? For example, in-product messaging on a login screen for web or mobile-first companies, messages surfaced to bank tellers for banks, or even the tape that seals packages sent in the mail for an e-commerce company like Amazon. This all forms part of your company context in adopting generative AI for marketing.

Now that we've identified some of the key trends and have your company context in mind, let's delve into some key principles that should govern your AI strategy for marketing.

9.3.1 Your data strategy

While you can apply generative AI in your organization to write more concise email copy or more interesting blog posts completely independent of your customer data, the results won't meaningfully scale your marketing team's personalization efforts.

> **TIP** "You can't have an AI strategy if you don't have a data strategy."—Tameem Iftikhar, CTO of GrowthLoop

Customer understanding, especially from first-party data, is absolutely essential to provide machine learning and generative AI models with the customer context they need to make informed personalization recommendations. For example, without knowing that a high-spending customer has returned every shirt from Ralph Lauren due to those shirts offering a poor fit, your campaign might have featured Ralph Lauren for all high-spending customers. With greater context, your marketing team's personalized campaigns could capture very refined nuances in customer behavior, such as the fact that a high-spending customer only purchases shirts and sweaters in red if they are patterned, or that they tend to buy clothes early or late for each season of the year. As a result, we believe generative AI for marketing can amplify the effect of a good first-party data strategy.

The good news is that all of the recommendations and best practices in the prior chapters of this book are the same ones needed to get the most out of generative AI. We recommend that you take control and ownership of your first-party data in a marketing data lakehouse to maximize its flexibility and extensibility. Decoupling your first-party data from marketing applications only becomes more important when your team is faced with rapid technology changes. With such an open architecture, your marketing and data teams are free to use your first-party data seamlessly in conjunction with an ever-changing set of upstream data sources, intelligent personalization tools, or downstream activation channels.

This open architectural approach offers the highest point of leverage for generative marketing because generative AI capabilities sit at the center of all your first-party data and can be used to direct campaigns across all your marketing channels. More specifically, this architecture unlocks insight generation, audience and journey suggestions, experiments, and measurement, all on a shared and comprehensive source of truth. If you have a strong activation component, such as a composable CDP, you can put these insights and suggestions into action seamlessly across all your marketing channels, as shown in figure 9.5.

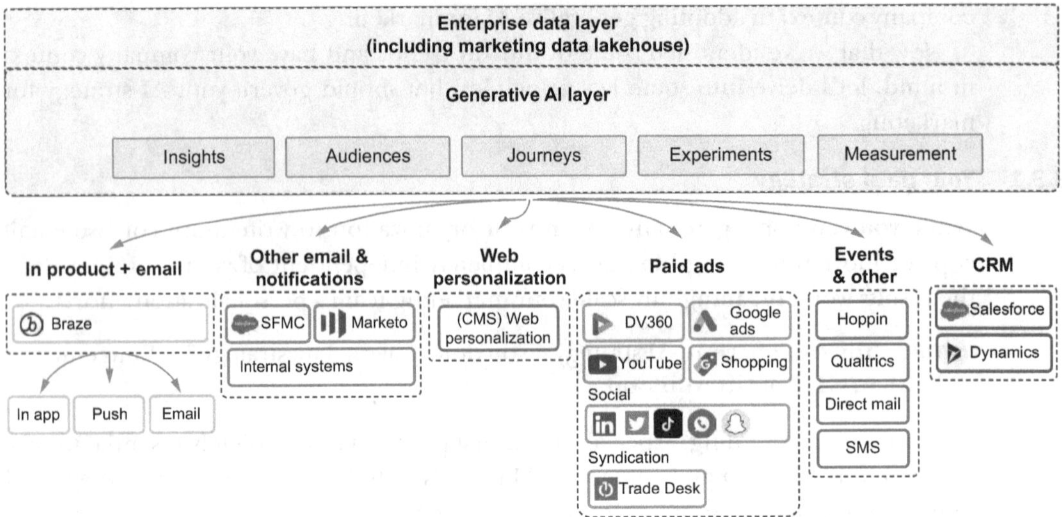

Figure 9.5 The centralization of generative marketing capabilities

There is an additional advantage to this cloud data warehouse or data lake architecture at the enterprise level, which is that your organization has the opportunity to use the entire ecosystem of partners to create new AI capabilities in each cloud platform. For example, Google Cloud BigQuery ML's row-level large language model capabilities are easy to integrate with your marketing data if they are already hosted in BigQuery or BigLake.

Once you establish the right architecture, there are several ways to incorporate your organization's specific data to customize your generative AI results:

- *Prompt engineering* involves crafting well-structured inputs (e.g., prompt templates) to guide the AI's responses with your company's context without modifying the model itself. It is cost-effective, easy to implement, and works well for quick adjustments but is limited by the model's existing knowledge and context window.
- *Retrieval-augmented generation (RAG)* combines a generative model with real-time data retrieval from external sources like databases or documents. This allows the

AI to access and use updated company knowledge without retraining, making it ideal for dynamic information but requiring a well-maintained retrieval system.

- *Fine-tuning* adjusts a model's parameters using company-specific data to improve accuracy and relevance. This method provides deeper customization (usually via API for most cloud-based generative AI models), but is expensive and requires lots of structured training data.
- *Embedding custom knowledge* is achieved by storing enterprise data as vector embeddings in a searchable database, allowing the AI to retrieve relevant information when responding. It enhances accuracy without modifying the model itself, making it a good middle-ground between fine-tuning and prompt engineering.
- *Training from scratch* involves building a custom generative AI model entirely from proprietary data, giving full control over its training and behavior. This requires huge amounts of proprietary text, structured data, and GPUs, so it is not recommended for most companies.

We've summarized these options in the table 9.1.

Table 9.1 Generative AI model customization using your organization's data

Method	Customization level	Cost	Latency	Best for
Prompt engineering	Low	Low	Fast	Quick, low effort adjustments
Retrieval-augmented generation (RAG)	Medium	Moderate	Slightly slower	Keeping AI responses updated with real-time company data
Fine-tuning	High	High	Slow	Tailoring AI for specialized domains (finance, healthcare)
Embedding custom knowledge	Medium-high	Moderate	Fast	Enhancing AI with large enterprise datasets
Training from scratch	Maximum	Extremely high	Very slow	Large-scale AI development with full control

Creating a unified first-party data layer for your organization can enable powerful new AI capabilities for your organization. Given the advent of generative marketing, this unified data layer has only become more urgent for data-driven marketing teams that want to take or hold leadership positions in their respective industries.

9.3.2 *Your technology strategy*

Most organizations will gain generative marketing capabilities provided by their marketing technology purchases. For most teams, this is easier than building new capabilities in-house because there are terms of service in place to govern legal, regulatory, and information security concerns. As this new category takes shape, we recommend seeking solutions that are composable, AI-native, and thoughtfully designed to fit with your team's bespoke needs to support your change management goals.

COMPOSABLE ARCHITECTURE

As you evaluate marketing technologies, your team should ask how the architecture of the technology supports generative marketing. For example, what data is made available to the generative marketing engine in the platform you choose? What does this imply for any biases or blind spots it may have? For example, if you are using a new personalization capability in your email platform that uses generative AI, it may not have access to web conversions driven by paid media. This may lead the model to underestimate the engagement of some of the most active customers who do not regularly use email.

On the other hand, the AI models embedded in that same email platform may have strong proprietary data to inform the most optimal send times for open and click-through rates for each message but lack key product usage metrics by customer.

How can you combine the best of both worlds, including customer-centric data and channel-centric data? You look for solutions that offer a composable architecture that connects the generative marketing capabilities to your marketing data lakehouse, which encompasses all of your organization's data.

There are two key attributes to this data architecture critical for AI:

- *Zero-copy* refers to the way composable solutions do not need to create multiple copies of the data hosted within each application to use it. This ensures you have a single consistent source of truth while reducing costs and security risks.
- *Open data model* refers to the fact that composable solutions do not need your organization's data to fit a predetermined data schema or data fields. This means the data can reflect your organization's true complexity, which provides AI models with more information than a predetermined data schema.

Despite the product messaging you may see for marketing technologies, these attributes are not binary. You may have a mostly zero-copy system that copies audience membership but not personalization fields, or you may have an open data model with minimal requirements to function with the product. Both of those are okay so long as your team keeps the design principles in mind and makes trade-offs intentionally. We covered this topic in more detail in chapter 4, but it's worth mentioning that the advantages of a composable choice are even more important as AI takes a greater role in marketing.

AI-NATIVE CAPABILITIES

By now, most popular marketing technologies have embedded some form of generative AI into their products, but they should not be mistaken for AI-native products. How can you tell the difference? AI-native products that will help you embrace the full potential of generative marketing have three key attributes:

- *AI at every layer*—This means that every capability is reimagined with AI in mind, even if it is a peripheral feature. For example, many CDPs are designed to help your team harmonize data from various sources to create a unified view of the customer. Traditionally, many CDPs would have users manually input data linkages using a series of menus and buttons, but AI-native products will proactively infer unified data models to show a result that users can adjust with natural language.

- *AI-driven workflows*—AI-native products are built to allow AI models to direct actions within the product itself and in other products via programmatic integrations (with governance and controls, of course). Some systems may make use of AI agents, which are instances of AI models assigned specific roles and contexts to make decisions and take actions on behalf of the system or its users.
- *AI user design*—This means the product design accounts for much more collaborative iteration with your team members in a natural way. Early examples of this may show a split screen, with the work product on a canvas and the dialogue between the human user and the AI in a separate panel.

AI-native architectural and design elements are important because it will be very challenging for traditional marketing technologies to be rewritten under the AI paradigm. For an example of what "AI-native" looks like in practice, on April 2, 2025, GrowthLoop announced that its platform is now "powered by agentic AI," delegating tasks to the following AI agents:

- "Data Agent learns and understands the data in your cloud to provide user-friendly field descriptions while assessing what data would be most useful for each audience.
- Audience Agent creates precise audience segments for your campaigns based on campaign history, traits, and attributes, and suggests additions to the segment as insights arrive.
- Journey Agent builds personalized omnichannel journeys, choosing the optimal channels and timing based on historical performance data, and provides optimization options based on performance.
- Insights Agent references historical and real-time performance data and helps other agents provide actionable recommendations for rapid improvement.
- Research Agent acts as your personal brainstorming partner who searches the internet to retrieve contextual answers about campaign decisions.
- Supervisor Agent oversees all other agents, making real-time assessments of when it's time to activate one or multiple agents to perform growth-driving actions for you."[1]

Locking your team into noncomposable, non-AI-native technologies means you risk following a vendor on a path to a dead end in innovation.

9.3.3 User-design considerations

The most successful capabilities augment existing marketing operations seamlessly rather than add cumbersome new steps. Is it possible to incorporate new generative

[1] GrowthLoop, "GrowthLoop unveils its Compound Marketing Engine, Revolutionizing How the World's Leading Enterprises Drive AI-Powered Growth," *PR Newswire* (Apr. 2, 2025), https://mng.bz/15jZ.

marketing capabilities into an existing workflow for its core users, or does it require changing the context from one marketing tool to another? It is generally much easier to drive change management for a team when you can make the new workflows easier to use than the previous ones, and maintaining a sense of familiarity usually helps with this.

Most generative marketing features produce outputs that need to be reviewed by marketers to mitigate the risk of "hallucinations" or malformed outputs. In many cases, these outputs may simply be inputs to designers or campaign planners who will make further refinements. Ensure that your technology choices support a strong approval and feedback process to minimize any risk to campaigns in production. We'll cover this in more detail in section 9.3.4.

9.3.4 Managing organizational risks

AI without governance is like driving without a steering wheel: acceleration without control. Generative marketing is an emerging new technology, which means that regulations and policies to govern it are still under development. Marketing teams that wish to use generative marketing will need to navigate a variety of problems. We have listed some examples here, but there may be others depending on your organization's goals and risk tolerance:

- *Legal problems*—Is it legal to use generative AI models on your company's datasets? Is your organization comfortable using intellectual property developed by AI models?
- *Cost scaling problems*—Generative AI model costs have come down dramatically but are still a major concern when they are used at scale.
- *Regulatory problems*—Does the use of generative AI comply with your company's privacy regulations? Do you consider the generative AI technology a subprocessor of PII (personally identifiable information) as defined in GDPR or similar regulations?
- *Ethical problems*—Is your use of AI biased in ways that run counter to your organization's values?
- *Organizational problems*—How do you navigate training on new technologies to keep the team up to date? How do you mitigate fears of job loss or redundancies?

As you can see, the risks of adopting generative marketing are numerous, but they are surmountable. The following subsections look at specific ways to mitigate the risks as you seek to utilize this emerging technology for its benefits.

CONSIDER COMPLIANCE AND DATA SECURITY

Before you adopt generative marketing capabilities, make sure your team consults the right compliance teams to avoid falling afoul of any regulations or policies. Most generative marketing capabilities must send data to third-party generative AI providers, such as OpenAI or Google Cloud, which means you may need to list them as a subprocessor for PII. Ensure your security and/or compliance team is comfortable with the data being sent to these services. Consult your legal team to ensure your organization is comfortable using the intellectual property generated by AI models to run marketing campaigns. If you do so successfully, your team should not need to worry about terminating successful marketing workflows powered by generative AI at some later date.

Folks who recall the days before cloud computing and software as a service (SaaS) may recall objections to those technologies compared to software that would be installed and run on local computers (since most risk models assumed company data would stay on company-owned machines). A majority of large enterprise organizations have since adopted cloud technologies and SaaS platforms by addressing a similar set of problems in partnership with their legal, compliance, and information security teams. We've seen marketing and technology leaders use this as a precedent for the adoption of generative AI technologies. In some cases, it may be easier to use generative marketing capabilities embedded naturally in SaaS platforms that are already approved for use.

If your security or compliance teams do not approve the use of third-party generative AI technologies, we have seen companies take the following additional measures:

- *I/O controls*—Security-conscious companies have begun to build or buy wrapper applications that control the input and output of data to and from generative AI models. This prevents any prohibited company information (e.g., sensitive PII, trade secrets, and confidential information) from being shared externally because the wrapper application acts as a filter for outgoing data. Then, the wrapper application acts as a filter for any prohibited or noncompliant results or incoming data from the AI models.
- *Isolation*—Alternatively, some companies have opted to fully develop and host their own generative AI model with on-premise deployment, private cloud hosting, air-gapped environments, and secure data pipelines. This is a major undertaking that requires dedicated engineering resources to build and maintain bespoke generative AI models.

Understand the AI model's bias and limits as part of ethics

While generative AI providers make a strong effort to remove bias from their models with reinforcement learning from human feedback (RLHF), no model is perfect. This may include bias based on race, disability, age, or other protected classes. Furthermore, any AI model is limited by the data you provide to it, which means that generative marketing capabilities found inside specific tools may offer suggestions that are inherently constrained by the data available to them in those tools.

Review and approve outputs

We believe human-in-the-loop models are likely to continue as the leading paradigm in using generative marketing for the foreseeable future. As a result, we recommend strong review and approval processes for AI-generated marketing outputs before they're put into production. This should be relatively straightforward for campaign-level targeting and assets, but you may need to use sampling in the case of 1:1

personalized content and contend with some level of risk for unreviewed content. This is so important to get right that we dedicate section 9.3.5 to covering roles and workflows in greater detail. Ultimately, each organization will decide on its own process and policies for AI-generated content, but your organization should proactively decide how it plans to handle this problem.

DETERMINE ORGANIZATIONAL READINESS

One of the most common setbacks hindering the adoption of AI in many organizations is a lack of understanding and training across the organization about AI, which may result in a blanket rejection of its capabilities. In addition to offering hands-on training for those who will use these generative marketing tools, make sure your team distills the key concepts for the leadership team that has decision-making power over company policies and AI adoption more generally. This represents a major change for many, and there is plenty of fear about AI in the media that may make it difficult to advocate for smart AI-driven solutions in your marketing workflows.

> **NOTE** A full deep dive into the privacy regulations, security, and ethics of AI falls outside the scope of this book. For further reading, we recommend *AI Data Privacy and Protection* by Justin Ryan and Mario Lazo (Technics, 2024).

9.3.5 *Designing new team workflows and roles*

As a marketing leader, you will need to drive the change management that brings your team along to embrace generative marketing. Setting a series of principles to govern your strategy will also give your team confidence that you are thoughtful about this emerging technology both for the benefit of the company and the benefit of your team.

Introducing generative AI to your organization will require new approaches and a transition of marketing roles, moving from creating everything manually to working with AI-sourced suggestions for approval to eventually being an AI advisor.

MARKETER AS CREATOR

Marketer as creator is the most familiar role to most marketing teams. They may have individuals, agencies, or a mix of both creating campaign ideas, determining target audiences, designing experiments, developing creative, and then executing marketing operations. Weeks or months later, they may have campaign results that they interpret with the assistance of data teams.

Several point solutions, such as those covered in section 9.2.1, can be integrated into your marketing workflows to augment each marketer's insights or output. For example, a marketer can use Typeface to generate several more display ad formats from a single creative example.

At this stage of adoption, AI tools effectively serve to extend or accelerate the marketer's role as a creator of marketing campaigns, so there's no strong need to modify your workflows other than to set policies around the ethical and compliant use of AI, covered previously in section 9.3.3.

Marketer as approver

As generative marketing systems become more autonomous, marketers may choose to enable proactive suggestions for campaigns that are not a direct result of a marketer's direct request. These may be variations of previously successful campaigns that AI models identify as having high potential.

For example, on April 4, 2024, GrowthLoop expanded its AI audience suggestion offering from response-based audience suggestions based on specific marketing prompts to GrowthLoop Audience Discovery. This new capability "proactively generates audience suggestions based on the user's most active, engaged audiences" (https://mng.bz/PwW2).

At the marketer as approver stage, the marketer's role changes in nuanced ways from creator to approver, so it's important that workflows incorporate the following:

- *Notifications*—These need to reach a marketer to solicit review of suggestions that may be generated at any time.
- *Inspection capabilities*—The marketer must be able to review and question the AI model to explain its recommendations. (One of the advantages of generative AI systems, more broadly, is their ability to explain their actions.)
- *Guidelines and rules for the AI model*—The AI model should follow these in generating useful, compliant recommendations. The good news is you can likely start by sharing the marketing guidelines your team uses to train new team members with the generative AI model.

Marketer as advisor

Finally, as marketers enable AI-generated campaign development that surpasses a human's ability to review each and every instance, the marketer's role may change again to that of an advisor. At this stage, your team may consider using AI capabilities to automatically generate target audiences, creative, channel distribution, and experimental design and then perform the marketing operations needed to launch those campaigns in production. This is likely to be made possible as early as 2025, as end-to-end generative marketing systems are made available.

As an example, consider mass personalization tools that enable the creation of a bespoke message for each and every customer (e.g., Google Cloud BigQuery ML's row-level LLM capabilities mentioned in section 9.3.1). In order to use such 1:1 personalization, your team will need to set the guidelines for generation as well as review anomalous or high-risk messages to meet the massive scale of personalization.

At this stage, the marketer must have a way to provide the generative marketing platform with the following:

- *Business objectives* on which to optimize the AI model's activities (e.g., specific goals in terms of retention, lifetime value, and their respective priority).
- *Marketing strategies* that align with those business objectives (e.g., how the marketing team plans to reach those goals, such as by identifying an ideal customer profile, ideal customer paths, or differentiated positioning).

- *Comprehensive guidelines* and rules on the generation of marketing (e.g., brand guidelines, content policies, etc.), such as might be available to new team members in a way that assumes very little oversight.
- *Governance and review guidelines* that set clear boundaries for what the generative marketing system is authorized to run on its own without human supervision versus actions that require human supervision. We recommend establishing a clear escalation path for actions that may require human supervision based on identifying marketing approaches or assets that exceed guidelines, represent anomalies, or otherwise pose significant risk to the business.

Leading the design of your marketing workflows with AI to intentionally align to these roles—or to a comparable set of roles, such as the well-known RACI framework (responsible, accountable, consulted, and informed)—will set your team up for success at each stage of the adoption curve of generative marketing.

Developing a unified AI strategy for marketing should not only account for a data strategy, a technology strategy, organizational risks, workflows, and roles, it should also account for the dependencies between those areas in service of your organization's business objectives. For example, if your organization has poor data maturity (see chapter 5) or operates in jurisdictions with high privacy compliance requirements (see chapter 2), it should inform the technologies you choose and the workflows and roles you prioritize.

Given how early it is in the development of generative marketing, however, we recommend taking a flexible and extensible approach centered around a strong first-party data strategy and the composable solutions presented in this book.

While you could adopt a fully hosted suite like Salesforce, we believe that the centralization of your company's data (especially first-party data) in a marketing data lakehouse or equivalent will deliver your marketing team a durable competitive advantage in using AI. Furthermore, decoupling your data from specific marketing systems and channels will give you the flexibility to change downstream technologies as innovations force you to revisit which email platforms, CRM systems, and paid ad vendors you use.

Summary

- Historically, marketing teams have used AI (specifically machine learning) to predict specific outcomes using structured input data (e.g., churn likelihood or lifetime value predictions based on engagement data).
- Today, marketing teams are applying new generative AI models to marketing, which we refer to as generative marketing.

- Generative marketing will help describe first-party data, create insights from first-party data, harness those insights to suggest targeting and personalization, generate creative suggestions, suggest measurement models, and help interpret marketing results.
- Successfully adopting generative marketing requires a holistic strategy that encompasses data, technology, organizational risk, and team workflows.
- Generative AI models are constrained by the data made available to them, so companies that embrace a holistic and unified first-party data strategy—like the one we have recommended in this book—stand to gain a competitive advantage.

appendix A Integrating GrowthLoop with Klaviyo

This appendix provides step-by-step instructions for connecting GrowthLoop to Klaviyo, ensuring that your first-party data segments remain in sync and enabling you to run targeted personalized email campaigns.

A.1 Prerequisites

Before you begin, ensure you have the following:

- A GrowthLoop account with appropriate access permissions
- A Klaviyo account with administrative privileges
- An API key from Klaviyo (available in your Klaviyo settings)

A.2 Step-by-step guide

Follow these steps to connect GrowthLoop to Klaviyo:

1. Access the Destinations tab in GrowthLoop:
   a. Log in to your GrowthLoop dashboard.
   b. Navigate to the Destinations tab in the main navigation menu.
2. Add Klaviyo as a Destination:
   a. Click the New Destination button in the top-right corner.
   b. In the Select Destination window, locate "Klaviyo" and select it.

   c. Provide the required information: for Destination Name, give a clear, recognizable name (e.g., "Klaviyo - Marketing Campaigns"); for Sync Frequency, choose how often you want to refresh your audience data (e.g., daily, hourly); and for API Key, paste the API key from your Klaviyo account.
   d. Click Create to complete the setup.
3. Verify the connection:
   a. After you create the Klaviyo destination, it will appear in your list of destinations.
   b. Confirm that the connection is active (e.g., a green status indicator).
4. Export an audience to Klaviyo:
   a. In GrowthLoop, navigate to the Audiences tab.
   b. Select the audience segment you want to sync with Klaviyo.
   c. Click Export and choose "Klaviyo" as the destination.
   d. Click Start Export to initiate the data sync.
5. View the synced audience in Klaviyo:
   a. Log in to your Klaviyo account.
   b. Navigate to the Lists & Segments section.
   c. Locate the newly synced GrowthLoop audience list.
   d. You can now use this list for targeted email campaigns, automated flows, and personalized messaging.

A.3 Next steps and best practices

To make the most of your integration, follow these best practices:

- *Testing*—After the first sync, consider running a test campaign to ensure the data transfers and the audience is updated as expected.
- *Ongoing optimization*—Adjust the sync frequency and segmentation criteria based on campaign performance and engagement metrics.
- *Privacy and compliance*—Ensure your data collection and communication strategies comply with all relevant privacy regulations (e.g., GDPR, CCPA).

A.4 Troubleshooting tips

If you encounter issues during the integration, try the following troubleshooting steps:

- If the audience doesn't appear in Klaviyo, double-check the API key and sync frequency settings.
- Ensure your Klaviyo account has the necessary permissions to create and update lists.
- Contact GrowthLoop support if persistent issues arise.

appendix B Creating customer journeys in GrowthLoop

GrowthLoop's Journey Builder enables marketers to design cross-channel, multistep customer journeys using a visual drag-and-drop canvas. A journey typically begins with a defined audience segment and then guides customers through a sequence of actions, delays, criteria-based branches, experiments, and destinations such as email platforms or paid media channels.

The full GrowthLoop documentation provides detailed, regularly updated instructions covering

- Creating a new journey and setting up entry criteria and scheduling
- Building workflows with entry, criteria, delay, destination, and experiment nodes
- Configuring journey re-entry settings and advanced delay options
- Saving, publishing, and managing journeys over time

For step-by-step instructions, best practices, and the latest platform updates, see the GrowthLoop Journey Builder guide: https://docs.growthloop.com/docs/build-a-journey.

index

A

B

C

D

E

F

G

H

I

K

L

M